SPIRAL OF CYNICISM

⟫ SPIRAL OF CYNICISM

The Press
and the
Public Good

Joseph N. Cappella

Kathleen Hall Jamieson

NEW YORK   OXFORD

Oxford University Press

1997

OXFORD UNIVERSITY PRESS

Oxford   New York   Athens   Auckland   Bangkok   Bogotá
Bombay   Buenos Aires   Calcutta   Cape Town   Dar es Salaam
Delhi   Florence   Hong Kong   Istanbul   Karachi   Kuala Lumpur
Madras   Madrid   Melbourne   Mexico City   Nairobi   Paris
Singapore   Taipei   Tokyo   Toronto
and associated companies in
Berlin   Ibadan

Copyright © 1997 by Joseph N. Cappella and Kathleen Hall Jamieson

Published by Oxford University Press, Inc.
198 Madison Avenue
New York, New York 10016

Oxford is a registered trademark of Oxford University Press

All rights reserved. No part of this publication may be reproduced,
stored in a retrieval system, or transmitted, in any form or by any
means, electronic, mechanical, photocopying, recording, or otherwise,
without the prior permission of Oxford University Press.

Library of Congress Cataloging-in-Publication Data
Cappella, Joseph N.
   Spiral of cynicism / Joseph N. Cappella, Kathleen Hall Jamieson.
      p.   cm.
   Includes bibliographical references and index.
   ISBN 0-19-509063-2 — ISBN 0-19-509064-0 pbk.
   1. Press and politics—United States.   2. Government and the
press—United States.   3. United States—Congress—Reporters and
reporting.   4. Mass media—Influence.   I. Jamieson, Kathleen Hall.
II. Title.
PN4888.P6J36   1997   071'.3—dc20   96-24735

9 8 7 6 5 4 3 2 1

Printed in the United States of America on acid-free paper

To Joe's father, Joseph Cappella
To Kathleen's sister, Anita Jeanne Hall

ACKNOWLEDGMENTS

THIS BOOK is a true collaboration between the authors. One cherished what the other wanted to excise; conclusions obvious to one were elliptical to the other; one was thrilled by technical discussion the other found tedious; one thinks inductively, the other deductively; one is always interesting and sometimes right; the other is always right and sometimes interesting. One was trained as a physicist; the other as a rhetorical critic. The thinking, planning, plotting, arguing, proving, and writing never suffered from a lack of diversity of opinion or style. It will probably show.

The research also did not suffer from a lack of dedicated and smart assistants. We had graduate and undergraduate research assistants who contributed at every stage, making important contributions to our thinking to say nothing of coding until the wee hours or traveling cross country during blizzard conditions. The graduate research assistants included Robin Nabi, Fawn Johnson, June Woong Rhee, Cass Conrad, Douglas Rivlin, Melinda Schwenk, Susan Stone, Emory Woodard, Tony Pals, Kevin Terpstra, Sean Aday, Kiersten Stewart, Chris

Ferris, Doug Battema, Shannon Kokoska, Thomas Timperio, Sheila Collins, and Byron Colby. A few of the undergraduate assistants who survived long-term commitments to our research were Rita Ventresca, Tamara York, Robert Giacopetti, and Nicole Rosenblum. Without their complementary skills, our projects would not have been possible.

The research could not have been completed without the support and encouragement of Lloyd Morrisett of the Markle Foundation; Frank Karel, Paul Jellinek, Jim Knickman, and Mark Kaplan of The Robert Wood Johnson Foundation; and Richard Leone of The Twentieth Century Fund. The Markle Foundation encouraged our studies of election campaigns, while the Robert Wood Johnson Foundation made possible research during the Health Care Reform policy debate of 1993–94. Without the generous funding from both groups it would not have been possible to carry out the surveys, content analyses, and field experiments we report here.

Released time to write up results on public cynicism and the press was made possible by the Twentieth Century Fund. They also provided a forum in which we could test our thinking with a skeptical (but certainly not cynical) audience of journalists and academics.

Professors John Zaller of UCLA and Richard Brody of Stanford read a draft of the manuscript and provided detailed comments. We thank them for their careful critique. Where we have failed to follow their advice, the fault is ours.

Our colleagues at the Annenberg School for Communication have been unwitting accomplices. Their patient listening to zany arguments and fragmentary evidence in hallway conversations often led to reconsiderations and alternative structures.

The editor, Tom LeBien, and the staff at Oxford tolerated our delays and revisions amiably and still undertook yeoman efforts to bring the manuscript to press quickly. Our special thanks and sympathies to our copy editor Rosemary Wellner, who had to tame the prose of authors who spoke in two rather different voices. Kathleen wants to offer special thanks to Laura Brown, who has participated in every one of her Oxford Books.

With good humor and minimal complaint, our spouses, Elena and Bob, shared us with this book manuscript. As important, they have put up with us for over twenty-five years and appear to show a willingness to continue to do so.

CONTENTS

SPIRAL OF CYNICISM

≫ 1

THE PRESIDENT,

THE SPEAKER,

AND THE PRESS

AFTER THE fall 1994 election, the Republican leadership visited the Clinton White House for an introductory session. Their meeting was, in the words of newly elected Speaker of the House Newt Gingrich, "great." The Democratic president and Republican congressional leaders acknowledged the need to minimize unfunded mandates and apply the laws of the land to Congress as well. They also agreed on the need for a presidential line-item veto. In sum, the meeting was constructive and cordial.

On the White House lawn afterwards, the Republicans told the assembled journalists just that. "We say to the White House press corps: We had a great positive meeting," recalled Gingrich. "We're going to be able to work a lot more than people think. And we began to list these [areas of agreement]. The second question we were asked [was] 'What do you think it will break down over?'" That question was symptomatic of a widely documented tendency of the press to focus on conflict, not consensus.

Republican Senate leader Dick Armey and Gingrich "got mad,"

recalled the Speaker. "So I just said to the reporter—I said, you just heard the leaders of the Republican Party say that the Democratic President today had a wonderful meeting on behalf of America; we're trying to work together. Couldn't you try for twenty-four hours to have a positive, optimistic message as though it might work?"

Gingrich told this tale in an unprecedented public forum that he and Clinton held more than a year later. In that event, the two leaders engaged in behavior that was both in their own self-interest and in the public interest, a notion incompatible with the one pervading much of contemporary press coverage.

The forum itself probably would not have occurred had it not been for Gingrich's explicitly stated willingness to exploit the press's preoccupation with his own "strategy." Their meeting attracted high-profile press attention in part because Gingrich had hinted that he might have presidential aspirations. The hints, he said, were a ploy to ensure that his ideas continued to draw press notice. On the *Today Show*, he admitted, "Of course it's manipulative, because the only way I can convince your editor and your producer that it's worthwhile covering my ideas is to convince them that I need to personally be ambitious."[1] As we will show, many press reports reduced the meeting to the sum of the leaders' self-interests and a chronicle of who won and who lost.

The Clinton–Gingrich meeting provides an optic through which we can view both political and press behaviors. In our analysis we will ask, What is the tenor of contemporary political discourse and the texture of journalistic accounts of it? We will argue that, faced with amicable argument, reporters demonstrated the hold of a strong tradition that reduces leaders to their presumed motives and substance to its strategic intent, bypassing consensus for conflict. But some journalists broke from the pack to demonstrate an ability to both recount and also contextualize argument in ways that were more conducive to contemplation than cynicism.

The Clinton–Gingrich meeting occurred almost by chance. On Thursday June 8, 1995, President Bill Clinton "light-heartedly"[2] told a reporter for the *Concord Monitor* that he would like to take House Speaker Newt Gingrich around New Hampshire and "have some joint meetings and let the citizens come in and ask us both questions." Interpreting the statement as an invitation, Gingrich accepted. The town-hall-like meeting was scheduled for the following Sunday, June

11, as part of an already planned Clinton picnic with senior citizens at the Earl Bourdon Senior Center in the old mill town of Claremont.

That Sunday afternoon at 4 P.M. EST, in an encounter televised live on CNN and C-SPAN, President Bill Clinton and House Speaker Newt Gingrich, seated on bentwood chairs on a small stage with two American flags, met with an audience of 200 to 300 senior citizens for what papers billed as a "showdown."[3] Some in the audience brought the same expectations. Among the signs lining the parade route was one saying "Kick Newt's Butt."[4]

When New Hampshire's Channel 4 (WBZ-TV) preempted the Kemper Open for the Clinton–Gingrich event, golf fans called to complain. WCVB-TV didn't have the same problem — the Detroit Grand Prix had ended before the Claremont forum began. WHDH-TV decided not to preempt the Senior BellSouth Classic for the Claremont exchange. Nationally, every network except CNN and C-SPAN continued with scheduled programming.

The meeting occurred as part of a New Hampshire trip designed by Clinton "to stave off Democratic challenges in the February 20, 1996, primary."[5] But the event failed to meet those expectations. "It was no showdown; it was a display of mutual respect," recounted the *Austin American-Statesman* later.[6] Throughout the encounter, the two were consistently civil and cordial. Each granted the good will and integrity of the other. Each praised the other when praise was due. They disagreed without being disagreeable.

Indeed, that was their explicitly stated intent. The day before the event, Gingrich had said that he "did not think he or the president should try to score points on one another, but instead should have the opportunity to lay out their differing positions on a range of issues."[7] "I would hope," said Gingrich, "it is a very friendly, very positive dialogue and the people say afterward that it's nice to see that leaders who belong to different parties and different branches can actually find some way to deal with each other that isn't hostile."

Both the president and the Speaker characterized the event in metaphors based in talk, not the physical encounter of sports or war. "I think just having your leaders *chat rather than fight* is a good thing," said Gingrich in the meeting (emphasis added). "It wasn't a *contest*; it was a *conversation*," Clinton observed afterward.[8] (emphasis added). So too did their representatives. "They weren't fighting each other; they were laying out their thoughts," said Gingrich's spokesman after the forum.[9]

Meanwhile, reporters struggled to find words to characterize the event. The *Boston Globe* called it a "joust." Gingrich aides reportedly laughed when one reporter opined on the day before that "Newt Gingrich came to New Hampshire to see a moose and ended up bagging a president."[10]

But behind the scenes the political followers of both leaders were "handicapp[ing] the stakes." "The Gingrich loyalists, agog that the president let their man sit chair-to-chair with the Commander in Chief, likened Mr. Clinton's unpredictable willingness to let the Speaker join him to the White House's Bosnia policy."[11] "For a lot of different reasons it fits our game plan," commented the White House press secretary. "It's a serious deal. It will get a lot of attention."[12]

In their opening remarks, the president and the Speaker set the tone of the hour-long discussion. "We have a lot of differences," Clinton said in his opening statement, "but we also have some areas in which we can work together. I think the most important thing is that we try to identify clearly the places where we disagree, but then make our best effort, our dead-level best effort, to work together to move this country forward." The audience applauded.

"I believe all Americans can be told the truth and can actually watch their leaders have honest, open disagreement and talk things out and find common solutions," noted Gingrich in his opening remarks. "So I hope with your permission, the president and I will now have a dialogue with you, and maybe the country can learn a little bit about working together and not just buying commercials and attacking each other. Thank you for letting me be here." Again the audience applauded.

Although news reports focused on the tone of the encounter, its content was also remarkable. In response to each question, the two indicated either their areas of agreement or granted that their differences were philosophical, not personal. Speaking of Clinton's Americorps, Gingrich said, "Let me say, this is an area where I think the president has a good idea, but we disagree. But it's not a bad idea.... I have two concerns that I think are a different direction philosophically." The Speaker then discussed a taxpayer credit for contributions to charities that would perform the same functions as this government program. "I believe we want to have less Washington-based bureaucracy and fewer decisions made in Washington. And we want to strengthen the private charities."

Instead of simply attacking, each specified an alternative and then provided a justification. In other words, where contemporary politics is typically carried on in assertion, both engaged in traditional argument, marshaling evidence in support of claims. "I agree with the president that there are a number of things that have to be changed about health care in America," said the Speaker. We ought, for example, to "guarantee tomorrow morning that you have portability that you can change insurance and change jobs, and there are no preconditions.... I think where we disagreed strategically is, I think you can do those one building block at a time and get them through and get them signed. I think it's very hard as a practical matter to get a big comprehensive bill through because it seems to break down of its own weight."

As unprecedented as the encounter itself was the level of engagement. One is hard-pressed to recall another recent instance of a political leader acknowledging that evidence for a position is inconclusive—indeed contradictory. Yet Clinton noted that "it is true that there [are] economic studies that say if you raise the minimum wage, you raise incomes for people who are at the minimum wage and a little above it too, who get bumped up, but it costs some jobs. There are other studies that say it doesn't cost any jobs because, for example, people on welfare or out of the work force will think it's more worth their while to come in and compete for those jobs and they'll want to work more. The reason that I am for it is that. . . ."

While it is unusual to witness such discourse in public, it is in fact the form that discussions often take in private. "[M]any of us were commenting afterwards," observed White House Press Secretary Mike McCurry the day after the Claremont exchange, "that the tone of the encounter they had with the senior citizens group in New Hampshire last night was very much like the bipartisan leadership meetings we frequently have here in the Roosevelt Room in the White House. It's that type of familiarity that they have in these discussions; it's that type of reasoned approach to issues. But it does reflect, I think, some differences — some philosophical differences in the approach of the Republican majority and the administration."[13]

As many reports indicated, the meeting "broke little new policy ground, apart from a handshake deal for a joint commission to look into lobbying and campaign finance."[14]

But it did point to areas of agreement on anti-terrorism legislation, the need to reform Medicare, and portability in health care insurance; it highlighted disagreement on raising the minimum wage, how to reform Medicare, the role and utility of the UN, and national service, specifically Clinton's Americorps program. And, as Clinton indicated in the forum, it showcased two dramatically different philosophies of government.

It also included a number of remarkable comments about the form of discourse that each was rejecting. "It is so difficult for us in Washington to communicate with people out in the country, that often the only way to break through is with some fairly extreme statement," noted Clinton, adding, "Speaker Gingrich is real good at that. He can break through like nobody I've ever seen." In the debate over Medicare Clinton could break through by claiming that Gingrich would excessively cut benefits and Gingrich could do the same by saying that Medicare would not be saved under Clinton. "The truth is," Clinton observed, "we both believe that but it's more complicated than that." In the exchange each indicated his position on Medicare, differentiated it from the other's, and argued for the value of one over the other.

"There are very often no simple answers to complicated problems," said Clinton. "But simple answers move the electorate. If you don't want that, if you want a reasoned debate, then when your congressmen and senators come home on weekends, you need to tell them that."

The difference between the discourse in Claremont and political rhetoric as usual was evident in the kind of talk that bracketed the event. Hours before, on *Meet the Press*, the White House Chief of Staff had said, "I think they [the president and the Speaker] have a very different version of where this country should go. I think the Speaker basically thinks it's survival of the fittest, and that basically a few key people can get what they want and special interests can get what they want and everybody else has to kind of fight for crumbs off the table. The President thinks that we ought to be a family, working together to give everybody a part of the American dream."

The morning after contained both less sweetness and less light. On a conservative radio talk show (the *Dan Pierce Show*), Gingrich responded to a caller's question asking why he did not favor an independent counsel to investigate ethics complaints against him by attacking House Minority Whip David Bonior. "What you've got is a group of very bitter left-wing Democrats led by David Bonior, who don't have any ideas about welfare. They don't have any ideas about balancing the budget. All they've got is 'Smear Newt Gingrich' and I think it's absurd to say that anybody who can make up a good smear automatically gets to appoint an independent counsel."[15] Gingrich also "also took a swipe at Clinton on Medicare, contending the president Sunday had conceded the GOP budget would increase Medicare spending after weeks of the Democrats attacking Republicans for proposing sharp cuts. 'Maybe we need more sessions where we've got a liberal and a conservative without a moderator at the same place,' he declared. 'It is a lot harder to say something that is not true when you have the other person sitting next to you.'"[16] In a speech to a conservative group the same day, Gingrich said that Republicans "believe that this is a great country filled with good people, and our job is to educate, empower and liberate the good people.... The president seems to believe that this is a great government that hires good bureaucrats."[17]

The contrast suggests that politicians typically provide a discourse more conducive to the strategy and conflict frames than that offered by the discussion of that Sunday in New Hampshire. Indeed, what the press found most newsworthy about the Claremont forum other than the agreement to form a commission on lobbying reform was the cordiality of the event itself. "All in all," said ABC's Jim Wooten, "it was one of the more remarkably congenial and cordial moments in the politics of America" (6/11).

News reports contrasted what they portrayed as the standard discourse of Gingrich and Clinton with this unexpected alternative. "The partisan sniping that dominates relations between the two vanished into the soft afternoon air," said the *Boston Herald*. "Time and time again," wrote Todd Purdum in the *New York Times*, "Mr. Gingrich played against type, forsaking the jugular for the handshake, praising as worthy ideas even presidential programs that he has promised to cut or abolish, like the National Service Corps. And time and again, Mr. Clinton voiced his differences with Mr. Gingrich not in the sharp-edged sound bites that the White House has honed for months but in the respectful tones of a fellow policy jock" (6/12).

It is impossible to know which came first — the conflict-driven sound-bite-oriented discourse of politicians or the conflict-saturated strategy-oriented structure of press coverage. Whatever the answer, each now feeds the other with politicians providing a menu that includes what the press seems most likely to cover and the press arguing that it simply is reporting what it is being offered. This mutually reinforcing process creates what we will call a spiral of cynicism. Part of what made the Claremont meeting and its press coverage so interesting is that it gives us a chance to ask, When offered an alternative form of discourse, what does the press do? The answer is, in large part, "Fall back on the language of game, war, and conflict and frame the substance strategically."

Although some persisted in describing the two as "combatants,"[18] others struggled to find the language to characterize an encounter between two political leaders that could not aptly be captured in sports or war terms. The word "love-fest" appeared in accounts ranging from the one on NBC to those in the *Los Angeles Times* (a "bi-partisan love fest") and *San Francisco Chronicle*. "If people expected fireworks here today," wrote Dan Balz in the *Washington Post*, "they got a love-in instead" (6/12). On CBS, the meeting was described as "friendly, polite, even deferential." A reporter for the *Atlanta Journal and Constitution* characterized Clinton as "smooth and affable, loose as a moose," while adding that "conservative activists reared on the vinegar of Gingrich's partisan attacks must have retched at this dose of maple syrup" (6/12). Another mixed metaphor appeared in the *Washington Post*, where Ann Devroy noted that Clinton and Gingrich "coated their disagreements with a layer of sugar during a historic hour-long dialogue that illuminated their differences but did not emphasize them."

If confrontation anchors one end of the political spectrum, reporters seemed unable to locate the word or phrase that would characterize the other. "Comity" might have served if that word had not fallen from contemporary use to the extent that when it was used on CNN the transcriber rendered it "comedy."

Some of the coverage implied that reporters find it easier to identify and write about disagreement when it is carried on in hyperbole, simplification, and personal attack. The encounter, wrote a reporter for the *New York Times* was "so muted, so polite and so carefully conciliatory that it was often hard to distinguish the sharp philosophical differences between the two men" (6/12).

"If this had been a boxing match," opined two reporters for the *Boston Herald*, "it would have been called in the first round—for lack of action."

Charting the transformation in Gingrich in terms of motive and probable political effect, reporters shifted from the predator to the pet and from canine to feline. On *Capital Gang, Newsweek's* Howard Fineman sketched the advantages for Gingrich. "[H]e gets to demonstrate that he doesn't have horns, that he can actually have a polite discussion. He's not just an attack dog." For those who disapproved of Gingrich's behavior, he had instead become a pet — or, as the *Manchester Union Leader* described him, "a lap dog.""The only ones likely to be upset by Gingrich's performance are the conservative activists who must have grimaced each time he praised Clinton or declined to go for the president's jugular," noted the *San Diego Union-Tribune.* "This pussycat was not the Newt they had come to love."

The alternatives demonstrated that reporters are so unaccustomed to civility that they could render it only in hyperbole. The event "more closely resembled a love fest than a confrontation" said the *San Francisco Chronicle* in a characterization that ignored the clearly drawn areas of disagreement at the meeting. Nor, despite claims by reporters for the *Washington Post* and the *San Francisco Chronicle,* did the two sound like running mates; Ann Devroy's script in the *Post* had Gingrich functioning as Vice President Al Gore in his praise for Clinton.

Other analogies were comparably strained. In the *Atlanta Journal-Constitution,* Tom Baxter trivialized the encounter by saying that it had "the look and feel of a Regis-and-Kathy Lee knockoff on a local affiliate"(6/12). Some phrasings that were accurate were also awkward. ABC's Morton Dean described Gingrich and Clinton as "on the same stage and the same wavelength, not politically or philosophically, but politely" (*Good Morning America,* 6/12).

And some descended dramatically into the colloquial. "Were you a little put off by the fact that Newt Gingrich was so kissy face with the president," the *Washington Post's* Jim Glassman asked Mona Charen on *Capital Gang.* "Yes," Charen replied.

At a loss to describe what it was, reporters fell back on defining what it was not. "Confounding conventional wisdom," wrote the *San Diego Union-Tribune,* "the much-anticipated political showdown between the two political foes was neither a slugfest nor a cat fight." By contrast, here reporters could call on a highly developed vocabulary, one in marked contrast to the strained sparse one available for describing the civility of the discourse. "It was the lack of acrimony, the lack of pot-shots between the two men that was so unusual," observed a

CNN reporter. "Disdaining the harshness and hyperbole common to contemporary political discourse," wrote Bob Shogan of the *Los Angeles Times*, "Clinton and Gingrich took every opportunity to find points of agreement" (6/12).

Competition remained an underlying frame of reference for columnist William Safire. "[T]wo men with basic differences in political outlook competed only in degrees of conciliation," he wrote.[19] Pugilistic metaphors abounded. "They wore pillows on their fists," wrote Safire. They "faced-off," said the *New York Times* (6/12). They "square[d] off," said the *San Francisco Chronicle* (6/12). "There were a few jabs," noted *Newsday* (6/12). White House aides shared the notion that at its worst this would be a fight out of control. "[T]he White House was nervous beforehand that Clinton might lose his ability to remain 'presidential' in a brawl with Gingrich," noted the *Boston Globe*; "Clinton came armed with barbs" (6/12). "There were few sparks. Mostly bouquets," said the *Boston Herald*.

In the process, they created oxymora. Gingrich and Clinton "sparred politely," said a report in the *Dallas Morning News* (6/12). The "pair wrestled gently," the *Boston Herald* observed. They "joined lengthy battle, ever so politely," said the *Financial Times* (6/12).

The journalists knew how to describe Clinton and Gingrich in their other incarnations. "President Clinton and House Speaker Newt Gingrich, two men schooled in attack dog campaigning and killer sound bites, yesterday exchanged compliments instead of jabs," said the *Boston Herald*. "Mr. Gingrich was decidedly gentle in his criticism of the United Nations, which he has *vehemently attacked* in the past several days as a 'disgrace to civilization,'" noted a report in the *Baltimore Sun* (6/12). "The House speaker even praised Mr. Clinton's national service program, which he has *denounced harshly* in the past" (Emphasis added). For *The Independent*, "the remarkable encounter seemed to propel the normally sharp-tongued Speaker and an increasingly defensive president into uncharted waters of civility at least in public" (6/12). The language of the press reports suggests that this territory was uncharted for reporters as well.

Reporters scrambled to attribute the civility to political self-interest. And embedded in most reports was the assumption either that the public interest was not at issue or that both the leaders and the public could not win. On *Fox Morning News*, Charlie Cook noted that they both needed to lower their negative ratings — "it's in their own best interest [note that he does not add "and also in the interest of the public and the political process"] — so I think they were looking to come across as warm, decent guys [not that they *are* warm, decent guys] who were just working to try ... to achieve some solutions" (6/12). "[W]hat may have been most significant about the dialogue in Claremont was that these two gifted and driven politicians each evidently concluded that the best way to win support from an increasingly restless and suspicious electorate was to convince voters that they take the job of governing seriously," wrote Bob Shogan in the *Los Angeles Times*. Public interest apparently played no role in the decision. "Indeed, even after it had happened," wrote the *New York Times*'s Todd Purdum, "it was hard to believe that it had. That it did was a testament to the wary self-interest that made Mr. Gingrich leap at the chance, and led Mr. Clinton to take the risk of letting him."

Among the questions populating the coverage was — Who won and who lost? Most focused that question on the fortunes of the Republican primary contenders, or Gingrich and Clinton, but not the public at large. Late-night PBS host Charlie Rose opened a segment on the New Hampshire meeting by asking, "Who won this nondebate? Who gained and who lost? We'll ask our panel this evening" (6/12). Former congressman Tony Coelho noted that "Newt got what he wanted, and that was basically to come off as someone credible to be on the same stage with the president."

One question often asked by those "gaming" a political event is, Who appeared better suited for the job he sought? This posture permits journalists to retain the form of objectivity—they are after all not indicating who *is* more presidential or competent — and at the same time advances the analysis of tactical advantage. Some of those moments are almost absurdist. On Charlie Rose's show, ABC's Jeff Greenfield literally concentrated on appearance. "[N]ext to Gingrich, Clinton looks very slim." An extended moment of late-night silliness follows:

Rose: "Yes."
Greenfield: "I have a feeling he'll want him on stage for the rest ..."
Rose: "This is the physical—"

Greenfield: "of the ca—He looks buff."

Howard Fineman (*Newsweek*): "Yeah. I was going to say. I saw Newt in his blue jeans the other day and Clinton wins that one hands down."

Rose then returns to serious talk about strategic advantage. "Let me raise this question raised by Bill Safire, in fact, that Bob Dole is the winner in all of this because Gingrich's presence freezes out anybody, any other contender rising to form a sufficient challenge against him." "Let's cut to the chase," Safire had written in his day-after column. "[I]n the debate between two men trying desperately to lower their high negative ratings, who won?" Safire then focused on appearance and effect while implying that for Gingrich, at least, what separated appearance from reality was hypocrisy. "Gingrich came across as a man trying hard to come across as someone other than himself." And so, Safire concluded, "Bring back back-biting. Sorry, zero sum gamesters, the snap judgment in this corner—too soon to be influenced by polls or spinmeisters — is that they helped Bob Dole." On CNN's *Capital Gang*, Martin Walker of Britain's *Guardian* agreed. "There's only one loser in this and that's Senator Bob Dole" (6/11).

The assumption that appearance and reality differ was at play as well. "[B]oth seemed intent on appearing above the political fray and said the country would be better served if politicians stopped their sound-bite bickering," noted the *San Francisco Chronicle* (6/12).

A few reporters broke from the assumption that the good of the candidates and the process are mutually exclusive. When asked after the event whether he thought that both men benefited, CNN's Bruce Morton observed, "Well, I think maybe they both were, and I think maybe the voters were helped. You now know in non-passionate, non-screaming, non-30-second attack ad terms where Bill Clinton stands on a number of issues, where Newt Gingrich stands on a number of issues—and that's kind of good for the process" (6/11).

At the close of the event, spokespersons for Clinton and Gingrich agreed that it was inappropriate to view the forum as one in which there were winners or losers. Before and after the exchange, Gingrich specifically rejected the notion that scoring points was the goal. Yet NBC's Jim Miklaszewski concluded that "the fact that Gingrich was even here means he won this round before it even started" (NBC's *Today Show*, 6/12). Writing for Copley News Service, George Condon identified Clinton and Gingrich as "big winners." The losers — the other nine Republican presidential contenders. *Wall Street Journal* reporters agreed that the other Republicans had suffered from being out of the spotlight (6/12). Dan Baltz of the *Washington Post* called it "the president's event but Gingrich's day (6/12). On ABC, Jim Wooten declared, "No hits, no runs, no errors" (6/11). "It was Clinton who seemed to have the crowd in his corner," noted Baxter in the *Atlanta Constitution.* "If Gingrich did the Republican presidential candidates any favors in this meeting, it was to remind them that Clinton, who looks so vulnerable in Washington, looks good on the stump." The debate was worth watching, wrote Safire, "not for what was said, but for the sight of two young old pros sparring publicly for the first time, one hand washing the other's political interests" (6/12).

Reporters quoted pundits who also assessed comparable advantage. From Clinton adviser James Carville: "Hopefully, it'll help Gingrich. The worst thing we could do is hurt him. Who knows? Miracles happen and he could get the nomination" (*New York Times,* 6/12). From the Christian Coalition's Ralph Reed came the conclusion on *MacNeil-Lehrer* that the meeting "was sort of a political version of rope a dope. I think they both went in there, and neither one wanted to get knocked down, and so there wasn't really the kind of slugging that you would normally see" (6/12). Former Reagan adviser Mike Deaver added, "[A]ny time that it appeared to the American public that the people in Washington were acting like adults, everybody, everybody benefitted."

Indeed, by answering rather than rejecting reporters' questions about strategic advantage, spokespersons for Clinton and Gingrich themselves invited what we will in a later chapter define as the strategic frame. "I can't imagine Bob Dole found many cameras in Iowa this weekend," said Clinton Press Secretary Mike McCurry. "That thought might have crossed some minds at the White House, but since we're not being overtly political, we're not overly preoccupied with such things."[20] Of course, implied by McCurry was that the White House was being *covertly* political.

Just at the edge of many press claims about self-interest is the implication that these are individuals unlike the rest of us, driven by needs and motives that bear watching. Psychological profiling occurred as well. "[T]his much seemed clear" to the *New York Times*'s Todd Purdum: "The President who so loves to be liked was at some pains simply to compete with the Speaker who so often seems not to care who likes him" (6/12). "[I]f there is one quality that marks each of the two men who sat on the platform here," noted the report in the *Los Angeles Times*, "it is ambition." "[A]t the risk of sounding cynical," wrote columnist Safire, "Mr. Gingrich's relentless obsequiousness struck me as insincere" (6/12).

The substance of the encounter between Clinton and Gingrich was largely lost in discussion of strategy in some news venues. But in others the substance was showcased. Where its pre-event coverage had been highly strategic, after the forum CNN ran well-edited excerpts highlighting the areas of agreement and disagreement. A number of newspapers boxed quotes from both to show similarities and differences. Some quoted extended sections of the exchange. There was, in other words, evidence that if presented with a civil engaged discussion, reporters could in fact report it.

This book examines the effects when they do not. In nine chapters we will explore the effects of strategy-driven, conflict-based press coverage on voters and citizens in both a campaign and a public policy environment. Our exploration begins in Chapter 2 by asking if, in the world of politics, cynicism is the only realistic attitude or if one can be a realist while retaining a trusting, if skeptical world view. In Chapters 3 and 4, we focus on the framing of news content since news frames direct and organize the way people think about events. We explain framing in general and then, in Chapter 4, propose how strategic news frames work on the audience's learning and judgment. Chapters 5 through 8 present new research on the effects of strategic news frames. Chapter 5 describes the kind of studies we carried out, discussing especially how we tried to ensure realism in the news articles and broadcasts used. Learning from strategy and issue news is the focus of Chapter 6, and Chapter 7 tests whether strategic news has the power to activate cynical reactions in the public. Chapter 8 supplements the findings on learning and cynicism by analyzing essays and stories and evaluating survey and time-series data on learning from and cynical response to news frames. We examine the public's reaction to the press itself in Chapter 9. The final chapter shows how the spiral of cynicism created when the press, the politicians, and the public come to expect low performance of each other can be broken.

》 2

CYNICISM OR REALISM?

"[C]YNICISM is epidemic right now," wrote nationally syndicated columnist David Broder in the *Washington Post* in early July 1994.[1] "It saps people's confidence in politics and public officials, and it erodes both the standing and the standards of journalism. If the assumption is that nothing is on the level, nothing is what it seems, then citizenship becomes a game for fools and there is no point in trying to stay informed." A July 1994 *Washington Post*–ABC News Poll seemed to justify Broder's concern.[2] It found that

- Overwhelming majorities say they think that members of Congress care more about special interests than about "people like you" and care more about keeping power than about the best interests of the nation.
- Large numbers say most candidates for Congress make campaign promises they have no intention of fulfilling and quickly lose touch with the people after coming to Washington.
- More than a third of those interviewed—37 percent—consistently offered the most negative evaluation when asked their perceptions of the work

habits, honesty and integrity of Congress. Less than one-fifth expressed few reservations.

This poll was consistent with nineteen earlier ones done in the past half-decade during the tenure of three Congresses and two presidents. In these, "the average scores for Congress have been 33 percent approval and 62 percent disapproval." The July 1994 poll showed 34 percent approval and 61 percent disapproval.

Similarly, a poll for the Associated Press (July 27, 1994) depicted more people agreeing that the parties to the health care reform debate were "mostly trying to gain political advantage" than trying to "do best for country."

Of course, the halcyon days of high public confidence in Congress are more based in myth than actual memory for, as Glenn Parker notes, "Congress has received more negative than positive evaluations in over 80 percent of the survey measurements of congressional popularity between 1939 and 1977; during this period, congressional unpopularity has a mean of 52 percent."[3] What is worrisome is the decline in public confidence from even that low point.

A *Time* magazine survey reported that while in 1964 60 percent believed that the government would generally try to do the right thing, in 1994, 10 percent did. "Distrust in government has increased over time," writes Eric Uslaner in *The Decline of Comity in Congress*, "and the correlation is almost as impressive, despite the much smaller sample size, as that for trust in people."[4]

Similarly, National Opinion Research Center Surveys from 1973 and 1993 suggest an increase in confidence in the people running the military (from 32 percent to 42 percent) but sharp drops in organized religion (from 35 to 23), education (from 37 to 22), banks and financial institutions (from 32 to 15), television (from 19 to 12), the executive branch (from 29 to 12), the press (from 23 to 11), organized labor (from 16 to 8), and Congress (from 24 to 7).[5] When asked about their confidence in the government as a problem solver, three-quarters in 1972 felt either a great deal or a fair amount of confidence. In 1993, that percent was 42.[6]

Occasionally, a prominent event will prompt a brief shift in public support for government. In the aftermath of the Oklahoma bombing in spring 1995 a *Washington Post*–ABC News poll suggested a resurgence in such support. In January 1995, 27 percent had reported that they were satisfied but not enthusiastic about the way the federal government works, but in mid-May, 45 percent answered that question affirmatively.[7] The increase did not persist. A *New York Times*–CBS poll conducted August 5 to 9, 1995, found 59 percent saying that there wasn't a single elected person they admired. Six percent of the 36 percent who did think of one named President Bill Clinton, 5 percent listed Senate Majority Leader Bob Dole.

At the same time, "seventy-nine percent, the highest figure in several decades, said the Government was pretty much run by a few big interests looking out for themselves.... And 58 percent said that people like themselves had little to say about what the Government did."[8] In July 1995, a *U.S. News and World Report* poll found 50 percent of those surveyed saying that the work the news media do conflicts with their and their families' goals, with 36 percent reporting the same thing about elected officials.[9]

Is Public and Press Cynicism Actually Realism?

The cynic tends to hold that the political system is corrupt; its players are Machiavellian partisans uninterested in the public good, its process driven by a concern with winning, not governing. Because we cannot know what motivates an individual and because any action can be recast to serve some selfish end, the cynic's position is ultimately not contestable. Sealed within her own self-reinforcing assumptions, the cynic can interpret even selfless actions as calculated attempts to create an image of selflessness.

Any action, however noble, can be reduced to some strategic intent. If a vote is consistent with the views of financial supporters, it was cast not because the member of Congress and the supporters are like-minded but because the conscience of the representative has been mortgaged. In this world, votes not correlated to contributions may nonetheless have been cast in search of future funding. We begin this discussion, in other words, confident that the cynic is not subject to conversion. If, as the cynic believes, nothing is as it seems, any evidence that leaders or institutions act in the public's interest can be recast as proof of the opposite claim.

The larger question is, Is the public's lack of confidence in institutions justified? If leaders are motivated solely or even primarily by self-interest and if an inherent conflict exists between their self-interest and the public good, then press reports of self-interested political action are not cynical but realistic, and the rising public lack of confidence in its leaders and institutions is a repudiation of Pollyannaism.

This conclusion seems supported by the finding that cynicism may be grounded in experience with those who are more active and more informed — more cynical. Herb Asher and Mike Barr's analysis of the 1978–1992 American National Election Studies data (ANES) suggests that Congress is rated more poorly among "the more politically active and attentive citizenry." And "those who were knowledgeable about control of the House were much more critical of Congress than were less informed respondents."[10]

Those who posit the self-interest–public interest dichotomy face a number of problems, among them the rarity of national or even elite consensus about what the public interest is. Indeed, some economists maintain that the very notion of public interest is "merely a cover for private interests." But as Peter Brown argues, those who take that position "cut themselves off from any grounds on which to oppose private interests except other private interests."[11]

Another problem with the dichotomy is that the nature of an elective system undercuts one of its central assumptions. If one is elected by responding to constituents' needs, then aren't supposedly self-interested actions designed to ensure re-election also consistent with the self-interest of the voters? Re-election is secured, in other words, when the elected official acts in the perceived self-interest of his or her constituents. When the self-interests of various constituencies clash, legislative action is less likely. When they coincide, they define the public's sense of the public good.

The notion that the politician's self-interest plays a role in governing is a long-lived one. "Few in public affairs act from a mere view of the good of their country whatever they may pretend," noted Benjamin Franklin, one of the country's first publishers, "fewer still act with a view to the good of mankind."[12] Nor is there anything new in laments that politicians posture and pander. "In all assemblies," wrote James Bryce more than a century ago, "one must expect abundance of unreality and pretence, many speeches obviously addressed to the gallery."[13]

But it is possible that both Franklin and Bryce are correct and that the presumption that political leaders are driven primarily by self-interest to the exclusion of the public interest is nonetheless wrong.

The notion that humans in general are self-interested was forcefully posited by Thomas Hobbes in the *Leviathan*, which argued that "a general inclination of all mankind" took the form of "a perpetual and rest-less desire of Power after power, that ceaseth only in Death." But, as Jane Mansbridge perceptively argues, "Today, in the interests of a mis-placed 'realism,' we often ... [claim] that if we can detect any self-interested reason to act in a particular way, that reason provides the only explanation we need. Self-interest does not automatically drive out duty, however, in spite of the conceptual opposition between the two."[14] The dichotomy between public-spiritedness and self-interest may in political life be a false or at least not a necessary one.

Three bodies of evidence run counter to the notion that cynicism is in fact realism about politicians and the political process. First, presi-dents more often than not try to keep their campaign promises. Second, members of political parties act in a manner consistent with their party's platform. And, finally, members of Congress vote and select committee assignments in ways that suggest that the public interest is a motivator.

Presidential Behavior

After a detailed analysis of the promises and performance of presidents from Kennedy through Reagan, Jeff Fishel concludes that "the main contours of presidential and candidate activity under examination here, from Kennedy through Reagan in a period reflecting vast changes in the political environment, lead to a conclusion different from the conventional wisdom of cynics and other nonbelievers."[15] "[W]hen presidential candidates make reasonably specific promises about future domestic policy, take those promises seriously! Most of the time."[16]

Party Behavior

The same is true of party platforms. After a careful analysis of the per-iod between 1944 and 1966 and 1968 through 1978, Gerald Pomper concludes that "pledges are indeed redeemed. In the earlier two decades, over half the commitments met by direct congressional or executive action were fulfilled. When similar actions or appropriate inactions are included, nearly three-fourths of all promises were kept. During the last decade [1968–1978] ... almost two-thirds of all promises were fulfilled in some fashion, with 30 percent directly enacted through congressional or executive initiatives."[17] Similarly, Ian Budge and Richard Hofferbert found "strong links between postwar (1948–1985) election platforms and governmental outputs."[18]

Congressional Behavior

Congressional action also belies the claim that politicians are motivated by a self-interest at odds with the public interest. So, for example, Paul Quirk points out in his analysis of deregulation of the airline,
trucking, and telecommunications industries that "despite the political
benefits available to committee leaders in their relationships with
interest groups, they have strong moral, electoral, and institutional
incentives to lead their committees to respond effectively to general
interests.... Committee leaders know that their decisions on legislation have major consequences for public policy and the condition of
American society. To some extent this encourages greater concern for
the public effects of those decisions and a greater disposition to decide
on the merits."[19] He concludes that "the capacity of Congress to
respond to general interests and to act on ideas about those interests is
not limited to rare episodes like the abolition of an anticompetitive
regulatory program or the adoption of a major tax reform bill. Though
often overridden by special-interest politics, this tendency is regularly a
prominent feature of congressional policymaking."[20]

Because issue positions play an important role in the selection and
election of candidates, there is a strong correlation between a member
of Congress's position on an issue and "the mean opinion of his or her
constituents," a conclusion borne out in a careful study of the Survey
Research Center's 1978 survey.[21] Still, it is clear that, as elections near,
politicians are more likely to vote the wishes of their constituents than
their conscience when the two collide. So, for example, senators usually
vote their consciences on regulatory matters when re-election is a more
distant prospect.[22] Since they are elected to represent those in their districts or states, however, it is conceivable that these votes are either
consistent or at least not at odds with the public's self-interest.

In a system of representative democracy, voters elect individuals to
respond to their local interests. The good of a member of Congress's
constituents is for them at least and undoubtedly for the member a
public good. It is unlikely that the so-called special interests will overwhelm the specific interests of those constituents when they are at
odds, regardless of the number of political action dollars flowing from
those so-called special interests into the member's campaign. Support for this position can be drawn from the evidence that "PACs' allo-

cations are dominated by local inputs — recommendations of active members of the PACs at the state, congressional district, and county levels."[23]

Studies of the impact of money on political behavior suffer from a number of methodological problems. Cross-sectional studies are plagued by what social scientists call temporal order problem. As a result, it is difficult to decisively dismiss the explanation that "PACs are merely helping out those members who have the wisdom to agree with their own quite defensible view of the public interest."[24] Time series analysis is also problematic because "changes in legislative voting that occur after changes in special interest contributions may signify that donors, on average, correctly anticipate which candidates will support their interests in the future."[25]

To answer the causality question, Stephen Bronars and John Lott analyzed 731 multiterm members of Congress who held office between 1977 and 1990. By 1990, 291 had left the House, with 95 of them retiring. They asked whether the voting patterns of those who had not received special interest contributions differed from those who had in their second-to-last and last terms. They concluded by rejecting "the notion that campaign contributions buy politician's votes." "While it is not possible for us to say that none of the congressmen ever sold their votes for donations," they add, "our estimates demonstrate a remarkable degree of stability in voting patterns over time."[26]

Other evidence corroborates that conclusion. In his important book *Inside Campaign Finance*, Frank Sorauf concludes that "using larger bodies of data — large numbers of roll-call votes, for instance — and more sophisticated measures of correlation, they [scholars] generally find little if any relationship between the money and the votes."[27] So, for example, John Wright's study of the PACs of the American Medical Association, the realtors, the American Bankers Association, the general contractors, and the automobile dealers concluded that their political contributions only shifted predicted votes slightly.[28] Contrary to the implication of news accounts, the influence of money is likely to be marginally felt and on matters not attracting high levels of media and public attention. After interviewing twenty-five former members of Congress on the role of money in politics, Martin Schram concluded that "members were in rare agreement on one seldom-spoken fact of legislative life: Special interests are generally most successful at achieving their goals in Congress on matters that are relatively minor and unimportant to the general public *and thus ignored by the news media*—but that can be of multimillion-dollar importance to a single corporation, or entire industry, or other special interest [emphasis added]."[29]

The notion that narrow self-interest drives attraction to and action in public office is undercut by many of the behaviors members engage in once they are elected. An examination of the committee assignments most coveted by members of Congress does not suggest that exercise of patronage and control of benefits are the highest motivators of service. "Nor are the most sought-after committees in Congress those that dispense benefits to constituents, such as Public Works," writes Steven Kelman, "or those that help members procure a stable of eager campaign workers, such as Post Office and Civil Service. They are, rather, the committees that deal with broad issues of national policy."[30]

A legislator's ideology does play a role in legislative behavior.[31] A casual glance at recent history confirms a number of key moments in which individuals took political risks with the confidence either that the outcome would not jeopardize re-election or that the principle involved was worth the risk. George Bush's acceptance of a tax increase after building a campaign bid on "Read My Lips No New Taxes" is one such instance. Another can be found in the votes by members of Congress for an assault-weapons ban in the last Congress. In some cases, members paid for those votes with their seats.

Indeed candidates who tell the electorate things it presumably does not want to hear have been rewarded with the perception that they are courageous, a phenomenon that benefited the candidacies of John Anderson, who advocated a gasoline tax in 1980, Paul Tsongas, who predicated his 1992 candidacy on the need for sacrifice, and Ross Perot who captured 19 percent of the votes cast in 1992 with a message of increased taxation, reduced deductions, and a need to balance the budget. Moreover, President Bill Clinton's support of NAFTA and his decision to intervene in Bosnia both bucked public opinion.

The existing agreement between the Republican Congress and the Democratic president that deep cuts in Medicare are required to balance the budget provides another such message. "Whether you agree or not with this year's freshman Republicans," writes the Washington bureau chief of the *Wall Street Journal*, "they certainly demonstrated that not every member of Congress panders to opinion polls. And any reporter who's spent time on Capitol Hill knows there are many more seasoned members who struggle daily with important national issues trying to do the right thing."[32]

It is, in short, not self-evident that congressional and presidential self-interest are necessarily incompatible with the public interest or that either electoral branch acts out of narrow self-interest in opposition to the public interest much of the time.

This analysis leads us to concur with Thomas Mann and Norman Ornstein that "the healthy skepticism that long characterized public attitudes toward the institution [of Congress] has degenerated into corrosive cynicism."[33] The distinction between cynicism and skepticism is an important one.

Skepticism or Cynicism?

Broadly translated, the Greek *skeptikos* means "inquirer." The skeptics were at direct odds with the dogmatists who believed that they possessed certain knowledge. Their philosophical posture dictated that skeptics be ongoing investigators who did not accept or reject final conclusions. Among other things, the philosopher Pyrrho of Elis, who founded Greek skepticism, "is credited with the fundamental skeptical rhythm of *isosthenia,* or the balancing of opposite opinions; *epoch,* or suspension of opinion."[34]

One form of skepticism holds that we lack knowledge, another that we have no knowledge at all.[35] The second form was embodied in the position of Arcesilaus who supposedly said "that he was certain of nothing — not even of the fact that he was certain of nothing."[36] The skeptical hypothesis "can be used to show that our beliefs fall short of being certain and it can be used to show that they are not even justified."[37]

In the seventeenth century, Pierre Bayle would hold that, since proof of truth or falsity is impossible, we should tolerate all beliefs and ideas. At the same time, Bayle believed that careful reasoning could expose error.

The skeptics are remembered for a series of analytic moves designed to ensure that one is not deceived. These included the principle that data from one's senses are unreliable; by contrast, the cynics are associated with a rhetorical form — that embodies a set of assumptions the skeptic would find problematic. Classical cynicism polished what was at the time a new rhetorical form, the satire.[38] Having embraced a model of ascetic virtue, cynics set out to draw converts to it by unmasking the false virtue of others.

One of the early cynics himself fell victim to the form of cynicism that defines contemporary use of the term. When Peregrinus illustrated his contempt for death by immolating himself, "Lucian assumes that his action was due simply to a love of notoriety"—a conclusion that causes the historian of philosophy Frederick Copleston to make one of the points we are advancing in this chapter. "The motive of vainglory may very well have entered in, but it may not have been the sole motive operative with Peregrinus."[39]

Centuries later, the original positive meaning of cynic has been replaced by a pejorative. The *OED* defines a cynic as "a person disposed to rail or find fault; now usually: one who shows a disposition to disbelieve in the sincerity or goodness of human motives and actions, and is wont to express this by sneers and sarcasms; a sneering fault-finder."[40] There were medical incarnations as well, including the "Cynic spasm, a convulsive contraction of the facial muscles of one side so that the teeth are shown in the manner of an angry dog."

The notion that newspapers are cynical is not new. In 1881, an analyst condemned "the bitter cynicism of the newspaper satirists."[41]

In saying that the press ought to be skeptical not cynical, we are adopting contemporary usage. Skepticism, *Webster's* states, is "the doctrine that all knowledge is uncertain; also, the method of suspended judgment, criticism, or doubt."[42] Alternatively, the cynic is "(1) one of a Greek school of philosophers who taught that virtue is the only good, and that its essence lies in self-control and independence. Later Cynics were violent critics of social customs and current philosophies. (2) Hence, a faultfinding, captious critic, a misanthrope; specif., one who believes that human conduct is motivated wholly by self interest."[43] *New York Times* columnist Tom Friedman phrases the distinction well. "Skepticism is about asking questions, being dubious, being wary, not being gullible. Cynicism is about already having the answers —or thinking you do.... The skeptic says, 'I don't think that's true. I'm going to check it out.' The cynic says, 'I know that's not true. It couldn't be. I'm going to slam him.'"[44]

Some see in the rise of cynicism the "weakening...of that world known as democratic civil society, a world of groups and associations and ties that bind."[45] Indeed, a growing sense of "stalemate, gridlock, cynicism ... [may promote] a spiral of delegitimation."[46]

The Meaning of the Rise in Cynicism

A rich tradition of inquiry asks what evidence of public mistrust or distrust means. In an early work, Arthur H. Miller saw decline in "trust of government" indicators as a sign of erosion in the legitimacy of the political system.[47] Subsequent research showed, however, that many who expressed low trust in institutions also expressed strong support for democratic norms.[48] A comprehensive survey, encompassing the jump in confidence during the early Reagan years, ultimately led Seymour Lipset and William Schneider to conclude that "the confidence gap never amounted to a full-scale legitimacy crisis. Americans retained their faith in the country's basic institutional order. The polls always showed a deep-seated allegiance to the values of democracy and free enterprise."[49]

Origins of Cynicism

How such indicators arose, also aroused curiosity. Some attribute the breakdown of the civil society to a corrosive individualism that has spawned what in earlier times would have been an oxymoron — the label "private citizen." "We are concerned," write Robert Bellah and his colleagues, "that this individualism may have grown cancerous—that it may be destroying those social integuments that Tocqueville saw as moderating its more destructive potentialities, that it may be threatening the survival of freedom itself."[50]

Others see it as a by-product of the age's preoccupation with psychological explanations. Robert Coles recalls the impulse to believe that a patient believed or thought that she believed what she said. "That self-serving afterthought is, of course, the heart of the matter for me and my kind," he writes. "It is our conviction that there is an ultimate or bed-rock psychological reality to whose depths and contours we are especially privy."[51] As communication scholar James Carey has argued, the primary mode of explanation for journalists is one that focuses on motive. Politicians are agents with intentions. Their intentions explain their actions. In this explanatory frame, what is seen most often to motivate politicians is gaining political power or political advantage.[52]

By supplanting the what of politics with the why, we have interiorized the process, making it about the psyche and self of individual politicians rather than about policies and their outcomes on the lives of the citizenry. By answering the question Why? through the assumption of self-interest in conflict with public interest, we risk casting everyone in political life as a venal schemer.

Political scientists explain cynicism as the by-product of failed promises, policies, and performance. Was public distrust, as Joseph Schumpeter's work would suggest,[53] a reflection of the delivery of services by the state, with overpromising undermining political support? Were voters dissatisfied with the policy alternatives set before them by the major parties,[54] with, as Miller showed, the most cynical the ones who disapproved of the policy alternatives offered by both Humphrey and Nixon in 1968? Was it, as Jack Citrin argued, that cynicism was the by-product of dissatisfaction with the incumbents not the policy alternatives they offered[55] a conclusion that seemed to be borne out by the correlation in 1972 data between approval of presidential performance, positive affect for the president, and trust?

Some in the press also see cynicism fueled by unkept campaign promises. "Certainly," writes George Will, "the president whose campaign promise of a middle-class tax cut was patently disingenuous should not be amazed if Americans (in his words) 'indulge in the luxury of cynicism.'"[56]

Others blame the discourse of politics with its reliance on sloganeering, negativism, and attacks on political institutions.

An Increase in Slippery Slogans. For decades, pundits and politicians have decried the corruption of public discourse. Politics is often conducted in a language whose evasions invite cynicism. "We live," noted Eisenhower in 1960, "in a sea of semantic disorder in which old labels no longer faithfully describe. Police states are called 'people's democracies.' Armed conquest of free people is called 'liberation.' Such slippery slogans make more difficult the problem of communicating true faith, facts and beliefs. We must make clear our peaceful intentions, our aspirations for a better world. So doing, we must use language to enlighten the mind, not as an instrument of the studied innuendo and distorter of truth. And we must live by what we say."[57]

Yet the discourse of Eisenhower's time was comparatively constructive and candid. Note the difference between the current debate about who is actually cutting the deficit and Eisenhower's statement in his 1960 annual message. "I repeat, this budget will be a balanced one. Expenditures will be 79 billion 8 hundred million. The amount of income over outgo, described in the budget as a Surplus, to be applied against our national debt, is 4 billion 2 hundred million. Personally, I do not feel that any amount can properly be called a 'Surplus' as long as the nation is in debt. I prefer to think of such an item as 'reduction on our children's inherited mortgage.' Once we establish such payments as normal practice, we can profitably make improvements in our tax structure and thereby truly reduce the heavy burdens of taxation."[58]

The Way Politicians Campaign. Running against government, Washington, insider politics, and Congress is a stock-in trade of federal elections. The result is an irony. Candidates are elected by undercutting the institution of which they are or aspire to be a part. "Members of Congress run *for* Congress by running *against* Congress," observes Richard Fenno. "The strategy is ubiquitous, addictive, cost-free and foolproof.... In the short run, everybody plays and nearly everybody wins. Yet the institution bleeds from 435 separate cuts."[59]

Nor does the pervasive negativism of contemporary campaigns inspire institutional confidence. "The good news for New Jersey," wrote George Will in 1989, "is that neither of the congressmen trying to become governor is the contemptible mudslinging, fear-mongering, character-assassinating, truth-shading, tendentious, trivializing demagogue that both seem to be. The bad news for the nation is that New Jersey's campaign illustrates a virulent, contagious sickness spreading through American politics, a plague of pre-emptive assaults and escalating tawdriness."[60]

"I wish Dole weren't running," opines a campaign consultant about the 1996 presidential race. "I do hate being against him. And in fact, I told Lamar [Alexander] I will never make an untrue, vicious, negative ad about Bob Dole. Gramm is another thing. And I will gut him like a catfish."[61]

All these factors — a corrosive individualism, a psychological impulse, negative, anti-institutional, sloganeering campaigns, and disjunctures between the promise and performance of leaders may have contributed to the escalation in public cynicism about institutions. To them, we wish to add a number of specific practices of the press.

The Press

Concerns about public confidence in politicians and the press have been around for a long time. Founder Benjamin Franklin, printer and publisher, was among the country's earliest press critics. "Those who follow printing are scarce able to do anything which shall not probably give offense to some and perhaps to many," he noted.[62]

Nonetheless, there is evidence that, in democracy's early days, the press contributed significantly to civic activity. After examining the role newspapers played in the Upper Connecticut River Valley from 1780 to 1835, William Gilmore concludes that they and the other print media "greatly increased interest and participation in rural public life."[63] Indeed, Tocqueville praised the country's newspapers for "maintain[ing] civilization."[64]

Still, a well-established contemporary tradition blames the press for public cynicism. "[T]he White House press is totally dedicated to screwing us rather than getting the facts and reporting them," reported Nixon aide H. R. Haldeman in his diary.[65] "I have fought more damn battles here for more things than any president has in 20 years with the possible exception of Reagan's first budget," noted Bill Clinton two and a half decades later, "and not gotten one damn bit of credit from the knee-jerk liberal press, and I am sick and tired of it."[66] Newly elected Speaker Newt Gingrich agreed. Campaigning against the press's "scandalmongering" and "pervasive cynicism," Gingrich observed in January 1995 after the White House meeting mentioned in the last chapter that "it would be nice for the national press corps to report accurately that it was a positive meeting, and not to rush off and immediately try to find some way to get a cat fight started."[67]

Republicans and Democrats, members of the House and the Senate offer confirmation. "You come out of a legislative conference and there's reporters standing around with their ears twitching," comments Wyoming Republican Senator Alan Simpson. "They don't want to know whether anything was resolved for the betterment of the United States. They want to know who got hammered, who tricked whom.... They're not interested in clarity. They're interested in confusion and controversy and conflict."[68] "I do not remember a time when the press was as negative as it is," says Massachusetts Democrat Barney Frank. "I am now enjoying the best press of my life. And it's because I am attacking people and being negative. I get much more attention for three wisecracks and a point of order than I get for a full compromise to a difficult legislative solution."[69]

It is axiomatic that the media are most influential in shaping our sense of the world in those areas in which we have little direct experience.[70] Few of us have close contact with our leaders, their campaigns, or performance. We learn about them primarily through news reports. This fact has led some to claim that the public's knowledge of major institutions is a "mediated reality."[71] In *The Confidence Gap*, Lipset and Schneider argue that the news media are "primarily responsible for conveying to the public an impression of how the nation's institutions are performing."[72] The media figure in Richard Leone's account of confidence in government as well.[73]

If our knowledge of leaders and institutions is a "mediated" one, one might well ask, What effect, if any, does *how* candidates and public policy debates are covered have on public cynicism about leaders and their performance? We will argue that both the contemporary journalistic culture and a focus on strategy, conflict, and motives invite cynicism. "Do we increasingly substitute snideness for skepticism — and smart-ass pontification for legitimately aggressive questions?" asks David Shaw of the *Los Angeles Times*. "The answer, too often, is yes."[74]

Unsurprisingly, political consultants concur. Former Bush aide Mary Matalin observes, for example, that political operatives should avoid complimenting a reporter for fair treatment of their candidate. "It's the worst thing you can do to a reporter," she notes. "Michael Wines of the *New York Times* wrote a piece during the general election campaign [of 1992] that just stuck out as totally and completely fair.... Torie Clarke and some others of us who were on the trail at the time went to Michael that day and said, 'Thank you for a fair piece.' He looked at us like we had the plague.... The next thing we heard, a bunch of other reporters were grousing about Wines and accusing him of being a shill for Bush, of being 'in the tank.' By paying him a compliment we had compromised him. Reporters will always warn you, 'Just don't say anything good about me, it'll ruin my career.'"[75]

ABC News correspondent Jeff Greenfield agrees. In the post-Vietnam, post-Watergate era "the worst, the most embarrassing, humiliating thing is not that you accuse someone falsely but that you can be 'taken', that you can fail to accuse someone of something he ought to be accused of, that you can be spun by him."[76] Indeed, reporters perceived to treat Clinton too kindly are singled out for condemnation in the *New Republic*'s "Clinton Suck-Up Watch."

The press is preoccupied with conflict. "Our habits of mind," writes former *Washington Post* reporter Paul Taylor, "are shaped by what Lionel Trilling once described as the 'adversary culture.'"[77] Indeed, political scientist Larry J. Sabato subtitles his book *Feeding Frenzy*, an analogy between journalists and sharks, *How Attack Journalism Has Transformed American Politics.*[78]

Those cast as combatants are then portrayed as self-interested Machiavellians unconcerned with the public good.""The media ascribes political motivation to all official activities," writes Matalin. "The campaign tries mightily not to feed into their suspicions, lest the candidate appear propelled by political, as opposed to good-government, impulses."[79]

One result is negative coverage. Al Neuharth, founder of *USA Today* says he wants to provide a "journalism of hope" rather than a "journalism of despair." "If you look at newspapers in New York and Washington day in and day out, you'll find that negative stories far outnumber the positive," he says. "I think there is too much cynicism on the part of the metropolitan press especially. And that's why readers are as critical of journalism as they are."[80]

"Journalists usually err on the side of negativity," writes former *Wall Street Journal* reporter Ellen Hume.[81] Scholars see corroborative evidence in their studies. For more than two decades researchers have found that in the news that was not neutral, more was negative than positive.[82] And in many instances, there was more negative than positive news.[83] In 1980, for example, Michael Robinson and Margaret Sheehan concluded that the major candidates garnered more negative than positive coverage.[84] The same held true in 1984.[85]

The notion that bad news drives out good is a long-lived one confirmed by a number of studies of press practice.[86] It is important to qualify these findings, however, by noting that most study the national rather than the local press. As Michael Robinson observed in 1981, "The intuition that the news media are increasingly hostile to Congress fits best the reality of the *national* press. The evidence abounds."[87]

Studies of both Congress and presidential campaign have shown a rise in negative coverage. After analyzing press commentary from the three major newsweeklies and three major daily newspapers during ten important periods since the second world war, Mark Rozell concluded that "since World War II, the press has generally held Congress in low esteem. Deliberative, unexciting, usually uneventful, and often riddled with conflict, Congress is easily either ignored or criticized by the press. Negative and superficial congressional coverage is nothing new. But in recent years the extent and tone have become more severe, more disturbing. . . . Over the years press coverage of Congress has moved from healthy skepticism to outright cynicism."[88] Similarly, Thomas Patterson found an increase in unfavorable references to the major party nominees in *Time* and *Newsweek* paragraphs during the 1960–1992 period.[89] "Reporters have a variety of bad-news messages," reports Patterson, "but none more prevalent than the suggestion that the candidates cannot be trusted."[90]

These tendencies are all part of what such scholars as Patterson and Kathleen Hall Jamieson have called the game or strategy structure of contemporary journalism. In the past twenty years, media critics of news have noted a fundamental change in the distribution of media coverage from issue-based stories to ones that emphasize who is ahead and behind, and the strategies and tactics of campaigning necessary to position a candidate to get ahead or stay ahead.[91]

Jamieson argues that strategy coverage is marked by several features: (1) winning and losing as the central concern; (2) the language of wars, games, and competition; (3) a story with performers, critics, and audience (voters); (4) centrality of performance, style, and perception of the candidate; (5) heavy weighing of polls and the candidates standing in them.

Patterson characterizes strategy in an almost identical fashion, emphasizing that (1) the game of the campaign provides the plot of a story; (2) polls promote and support strategy coverage; (3) the electorate is positioned as spectators of candidates who are performers. Because journalists are interested in stories, and since election campaigns evolve as the ebb and flow of position in the race, it is "natural" to the journalistic endeavor that the happening that is the race is one of the primary objects of coverage.

Strategy coverage is not just an aspect of media coverage of politics but is becoming its dominant mode. From 1988 to 1992, horse-race coverage of election events on the nightly news rose 8 percent from 27 percent in 1988. Tracking polls accounted for another 33 percent. Policy coverage was down from 40 percent in 1988 to 33 percent in 1992. Patterson's studies of the *New York Times* front-page headlines from 1960 to 1992 (see his Figure 2.1, p. 74) show a stark contrast after 1972, with policy headlines taking a backseat to strategy coverage.

Jamieson has argued that the strategy frame is being generalized by journalists from campaigns to governance and discussions of public policy issues. In the health care reform debate, our own content analyses of print and broadcast coverage in major media markets show that

67 percent of newspaper articles were primarily strategic while 25 percent were basically issue oriented or factual; 67 percent of broadcast segments were strategic, and 20 percent issue based.

Strategy Coverage and Cynicism

There is a simple theory of human behavior behind the strategy approach to coverage. The theory goes like this. People do things for reasons. Some reasons are simple, some complicated; some are self-interested, some altruistic; some are aimed at controlling others, some at being controlled. So too for politics and political actors.

In the eyes of the electorate, politics is not an abstract, rational process; it is people. As people, politicians can and should be understood in the same way that other people are understood — by their motivations.

The central goal of campaigns, candidates, and elections is winning. When actions are placed in this interpretive frame, the motivation for action (of any sort, whether a policy or personal choice) is reduced to a single, simple human motivation—the desire to win and to take the power that elected office provides. In such an interpretive frame, all actions are tainted—they are seen not as the by-product of a desire to solve social ills, redirect national goals, or create a better future for our offspring but are instead viewed in terms of winning. Winning is equivalent to advancing one's own agenda, one's own self-interest, so the actions stand not for themselves but for the motivational system that gives rise to them — narrow self-interest. In this way, actions are reinterpretable as serving the candidate's underlying motivations.

In the strategy structure, policy positions are interpreted as a means of gaining a voter block to advance the candidacy or retain a position in the polls. Candidates' words and actions are seen as outward signs of strategic intent and cast as maneuvers rather than forms of self-expression.

Clearly, there is a story to be told about the relative positions of candidates in an election. An election is, after all, a process whose outcome is an important feature. The problem occurs when strategy stories dominate the news, crowding out discussions more relevant to issues of governance.

Take, for example, a hypothetical election for mayor. One of the candidates seeks to solve part of the city's financial problems by privatizing city services. This story can be covered by emphasizing the problems the city faces and how privatization will help to solve these problems or make them worse. The same issue can be covered by focusing on how privatization alienates certain voting constituencies and appeals to others, positioning candidate *X* favorably and candidate *Y* unfavorably with the electorate. When the privatization issue is told from the latter perspective, an issue is treated in a strategic style that we hypothesize will increase cynicism.

The easiest way to show differences between issue and strategy is to point to their uses. Where an issue story might report, as one of our broadcast stories in our mayoral experiment did, that candidates "Ed Rendell and Joseph Egan took turns outlining how they would run Philadelphia without raising taxes. They made their pitches to residents of the Spring Garden section of Philadelphia," the strategy condition dropped the tax information into the middle of the story and led simply by saying that they "took turns tonight making pitches to residents of the Spring Garden section of Philadelphia."

In the televised version of the experiment, the anchor told those receiving strategy coverage, "As the race for mayor of Philadelphia heats up this week, channel X will be taking you behind the scenes in the campaign. We'll be looking at the trials and tribulations of the mayoral candidates . . . who's winning in the ad wars and who's losing in the polls." By contrast, those seeing an issue version of the same story heard the same anchor say, "Throughout the race for mayor of Philadelphia this Fall, channel X will be bringing you in-depth coverage of the campaign. We'll be looking at what the candidates are saying, how they are saying it, and what those positions mean to the voters of Philadelphia."

The contrast between strategy and issue conditions is evident in such headlines as

> Egan comes out fighting, with jabs flying at Rendell. (strategy)
> Rendell firm on privatization, Egan calls it "divisive." (issue)
>
> Rendell makes a sales pitch to black voters. (strategy)
> Rendell hints Williams will retain police job. (issue)
>
> In debate, four candidates urge change. (issue)
> No knock-out by Egan. (strategy)

Where one strategy lead suggested that the candidate was motivated by polls, the issue one said that he was trying to reach out to voters. "With polls showing him on the ropes in the black community," reads a strategy paragraph, "Edward G. Rendell said yesterday that if he were elected mayor, he would keep Police Commissioner Willie L Williams on the job and would support a black candidate for City Council president." The issue paragraph began instead by saying, "Reaching out to black voters in the final weeks of the mayoral campaign. . . ."

Where strategy articles analogized the process to sports contests and war, the issue condition used the more neutral language of agreement and disagreement. "Turning the other cheek," noted a strategy article, "Democratic front-runner Edward G. Rendell took punch after punch last night as Republican Joseph M. Egan Jr. pummelled him in a televised debate as a liar, a failed leader and someone whose approach to city unions would be 'divisive.'"

Under the headline "Egan's strategy: lure democratic voters," a strategy story said, "Portraying himself as a populist with his finger on the voters' pulse and demonstrating that he is in tune with the polls, underdog Republican mayoral candidate Joseph M. Egan Jr. said yesterday that he wanted to set up 10 mini-city halls throughout the city." Bearing the headline "Egan wants to set up neighborhood city halls," the issue version opened by saying "Joseph M. Egan took his campaign to a half-century-old town hall in historic Germantown yesterday to promote what he called his 'revolutionary' plan to decentralize Philadelphia government by establishing 10 little city halls around the city."[92]

Our hypotheses about the effects of strategy coverage are not meant to suggest that journalists reason this way or that they believe that candidates are only driven by a single motivation — self-interest and the desire to win. However, if candidates are presented as if this were the case and if people's experience of the political process is only through the vicarious experience provided by the media, then the perception of candidates, campaigns, and perhaps even governance may become dominated by this interpretive frame.

Patterson, Jamieson, and others have argued that excessive strategy coverage may activate cynicism in the electorate. Cynicism may result from the spectatorship that the strategy format engenders. Alternatively, it could be produced if strategy coverage engenders involvement with the story. The story has conflict, tragedy, pathos, and joy. But the story being told is one with a particular set of motivations propelling the characters. It is the story of men and women driven to win at all costs.

Strategic coverage may, in other words, invite the attribution of cynical motives to political actors in campaigns and public policy debates, not because voters are distanced from the process but precisely because they are drawn into it and, through a rational analysis of the politicians whose motives they have come to know, reject the actors and ultimately the process.

But do any of these subtle distinctions in news content make a difference? One scholarly tradition holds that neither the process by which politicians campaign[93] nor the way in which the broadcast and print press cover politics has much effect. Indeed, one analyst summarizes the existing literature by saying that he has not "found any evidence that these changes [i.e., horse-race coverage and sound-bite journalism] have affected the quality of American Democracy in any significant way."[94] To the contrary, we wish to argue that there are good theoretical and empirical reasons for being concerned about the effects.

If, as various agenda-setting, framing, and priming studies have shown, media coverage can shape how the public thinks about politics,[95] it seems plausible to see press coverage as a factor — albeit not the sole factor — in declining confidence in such institutions as Congress.[96]

In her 1994 Theodore White lecture at Harvard's Joan Shorenstein Center, ABC's Cokie Roberts recalled the belief of some that "the press won Watergate." She added, "My question now is, What have we won, lately? And have we made it harder for the system to work? And is that clash, between politicians and the press, undermining our institutions so fundamentally that their very survival is called into question?"[97] After four years of research that included extensive content analysis and several controlled field experiments, this book answers the question, Has the press made it harder for the system to work? in the affirmative. Making that case is our next task.

❱ 3

FRAMING THE NEWS

WHEN SCHOLARS speak of framing, those not steeped in the jargon may recall that builders speak of framing a house and photographers of framing their subjects. Each offers a way to explain our use of the word. Like the framing of a house, a news frame creates a structure on which other elements are built. There is much in a house that is not the frame, but without the frame there is no house. And the frame determines the shape of the house.

A photographer frames her subjects by setting boundaries, choosing contexts, selecting and manipulating light. The act of framing determines what is included and excluded, what is salient and what is unimportant. It focuses the viewer's attention on its subjects in specific ways. The objects in the photograph are presented in a setting and illuminated to create visual effects. The photographer's act of framing binds its subjects together in a distinctive way; another photographer framing the same subject would produce a recognizably different picture.

The news frame we focus on is an organized set of assumptions that implies and often explicitly state that leaders are self-interested to the exclusion of the public good, that their votes can be swayed by monied or special interests that do not serve their constituents' ends, and that they are dishonest about what they are trying to accomplish and driven privately by a desire to stay in power. Explaining what they are doing to "win" or why they are "losing" is the resulting form of campaign coverage. Hence the phrase "strategic coverage."

Some would call this structure a schema or a script. We reserve these terms for the knowledge that audiences have, and use the term "frames" to describe the structuring of texts.

Conceptualizing Frames

In a 1991 article, three political psychologists argued that the concept of "schema," typically understood as an organized knowledge structure through which information is processed by an audience, was overblown, overused, and little more than a new word to capture old ideas.[1] They lamented that research on how political schemata affected judgments was no different from research into ideology, attitude, public opinion, or evaluation and affect—concepts long a part of the conceptual tools of political scientists.

A similar claim can be made about the concept of framing. When applied to the structuring of news and other texts, this concept suffers from two problems. First, it has been used in different ways in several different disciplines to mean different things. A general definition of framing seems to reduce to "the way the story is written or produced," including the orienting headlines, the specific word choices, the rhetorical devices employed, the narrative form, and so on. Any production feature of the verbal or visual text would seem to qualify at least as a candidate for framing the news. This view is clearly too broad. Second, differences in framing have been assumed to yield differences in outcome.

The first problem produces conceptual indeterminacy. Framing would be so diffuse that any stylistic or thematic feature differentiating one text from another could be fairly described as a difference in framing. In this chapter, we review some of the ways framing has been used in the literature and conclude that news frames are those rhetorical and stylistic choices, reliably identified in news, that alter the interpretations of the topics treated and are a consistent part of the news environment. In our view, framing *is* a very general process, but one that deserves study where particular frames carried by specific stylistic and rhetorical devices are reliably identified and consistently utilized.

The second problem points to a confusion between the framing of news and the effects that framing can be shown to have. This simple distinction is crucial for scholars trying to understand the consequences of what may be small differences in texts potentially magnified over many people and many iterations. If there are no reliable and demonstrable consequences for news differing in its rhetorical and stylistic format, then critics and watchdogs should remain silent. Moreover, they should be skeptical of their own conclusions about the effects of news frames in the absence of evidence about consequences.

Framing Devices

In a 1967 book, Paul Watzlawick, Janet Beavin, and Donald Jackson made a distinction between the *command* and *report* aspects of communication — with command referring to *what is said* and report to *how what is said is said*.[2] The distinction was one of the central tenets of their theory of communication. It emphasized the assumption that how messages are understood and the responses they create are as dependent on how messages are formatted as on what the messages are about.

Although Watzlawick, Beavin, and Jackson offered few specifics to distinguish the "what" and "how" of messages, subsequent writers in the cognitive and decision sciences and in political science and communication have made much of the distinction while remaining unaware of its roots in the literatures of psychotherapy and anthropology that guided the Watzlawick group. Cognitive scientists have adopted the terminology of framing to capture the notion that reacting to and comprehending a set of propositions depends on the context within which the propositions are set.[3] These contexts provide the framework within which understanding and subsequent response occur.

Consider what is perhaps the classic example of two messages identical in what they say but differing in how they say it. In a widely cited study, Daniel Kahneman and Amos Tversky showed that simple word changes can produce significant differences in the choices people make.[4] Here is the task they posed:

> Imagine that the United States is preparing for the outbreak of an unusual Asian disease, which is expected to kill 600 people. Two alternative programs to combat the disease have been proposed. Assume that the exact scientific estimates of the consequences of the program are as follows:
>
> If program A is adopted, 200 people will be saved.
> (Chosen by 72 percent)
>
> If program B is adopted, there is a one-third probability that 600 people will be saved, and a two-thirds probability that no people will be saved.
> (Chosen by 28 percent)

A second group received the same instructions with two options that had slightly different wordings.

> If program A is adopted, 400 people will die.
> (Chosen by 22 percent)
>
> If program B is adopted, there is a one-third probability that nobody will die and a two-thirds probability that 600 people will die.
> (Chosen by 78 percent).

Notice that the first choices given to the two groups are formally identical, yet the change in emphasis from gains in the first wording to losses in the second reduces its selection from 7 in 10 to 2 in 10.

Kahneman and Tversky's effects have been described in the language of framing. Although what is said is formally identical in the two cases, how it is said changes. Substantial alterations in the choices made by readers follow.

These effects may be the result of differing interpretations of a text invited by one frame instead of another. The context in which a text is read can seriously affect how the text is understood. Consider the following paragraph invented for research about comprehension:[5]

> The procedure is actually quite simple. First you arrange things into different groups. Of course, one pile may be sufficient depending upon how much there is to do. If you have to go somewhere else due to lack of facilities that is the next step, otherwise you are pretty well set. It is important not to overdo things. That is, it is better to do too few things at once than too many. In the short run this may not seem important but complications

can easily arise. A mistake can be expensive as well. At first the whole procedure will seem complicated. Soon, however, it will simply become just another facet of life. It is difficult to foresee any end to the necessity for this task in the immediate future, but one can never tell. After the procedure is completed one arranges the materials into different groups again. Then they can be put into the appropriate places. Eventually they will be used once more and the whole cycle will have to be repeated. However, that is a part of life.

Most people find this paragraph incomprehensible. The words and sentences are simple enough but they do not cohere because they do not (or seem not to) refer to anything. However, when readers are first cued that the topic is "washing clothes," then there is no confusion. What seemed to be an incoherent text is suddenly unproblematic. The hint serves to provide a frame of reference within which unreferenced pronouns have reference and unconnected ideas are connected.

How do these unseen connections suddenly become obvious? A preexisting set of knowledge, including concepts, procedures, and, most important, their interconnection, has been cued and brought into conscious awareness. Once they are available, the passage immediately makes sense since it now has a clear interpretation previously absent. Framing provides context that in turn activates prior knowledge. The activated knowledge in cooperation with the text produce an understanding of the text that neither alone can supply. Framing then serves as an explicit context within which texts are interpreted (and through these interpretations judgments rendered), and information recalled.

Frames not only make the interpretations possible but they also alter the kinds of inferences made. The inferences derive from well-established knowledge structures held by the audience and cued by the messages read or watched. Under many circumstances, these inferences allow for an efficient form of communication where some things can be left unsaid while being readily supplied by the reader. Under other circumstances, the inferences may be misleading, misdirected, or simply false.

In one study, people read a passage about the struggles of a young woman to overcome difficulties in her life. Some were told the passage was about Helen Keller and others were not. Those believing the story was about Keller falsely indicated that they had read statements such as "She was deaf and dumb" as a part of the initial message.[6] Similar kinds of false inferences have been observed with commonly understood scripts such as sequences of events in restaurants. Readers falsely attributed to the text sentences describing what would have typically occurred in a restaurant but were not actually part of the text.[7]

Even small wording changes can alter judgments in significant ways if the audience has prior knowledge that is readily activated. Thomas Gilovich had subjects read a scenario about military intervention by the United States in defending a hypothetical foreign country from invasion by one of its neighbors.[8] One of the scenarios had phrases indirectly reminding readers of the Vietnam War by mentioning "chinook helicopters" and briefings taking place in "Dean Rusk Hall." In deciding whether intervention was a wise choice, respondents leaned away from that option. When the language indirectly cued memories of World War II through phrases like "blitzkrieg invasion" and briefings in "Winston Churchill Hall," greater support for intervention resulted, even though respondents did not see the scenarios as similar to Vietnam or World War II. What is surprising about these findings is that memories for historical events whose implications for intervention (WW II) and against intervention (Vietnam) could affect judgments even in the absence of directly activating memories for the events.

Racial and sexual stereotypes are often a well-established part of an audience's knowledge. When they are, they can also be readily activated by some simple framing devices with consequences for judgment and evaluation. Galen Bodenhausen asked people to role play jurors in a hypothetical court case.[9] All received the same information except for the type and timing of the defendant's name: a stereotypically Hispanic versus WASP name and before the transcript or after. Judgments of guilt were stronger for the Hispanic name when it occurred before the transcript. Mark Snyder and Seymour Uranowitz gave people a biography of a young woman asking them to recall information about her life.[10] When she was later identified as a lesbian rather than a heterosexual, the details recalled tended to fit the sexual framing. For example, those told she was a lesbian usually failed to recall an item from her biography indicating that she had dated boys.

The activation of stereotypes does not have to be as conscious as in the jury study or the lesbian-heterosexual study.[11] People were showed lists of words that were below the threshold of recognition and were associated with stereotypes of African Americans. The list included terms such as lazy, dumb, athletic, and musical but avoided any words suggesting violence or hostility. Others were exposed to a more neutral list. Both groups then read a story about a person who demanded his money back from a store clerk while acting in an ambiguously hostile manner. Those who had been exposed to the words cuing an African-American stereotype rated the hypothetical customer's behavior as more hostile than those getting the neutral list, even though 98 percent of the subjects could guess none of the words from the lists correctly. Both prejudiced and nonprejudiced subjects made the same judgments.

Frames may be explicit components of messages, implied by word or name selections in the text of the message, or even activated in the audience without the audience's awareness that activation has taken place. The consequences for what is recalled, how messages are interpreted, and how people and policies are judged can be serious.

These examples show that, in controlled conditions, small changes in wording or orientation can have significant effects on understanding and choice. Other research supports the same conclusion.[12] These examples also suggest that framing can either operate within messages or outside them, creating a context within which the message is understood.

Framing effects seem to be caused by a variety of techniques from explicit changes in titles to subtle selections of wordings and even to using cue words that are not explicitly recognized by readers. Are all these techniques equivalent manifestations of the same underlying framing procedure?

Framing the News

The way the news is framed by journalists and how the audience frames the news it consumes may be similar or different.[13] A news story meant to evoke an emotional identification by framing its characters sympathetically may instead evoke blame directed at the victims as Shanto Iyengar found in some of his research on episodic and thematic frames.[14] Most scholars agree that the interpretation derived from the reception of any message is a simultaneous function of both the message (and how it is framed) and the knowledge the audience brings to bear during the process of interpretation.[15] News should be no different from any other text. To understand how news frames function, they must be kept conceptually distinct from the audience's schemata, even though the interaction between the two is the locus of interpretation and judgment.

Erving Goffman, despite his roots in the disciplines of anthropology and sociology, locates frames in the audience's classifications and categorizations of the social and physical world rather than in the social rules themselves.[16] Todd Gitlin anchors the frame to news texts by identifying the "persistent patterns of cognition, interpretation, and presentation, of selection, emphasis, and exclusion"[17] *employed by journalists* that become the routine organizations for visual and verbal news texts.[18] The effects of news frames on the Students for a Democratic Society were explored in Gitlin's historical account of the rise and undoing of the New Left in the 1960s. The historical audience's acceptance of the frames imposed by the press was never in question in Gitlin's discussion. William Gamson conceptualized frames as central organizing themes in news accounts at least initially,[19] but in later work he argued that persons interact with the themes imposed by mainstream media constructing their own themes for understanding social and political events.[20]

Robert Entman's definition emphasizes selection and salience:

> To frame is to select some aspects of perceived reality and make them more salient in a communicating context, in such a way as to promote a particular problem definition, causal interpretation, moral evaluation, and/or treatment recommendation.[21]

Salience and selection emphasize that framing includes not only what is made prominent but also what is left out, treated as secondary, tertiary, or less. Other definitions elaborate what is meant by salience in the framing context: "The central organizing idea for news content that supplies a context and suggests what the issue is through the use of selection, emphasis, exclusion, and elaboration."[22] In both definitions, framing is a way of drawing attention to certain features of an issue while minimizing attention to others.

Frames may have an agenda-setting function by virtue of giving exposure to certain topics and their related subtopics and forcing others into the background. But, as Entman points out, framing is more than agenda setting. It is not simply putting topics in the forefront of public discourse and backgrounding others. Rather, framing provides a way to *think about* events. Entman puts it this way:

> Frames, then, *define problems* — determine what a causal agent is doing with what costs and benefits, usually measured in terms of common cultur-

al values; *diagnose causes* — identify the forces creating the problem; *make moral judgments* — evaluate causal agents and their effects; and *suggest remedies* — offer and justify treatments for the problems and predict their likely effects.[23]

In short, a frame provides a way to *understand* a set of events. But how frames invite sense-making through definition, diagnosis, judgment, and remedy while adhering to journalistic norms of the appearance of objectivity is less clear. The options are as open-ended as the processes of print and broadcast production.

Zhongdong Pan and Gerald Kosicki, using discourse analysis as their model, describe some of the options available to journalists for accomplishing framing.[24] The authors are careful to distinguish the frames that operate within news texts from those operating in the minds of news consumers.[25] News texts are a form of discourse subject to four broad organizing structures: syntactical, thematic, script, and rhetorical. Syntactical structures refer not to grammar but more to typical sequences of headline, lead, episode, background, and closure. Thematic structures represent a particular thesis pertinent to a problem; for example, the thesis that the accident at Three Mile Island was human failure rather than technology run amok. Scripts are standard story lines that create narrative tension. For example, the success of candidates doing "better than expected" in primaries (even with 17 percent of the vote) and the dismal failure of those doing "worse than expected." Rhetorical devices include stylistic choices to help convey the character of the account. For example, to give the impression of journalistic objectivity after the Simpson verdict — while replaying tapes of jubilant blacks and glum whites — polling results about the verdict by race might be displayed.

Pan and Kosicki's comprehensive approach to treating framing in terms of the available descriptions of any discourse invites us to think of framing in terms of the devices available to writers and producers for presenting newsworthy events. Entman's more abstract conceptualization of framing seems distant from Pan and Kosicki's discussion of the nitty-gritty of the creation of visual and verbal news texts. Yet, as we tried to show in earlier examples, both small wording changes and larger contextual cues can generate significantly different textual interpretations.

In fact, news frames can be quite specific. To understand and investigate their effects, these specifics must be spelled out. Content analyses and the study of news norms have revealed several specific news frames that occur regularly. The strategy or game frame, discussed in Chapter 2, is a prominent one and will be our main focus. Others include an emphasis on conflict, personality, specific events with human interest, and culturally defined story lines (e.g., the underdog).[26]

Frames may be able to activate knowledge, stimulate stocks of cultural mores and values, and create contexts within which what are typically called media effects are produced. Frames are not just ways of representing news content; they have implications for processing news, and are the predictive basis for observed effects of news formats on citizens.

News frames appear to be complex, achieving their effects, if any, simultaneously at both abstract and specific levels. We have no doubt that microscopic distinctions between news formats and abstract but arcane differences between news formats can produce different consequences in audiences' understanding and judgment (especially in tightly controlled experimental contexts). But the differences in framing news that have the potential to matter in understanding news effects must meet three criteria in our view. First, the frame should have identifiable conceptual and linguistic characteristics. Second, it should be commonly observed in journalistic practice. Third, the frames should be able to be reliably distinguished from other frames.[27]

The first criterion assures that the frame can be identified from features of the text, not just from its effects. The second criterion means that what is studied for its potential effects is a frequent and regular occurrence in the experience of the news- consuming public. The third assures that the frames under study are able to be recognized by news consumers and not just by the isolated expert re-running the video player frame by frame. Highly specialized or arcane aspects of discourse may indeed have effects on attitudes, judgments, and interpretations, but news frames that matter to public attitudes and behaviors must be common, regular, and reliably distinguished. Not every possible difference between news texts is a consequential difference in framing.

We believe that the strategy frame meets the criteria for being an identifiable and potentially consequential format for the presentation of news. In Chapter 2, we described and illustrated the strategy news frame in campaigns and public policy debates. In the health care reform debate, our research team coded both broadcast and print news about the debate from January 15, 1994, through October 15, 1994. More than 1900 print news stories and over 900 broadcast news segments were evaluated. Two-thirds of the broadcast segments and 62 percent of the print were reliably identified as primarily strategic in format. Other research on other topics confirms the observation that strategic coverage of politics is endemic — whether the focus is campaigns or policy debates.[28] The pervasiveness of strategy as a format raises questions about its impact on the public's interpretations of events and its political judgments. But questions are not answers.

Is Framing an Effect?

Establishing that framing operates in controlled settings with simple messages doesn't necessarily mean that it affects comprehension and outcomes in more realistic contexts where the messages are more complex and the audiences subject to a variety of influences. In the day-to-day world, other social, ideological, and psychological forces may simply wipe out the subtle differences that distinguish one frame from another.

Constructing, understanding, and proving the existence of framing in the news is in no way equivalent to determining its effects on the consumer. We make this claim for logical, practical, social, and psychological reasons. Logically, the mere existence of framing differences between two messages or message campaigns does not necessarily imply differences in effects. Effects are found in people's knowledge, attitudes, and behavior, or in the public's priorities and opinions. Frames are in messages or in the construction of those messages. The two worlds may be connected — indeed this book's thesis is that they are — but the connection is *not* a foregone conclusion. The framing of a message does not logically imply its consequences for receivers.

Practically speaking, all the pundits cannot be right at the same time. For every commentator or scholar who claims that negative coverage is undermining the public's confidence in social institutions is an equally credible spokesperson for the adaptability and sophistication of the news consumer. Listen to almost any discussion about media and politics among experts whether on C-SPAN or *Cross-Fire* or PBS's *The*

Evening News Hour with Jim Lehrer. If one pundit argues that media coverage will elevate the public's cynicism about Congress despite legislative successes, another will surely maintain that the public is sophisticated and able to separate the games of journalists from the substance of the achievements being described. Even political and media experts imply effects that flow from content without firm basis for their inferences.

Socially, framing of news is not and cannot be assumed to inevitably influence the public's attitudes, knowledge, and behavior. Even if framing effects are present and significant, the effects of personal experience, even indirect experience, or influence from others[29] can mask or even reverse the effects of framing alone.[30] Additionally, cynicism about the mainstream media can lead consumers to downplay the credibility of these messages or seek competing information as an antidote to the frames permeating coverage. Simply put, even if the effects of media frames are consequential, they are not the only sources of influence on the audience. Other sources may mask, amplify, or catalyze framing effects.

In one of the first books written on weaknesses in human decision making under limited information, Richard Nisbett and Lee Ross cited a comment by one of their colleagues that puts framing effects in perspective.[31] The colleague chided, "If we're so dumb, how come we made it to the moon?" The point is well taken. Analogously, readers, viewers, and listeners are assumed to be susceptible to the slightest changes in news coverage. They are viewed as incapable of seeing beyond the media's framing of an issue to the issue itself. They are treated as malleable vessels whose own framing of news is no match for that of the politicians and news institutions. This view underestimates the intellectual skills of news consumers who are capable of using cognitive shortcuts — heuristics — to arrive at accurate conclusions and are willing to construct their own frames in opposition to those offered in the news.[32]

We are not denying that framing effects exist; instead we are arguing that they cannot be established simply by claiming that since frames exist, framing effects thereby exist. Yet, this is what many scholars do. For example, Entman argues that if the news environment is dominated by a particular frame of reference to the exclusion of all others, receivers are "clearly affected" because no other interpretations or frames are available to them.[33] This view ignores people's ability to think through the issues by using their own knowledge or that gleaned from other sources. It assumes what is to be proven.

Patterson has carefully documented changes in news coverage of presidential politics in the past thirty years.[34] He is usually careful to avoid moving from description of content to assumed effects. But why study changes in the nature of the media's coverage of politics if such changes do not produce effects? Indeed, Patterson assumes they do: The game schema "directs attention toward certain activities and away from others but also affects the significance attached to these activities"[35] and

> when voters encounter game-centered stories, they behave more like specta-
> tors than participants in the election, responding, if at all, to the status of
> the race, not to what the candidates represent. On the other hand stories
> about issues and the candidates' qualifications ... cultivate more involve-
> ment.[36]

In the final paragraph of his chapter on horse-race coverage, the claim that the news media's focus on strategic coverage creates cynicism in the electorate is boldly displayed: "By emphasizing the game dimension day after day, the press forces it to the forefront, strengthening the voters' mistrust of the candidates and reducing their sense of involvement."[37] These plausible hypotheses are suppositions, but suppositions are not facts. Content differences are not effects.[38]

Framing and framing effects must be assumed to be separate until proven otherwise. And the proof must be as direct and realistic as possible.

Previous Research on Framing Effects

Research on framing effects in news is found in three broad areas: cognitive and decision science, question effects in public opinion polling, and what we call simulation studies in political science and communication. The research on framing in cognitive and decision science[39] is extensive, carried out in a wide variety of arenas from problem solving to health and consumer decisions. However, this research is not primarily about news or politics, and it tends to sacrifice realism for control.

The research on context effects in public opinion polling uses nationally representative samples on issues of immediate relevance to politics, policy, and governance.[40] However, it is focused primarily on the effects of question wording and question order in surveys and is not fundamentally concerned with the ways news is framed.

Simulation studies attempt to mimic exposure to realistic news, selected or edited to reflect one framing of an issue versus another, and observe the subsequent effects, if any. These studies typically sacrifice some control for realism, do not employ nationally representative samples (although samples are usually more representative than those in cognitive and decision science), and are expensive to conduct. There are very few simulation studies.

Agenda setting and Media Priming

Two important media effects — agenda setting and media priming — are sometimes viewed as framing effects. Scholars of agenda setting find a consistent relationship between the prominence that the news media give to a topic and the importance of that topic in the public mind. The effect shows up as a correlation between the frequency of a topic covered by the news media and its ranking in public opinion polls.

Agenda setting has a long and venerable history in survey research[41] and a shorter one in experimental studies.[42] The agenda-setting correlation has been found in cross-sectional surveys and time series analyses.[43] To call agenda setting a framing effect, however, stretches the meaning of framing beyond what is reasonable. Agenda setting results from the frequency with which a subject is discussed in the news media with no attention paid to how the subject is treated. For example, when the president's health care reform plan is discussed, it matters not at all to the researcher in agenda setting whether the news report focuses on universal coverage as necessary to the plan's functioning or on universal coverage as appealing to the president's constituency in the lower and middle classes. The way the issue is framed is not consequential to the agenda-setting hypothesis. Its presence as a topic is the only concern. In our view, agenda setting is an important and well-established media effect, but it is not directly relevant to framing.

Media priming is a relatively new hypothesis — compared to agenda setting — in the media effects literature. Its authors, Shanto Iyengar and Donald Kinder, refer to it as "priming"[44] but we will use the longer "media priming" to avoid confusion with a process called cognitive priming,[45] discussed later. Media priming is a cousin of agenda setting, but results in greater impact on overall judgments for topics treated by the media than topics given no or lesser treatment.

In their experimental and survey studies, Iyengar and Kinder found that political issues receiving more news attention were afforded greater weight in people's judgments of political actors who also had some direct responsibility for issues. For example, judgments of the president's performance may depend on his handling of a variety of economic, domestic, international, and political issues. The media-priming effect shows that if a particular domestic issue — say, balancing the budget — is receiving a lot of attention in the news, people's judgments of overall performance will depend more on how they feel the president is doing on balancing the budget than on an issue getting little attention. Unlike agenda setting, a priming hypothesis posits that the media are responsible both for the ranking of issue *importance* and also for the use voters make of the issue in judging their leaders.[46]

Media priming is a robust effect that has been successfully tested in experimental and survey contexts,[47] consistently supporting the claim that media alter the impact issues have on judgments by giving those issues more and less prominence. But media priming, like agenda setting, is not concerned with how issues are treated in news coverage, only with their relative frequency. Priming would treat a story about President Clinton's decision to send troops to Haiti described as a ploy to drum up support prior to fall elections as equivalent to a story about sending troops to Haiti to ensure the return of democracy. These two stories are framed rather differently, but they are equivalent from the viewpoint of media priming.

Iyengar and Kinder performed a variation on their priming paradigm aimed at intensifying the effect as a function of framing. Consider two news stories focused on the same issue to the same degree. One emphasizes, for example, the president's responsibility for the problem of health care reform while the other simply stresses the problem of health care reform. Of the two, the story emphasizing responsibility should produce a stronger priming effect. In this example, by making responsibility important, the news story frames the issue to maximize its impact on judgments of the president's performance.

Iyengar and Kinder's tests consistently show that emphasizing responsibility strengthens impact. However, these effects are not strong and often fall short of normal levels of statistical significance.[48]

Their studies deal primarily with agenda setting and priming rather than framing. When framing is invoked, the results are either weak or framing per se is not actually studied.

Attempts to manipulate perceived responsibility led to Iyengar's later work on framing, which asked whether episodic television news stories altered attributions of responsibility.[49] Iyengar conducted a series of studies in which viewers were exposed to one of two types of news coverage: personal, anecdotal reports focusing on concrete instances (episodic coverage) or thematic reports treating the topic in a more general or abstract way, sometimes called a "background" story. The question is whether these two frames lead to different attributions of responsibility for the problems depicted in the news story — toward the individuals involved or toward social conditions. Although not every topic worked as he expected, Iyengar obtained support for his claim that episodic frames tend to elicit attributions of responsibility to individuals rather than social conditions. Because episodic reporting tends to focus on individuals and their actions instead of on social forces, its effects may be due to an increased accessibility of person-focused words, concepts, and images. With such a focus, viewers could be biased toward making attributions to actors on newscasts much as they do in face-to-face situations. These biases take the form of the fundamental attribution error and the actor–observer bias — explaining others' behaviors in terms of their character and motive and one's own behavior as a by-product of the surrounding situation.[50]

Iyengar's research is among the best on framing effects in news, using, as it does, realistic broadcast news segments and a population broader than college sophomores. Although it is one of the very few empirical demonstrations of framing effects, its focus is on attributions of responsibility, and has no direct implications for our inquiry into strategy frames and cynical responses.

Framing Political Ads

The power of news to frame ads has also been studied. During the presidential campaign of 1992, major news networks reviewed political campaign ads using a "grammar" for displaying and criticizing the ads developed in part by the Annenberg School. Instead of running the ads full screen from beginning to end and, when they were over, offering some critical commentary, Jamieson suggested that the news reports place the ad in a mock television screen, move the screen into the background, attach a news logo and a notice that the ad was for a particular candidate, and put print correctors on the screen. Especially significant was that the ad was not played from beginning to end, but was stopped when criticisms were made.

The purpose of the ad-watch grammar and critique was to reframe the ad in the context of corrective commentary. There had been considerable speculation that merely replaying parts of negative political ads would effectively give free national air time to the very notions and images that were supposed to be contextualized.[51] At least one study later supported these speculations.[52] Another did not.

Stephen Ansolabehere and Shanto Iyengar had people view ad watches directed at ads by Clinton's presidential campaign and then President Bush's campaign.[53] In three studies, those who saw the ad watch *increased* their preference for the candidate who was the target of the critique by the CNN commentator. Here the ad watch seemed to boomerang, making the sponsor of the criticized ad the more rather than less desirable candidate in the eyes of viewers. This counterintuitive finding can be understood by focusing on the content of the particular ad watch. In each case, the ad watch *supported* the gist of the claims made in the ad and primarily offered small caveats and reservations. Unlike most ad watches, these did not accuse the ad makers of fundamental deceits. We believe that Ansolabehere and Iyengar's evidence shows that the ad watches worked as intended.

The consequence, in our opinion, is that these ad watches gave the ads — and the candidates whose campaigns they represented — credibility. The results were therefore consistent with the evaluative push provided by the ad watches. Instead of framing the ads critically, the ad watches used by Ansolabehere and Iyengar actually framed the ads in a supportive way, reinforcing instead of undercutting their credibility.

We conducted a study to evaluate the effectiveness of the reframing intended by the ad watch grammar on learning, attitudes toward the source and the target, and the perceived justification of the ad.[54] The offending ad was a misleading attack by Pat Buchanan directed at George Bush during the 1992 Michigan primary. The ad watch was done by CNN in several versions for our study. The study's actual design was somewhat complicated. In brief, study participants received a series of one-hour videotapes of television programming to view in their homes each day (some received six, some four, and some three hours). Every hour of tape included the Buchanan ad. Except for the control, every other group also received a version of the CNN ad watch once early in the viewing period. The content of the ad watch was highly critical of the Buchanan ad.

People exposed to an ad watch evaluated the Buchanan ad as less important and fair than those who did not see the ad watch. The ad watch downplayed the ad's significance in the eyes of the audience. One possible explanation for the effects of ad watches is interpretive reframing.[55] The ad watch may alter interpretations of the ad in ways that undermine the ad's impact. This process in turn affects attitudes toward the ad and its sponsors. This could account for the fact that the ad watch did not increase accuracy of interpretation for all in the study. The more educated (some college and higher) did show small but significant increases in interpretive accuracy; the least educated did not.

Another explanation is "on-line impression formation."[56] When people are required to make a decision as information comes in (that is "on line") and are exposed to a great deal of relevant but complex information, they are more likely to form an overall attitude on the spot rather than carefully process and retain the information pertinent to the decision. When on-line impression formation occurs, an impression can be formed and reported even though there is no indication that the subject has retained the information on which it is based. This shows up as a lack of correlation between the information retrieved and the impression formed. People exposed to the ad watch altered their attitudes toward the ad and its sponsor, but were unable to recall the interpretations that could have presumably produced these effects.

When exposed to the ad watch, those with lower levels of education may pick up the tone of the ad watch, ignoring or forgetting many of its informational details, and later apply the impression to the ad without modifying the specific interpretations of the ad's content.

From Ads to Press Coverage

If, as various agenda-setting, media-priming, and framing studies have shown, media coverage can shape how the public thinks about politics,[57] it seems plausible to view press coverage as a factor in declining confidence in such institutions as Congress and the federal government.[58]

Michael Robinson's analysis of 1968 Survey Research Center data found that those who reported relying solely on television for news content were 23 percent more likely to hold that members of Congress quickly lose touch with their constituents than those who relied on media other than television for their news.[59] What Robinson could not know was whether those who were more cynical to begin with were more likely consumers of television news. Those reliant on television for news were distinguished from those reliant on newspapers but the study could not know what those likely watchers of television news were actually watching or what they were gaining from network newscasts.

In an attempt to overcome some of these methodological obstacles, Arthur Miller and his colleagues tied the self-reports contained in a survey to an analysis of the content the respondents reported focusing on. Their analysis of the 1974 American National Election Study data and the front-page content of ninety-four newspapers found that "readers of highly critical papers were more distrustful of government; but the impact of criticism on the more stable attitude of political efficacy was modest."[60] To draw this conclusion, the researchers matched respondents with the paper they actually reported reading. The model they offered posited that criticism by news mediated people's political understandings, ultimately affecting political malaise. Again, it is difficult to posit causality. Perhaps cynics were drawn to the more critical coverage. Nor could the researchers actually know that it was the front pages of these papers that these readers were actually reading.

Establishing causality requires knowing the cynicism level respondents brought to the study and being able to accurately characterize the content they actually read and watched.

Summary

The concept of framing has influenced the study of message effects for several decades in communication research and political science. Framing is a very general phenomenon whose specific effects cannot be anticipated until the nature and structure of a particular message frame have been uncovered.

Content analyses and critical assessments of news practices have been indispensable in guiding research toward the potential effects of news frames. It makes little sense to conduct expensive research into news frames that are infrequent, insufficiently described, or not a consistent component of the news environment.

Strategic frames for news have also become well established in research content analyzing and critically assessing the news. At the same time, the existence of a common frame — the strategic frame — for reporting campaigns, governance, and policy debates is not sufficient to imply its effects. Establishing the effects of any mediated message is a difficult task requiring the balancing of control, realism, representative samples, and representative messages. These problems are especially difficult when studying framing effects. Framing the news is a question of slant, structure, emphasis, selection, word choice, and context. The effects of framing, if any, will be subtle ones. They require direct access to the messages processed by news consumers, not long inferential leaps from assumptions about what is being read and watched. Although much speculation has championed the significance of framing for bending and shaping public opinion, too little research has been done to support such speculations.

Media priming and agenda setting are two effects well established in the research literature. Their far-reaching implications suggest that what is covered in the news affects what the public thinks and how it judges its leaders. Some have suggested that strategic news formats — focusing as they do on competition, conflict, performance and artifice, hidden motivation, and self-interest — may also have consequential effects on the public's attitudes toward its leaders and its government. Can public cynicism be attributed in part to the fourth estate? Not, in our opinion, without first establishing that such effects exist.

We next turn to a theoretical account of how the effects of news frames might be produced in audiences and, specifically, how strategic news might activate cynical reactions.

》 4

THE COGNITIVE BASES
FOR FRAMING EFFECTS

HOW AUDIENCES process news cognitively is central to understanding the effects of news content and news frames. In this chapter we offer an account of the psychology of the audience to set the groundwork for our studies of the effects of news frames on learning, cynicism, and understanding. Our discussion focuses specifically on the strategy frame and how it might interact with the audience's knowledge and normal cognitive functions.

News frames make salient certain features of a news event and depress others. What is salient in a story primes mental associations in the receiver and, through a process of spreading activation in the knowledge system, stimulates other, related concepts as well. Strategic frames invite negative attributions about political actors because the stories suggest that politicians are motivated by self-interest. These attributions may be automatic in the sense of being effortless and, after repeated application, may become the accepted narrative account organizing thinking about a politician or politicians in general.

We proceed first by discussing some general principles of the organization of knowledge and information processing; second, we discuss the importance of stories and narrative to understanding, recall, and the organization of knowledge; third, we take up the role of news in creating impressions of the political actors it discusses; fourth, we build from news and impression formation to account for the way strategic news frames might affect trust; finally, we explain existing findings on agenda setting, media priming, and framing in terms of our model of the psychology of news processing.

Previewing the Theory

Our theory may be summarized as follows:

1. Knowledge of politics is organized as connections among concepts or constructs in memory (sometimes called "nodes") that differ in how easily they can be accessed. These nodes hold substantive, emotional, and personal trait qualities.

2. The pattern of connections is through associations (sometimes hierarchical ones); activation spreads through the knowledge store along these lines of association.

3. Access to knowledge depends on activation, which in turn depends on recency and frequency of prior activation, chronic ease of access, and current external stimulation.

4. Framing makes certain information in a news story salient and depresses the importance of other information. News frames stimulate access to certain information, making it more accessible at least temporarily. Priming and the spread of activation are the mechanisms through which news frames stimulate thought processes and emotional reactions.

5. The knowledge activated by news frames accomplished through priming and spreading activation alters the accessibility of beliefs through changes in the ease of activation and through cuing scripts (or stock stories) pertinent to the topic.

6. The judgments activated by news frames take place in two ways: recall of information as the basis for political judgments; tallying the affective implications of information as judgments (i.e., on-line).

7. News frames that describe the behavior of a political actor or entity invite inferences by the citizen about the character of the actor (sometimes called character traits). These traits are both knowledge about the entity and have evaluative implications for how the person feels about the actor. When a single trait is implicated again and again, it can become the organizing "theme" for the person's theory about the actor or about political actors in general.

8. Strategic frames describe the behavior of politicians, make salient the self-interest of those actions, invite negative character attributions, cue stock stories about "politics as usual," and reinforce cynicism (as mistrust).

9. News stories, even those strategically framed, often carry substantive information about issues, albeit set in the context of self-interested manipulation. Attentive exposure can alter political knowledge by increasing the accessibility of information, changing the associations among constructs, and cuing and strengthening existing localized networks of concepts.

In the following sections, we develop the components of the explanation.

Knowledge, Association, and Spreading Activation

Any serious explanation of the process of learning and political judgment must begin with assumptions about how people organize the information they have and how they organize information about politics in particular.[1]

Models of how knowledge is stored in memory are numerous and diverse. Some assume that there are both visual and conceptual bases to knowledge,[2] others argue that propositional structures are all that we need.[3] Some models adopt the view that constructs are linked through networks of association that are hierarchical,[4] associational without hierarchy or differentiation,[5] or associational with some hierarchical structure.[6]

We cannot determine which model of knowledge storage is correct because current research tools do not allow direct access to the mental storehouse of knowledge. So the best assumptions are those that work to solve problems and paradoxes in observable data. We assume that knowledge is stored as a network of associations between nodes where the linkages vary from no connection to strongly connected. Nodes can be concepts such as "health reform" and "HMO," character traits such as "aggressive" or "intelligent," and affective components such as "liked" or "enthusiastic."

A key principle of an associative knowledge network is *spreading activation*.[7] This principle holds that whenever a focal node is brought into conscious awareness (i.e., is activated), some of its activation is then transferred to nodes that are linked to the focal node. The stronger the association, the greater the likelihood that a neighboring node will also be brought into awareness.

Positing an associative network with spreading activation as the basis of knowledge systems allows the explanation of three pervasive processes: cognitive priming, distortion, and inference-making. Cognitive priming refers to the well-established fact that activation of a construct stimulates neighboring constructs so that subsequent recall of the neighbors is easier than if no previous priming had taken place.[8] Another way to describe priming is that associates of the activated construct are made more accessible for later recall. For example, after reading newspaper stories about candidates for mayor during the previous week, people later asked to recall information from a televised debate among the candidates should find it easier, argue proponents of priming, to retrieve information from the debate than people who read news about something else. The principle is that using one's knowledge not only makes recall of the activated knowledge easier but also facilitates recall of related information.

Distortion and inference-making are closely related phenomena. They both require inferences, but distortion typically implies logically or pragmatically unacceptable inferences while simple inference-making does not. Stereotyping[9] can involve both distortion and inference-making. A study by Thomas Gilovich[10] described earlier shows how patterns of association can yield inferences that go beyond the information presented. Participants chose a more interventionist and aggressive solution to a military problem when the language cued World War II rather than Vietnam. One account of these findings argues that by priming World War II, inferences associated with avoiding the errors of appeasement were activated, whereas such notions as the hazards of foreign entanglements were primed by Vietnam inferences.

A substantial body of research suggests that the cues a text makes salient can alter what is recalled, what is inferred, how events are judged, and how events are interpreted. This research has focused on social stereotypes,[11] sexual minorities,[12] person perception,[13] and even biographies of famous personalities.[14] These inferential processes are central to our ability to understand texts. Without inference, only excruciatingly detailed texts would be easily interpreted.[15] These same necessary inference processes all show that simple cues activate related knowledge, altering what readers attribute to texts and the actors portrayed there.

The point of this excursion into inference, distortion, and priming is to make clear their centrality to ordinary information processing activities. Associative networks and spreading activation provide the outlines of an explanation of these important processes. Some treatments of mental models have adopted the script or schema view of knowledge organization to explain inference-making, person perception, and stereotyping.[16] Although we have no quarrel with this approach to the modeling of knowledge (and invoke it later) it is an unnecessary complication to the associative network with spreading activation. One way to view scripts and schemas is as specific patterns of linkage within an associative network of constructs. Priming, distortion, and inference-making can be explained by assuming that knowledge is organized as scripts or schemas. Parsimony suggests that associative networks governed by spreading activation are to be preferred.

Stories Organize Associative Networks

These networks of knowledge may also be the repositories of the stories people have acquired about politics that allow them to make sense of their too often confusing political and social worlds. We have labeled this the cognitive-narrative approach. Evaluations and judgments are the mediators of political outcomes. They are, however, a small part of the public and private discourse about politics. People do not only emote about politics, they lament it, explain it, and reason about it with other citizens.[17] Once they have stated their opinions and perhaps expressed their dismay, what do they say? Evaluations and judgments once stated may lead to a memory search for supporting information so that the judgments are seen by the interlocutor as having sufficient reason. They may also be supported by stock stories that help people make sense of their political and social worlds.

The study of narrative has a rich history in rhetoric and in litera-ture[18] but its treatment in cognitive science has been spotty.[19] In their recent essay, Roger Schank and Robert Abelson[20] have sought to change all this, arguing that:

1. Virtually all human knowledge is based on stories constructed around past experiences.

2. New experiences are interpreted in terms of old stories.

3. The content of story memories depends on whether and how they are told to others, and these reconstituted stories form the basis of the individual's remembered self.

Three propositions from this essay are important to the model we are proposing: (1) stories are the basis for understanding and making sense of events; (2) organizing information in the form of stories facil-itates retrieval of information; (3) salient cues in the environment can bias which story is activated.

Research in comprehension has long held that understanding new information depends on integrating the new into previously stored information that is itself already understood.[21] Schank and Abelson take this claim a step further by noting that what people know and understand best are stories; as a result, much of successful understand-ing is embedding new information in a story meaningful to the hearer: "Because we can only understand things that relate to our own experi-ences, it is actually very difficult for us to hear things that people say that are not interpretable through those experiences."[22] The new is understood in terms of the old:

> When a new story appears, we attempt to find a belief of ours that relates to it. When we do, we find a story attached to that belief and compare the story in our memory to the one we are processing. Our understanding of the new story becomes, at that point, a function of the old story.[23]

Little research has been done to evaluate Schank and Abelson's claims about stories and understanding. Nancy Pennington and Reid Hastie have shown that jurors try to comprehend the complexities of a criminal case by reducing the evidence to a story about the crime.[24] Their stories involve episodes from the evidence presented in the case, are usually consistent with legal norms, emphasize the motives of the accused, and mediate the jurors' confidence and decisions.

Many other decision-making contexts also yield stories as a part of the decision-making process,[25] but not all do. When specialists make decisions in their areas of expertise, the nature of the language, reasoning, and description is not particularly story-like.[26] Hastie and Pennington predict that stories are especially common when it is necessary "to organize a large, complex, conflict-filled collection of evidence as a temporal narrative summary . . . especially in social situations where communication, argumentation, and revision of both the evidence and decisions based upon it are sure to follow."[27] Even though they are not the only structures of knowledge used, stories can be a framework within which to bolster understanding.

Stories can also enhance the recall of information from memory by "preserving the connectivity of events that would otherwise be disassociated over time."[28] To do so, "they must be stored away in a fashion that enables them to be accessed as a unit. If this were not the case, stories would have to be reconstructed each time they were told, a process that would be more and more difficult as the connections between events fade from memory."[29] This view of the representation of stories in memory is quite speculative and we know of no empirical evidence to support or refute it.[30] A plausible alternative is a set of associations among constructs and personal episodes[31] that is activated when an appropriate cue is present in the environment, and that fades with disuse.

Less speculative is the facilitating effect of story memory on the retrieval of information. Those instructed to organize a set of unrelated test words into a story had five times the recall of a group told simply to remember the words.[32] Texts that have a strong narrative structure are read more quickly and material from them recalled better than when expository ones are used.[33] Stories also invite causal and motivational thinking that enhances recall. When readers report what they are thinking when they read stories, they sometimes report attributing causes and motives to the character. The more they do so, the better their later recall of the content of stories.[34]

The conditions that enhance memory are not well known, but narratives are certainly more likely to organize knowledge when the information being communicated is organized in a story format. The art of telling a good story is much of what is behind interesting journalism, good teaching, and being socially adept. It may also be part of the basis for remembering news, lessons, and people.

Which stored stories are activated depends in part on the subtle cues in the environment. What is made prominent by those who manipulate the symbolic environment activates and primes what is retrieved from memory. Schank and Abelson suggest that activation and priming apply not only to information retrieved from memory but also to entire stories. Some evidence supports the claim that scripts (or stereotypical stories) can be cued by sentences,[35] and proverbs primed by other proverbs with similar themes.[36]

If stories and story cues have the capacity to elicit stock stories existing in an audience, then in studying political news it is important to understand what kinds of stories about politics people hold and what categories of stories exist in the news environment. Such inquiry will help us understand how people make sense of their political worlds.

Stories About People

Central to a citizen's understanding of the role of stories in making sense of the behavior of political actors is understanding stories about people — what they are like, how they are organized, and what they imply. Most brief stories, whether or not they are about people, are organized around some theme. That theme may be the story's point or moral or it may simply be an organizing proposition. Themes organize stories and assist in the recall of information from the narrative.[37]

In stories about people, traits may play a role akin to themes in more general types of stories. Bernadette Park asked people to write open-ended descriptions of one another as they got acquainted over a seven-week period.[38] She found that individuals attributed traits to one another more frequently than anything else, including describing others' behavior, their physical attributes, attitudes toward them, and demographic characteristics. They did not begin by describing behaviors and other more directly observable features and then move to traits — traits organized their views right away. Later essays by these individuals considered whether the early trait attributions were correct and adjustments were made as writers deemed necessary.

Park concluded that traits organized people's impressions by combining in a shorthand way various behaviors and events.[39] To show this more rigorously, she took advantage of a cognitive process known as the fan effect.[40] As the number of pieces of disconnected information to be remembered increases, so does the response time to verify what has been previously learned. But the effect is reduced when the pieces of information to verify are conceptually organized. The organizing theme effectively interconnects the facts.

Park's studies of traits and behaviors indicated that when learned behaviors were organized around traits, the fan effect was reduced. This conclusion implies that traits organize behaviors and events and, in this sense, may be an organizing principle for our information about people.[41]

When people try to understand stories, they usually make inferences that allow them to bridge events whose connections are only implied. The kinds of inferences made during comprehension are ones that explain what is happening and these explanations are often motivations and causal antecedents for action.[42]

Stories about people are often concerned with their traits and their motivations. Persisting motivations can come to be seen as character traits. When research on understanding stories about people is combined with research on character judgments in evaluations of political candidates, it follows that character traits may organize impressions about political actors in the same way that they organize impressions about acquaintances.

Political Knowledge and Political Impressions

So far, our discussion of knowledge has been general and not involved its contents. The content of political knowledge — specifically, knowledge about candidates and elections — seems to revolve around two broad clusters: policy and position, and character and competence.

Richard Lau's 1986 analysis of the open-ended NES data from 1972 and 1976 concluded that voters organize political information in four clusters: issues, groups, personality, and party, with the same voters tending to rely on the same types of information when responding to different political stimuli.[43] So, for example, those with well-developed party information see party identification as more central to candidate evaluation than those without. Arthur Miller and his colleagues also analyzed the open-ended NES questions found broad groupings similar to those uncovered by Lau.[44]

These conclusions are consistent with others finding that policy positions and personal attributes formed two distinct clusters in memory.[45] Lau's analyses are consistent.[46] The position and person clusters become related when voters draw inferences about candidate traits from the candidate's position on issues. So, for example, voters in 1984 may have seen Mondale and Reagan's stands on defense spending as a sign that the individual candidate was strong or weak, competent or incompetent. Policy positions carried implications about candidates' character.

The process more often moves from issue to trait, from position on defense for example, to a self-interested reason for position on defense.[47] This direction of movement is consistent with both experimental and survey work, which suggests that people are more likely to draw inferences from issues to traits than vice versa.[48] The reasons are several. Just like everyone else who has to handle large quantities of information, voters are "cognitive misers." Instead of holding onto various detailed issue positions, these are reduced to personal qualities that are more familiar to the voter and can be further reduced to simple evaluations of the candidate in pro and con terms.

Second, impression formation is a common and continual daily activity in ordinary social encounters. Political decision-making is in many ways little different from forming impressions and making judgments about liking, competence, ability, and integrity. Donald Kinder and Susan Fiske argue that candidate appraisals are similar to personal appraisals.[49] Wendy Rahn and her colleagues present evidence showing that policy positions affect judgments of candidate competence and integrity.[50] This in turn affects overall evaluation of the candidate and likelihood of voting. In short, positions are the basis for impressions and impressions the basis for voting.[51]

Impressions — specifically, those relevant to emotional evaluation and voting — are central determinants of political judgments and may be a significant component of people's political knowledge, even that of sophisticated consumers. Knowledge of policy and position is not absent from the cognitive storehouse; instead it is mediated through impressions of personal character.

Automatic Inferences

The impressions that people form about politicians from their positions and their behaviors are kinds of inferences, specifically called *trait* inferences.[52] Trait inferences are an everyday process in ordinary social interaction. They are based on the behaviors people engage in and how those behaviors are represented.[53]

For example, if a candidate is described in news accounts as changing what he says depending on who is listening, performing for the cameras, and using equivocal language in position papers, one might infer that he is manipulative. This description is the larger category in which the other behaviors fit, but, more important, is an attribution about the candidate,[54] serving both to group his behaviors and explain them. The grouping is cognitively efficient and the labeling allows the audience to understand the candidate's behavior in ways consistent with ordinary interpersonal judgment.

One common assumption people make in explaining the behavior of others is what has been called the fundamental attribution error.[55] This "error" biases explanations of others' behavior toward personal interest or motive and away from situational or contextual reasons. The result is that trait inferences too readily become trait explanations, with the categorization of behaviors becoming the reason for behavior.[56]

Recent research has provided evidence that trait inferences from very simple texts are automatic. This means that people are allocating limited cognitive energy to this kind of inference while making the inferences without conscious awareness. The presence of automatic thought processes is generally based on solid evidence that is growing in depth and breadth.[57] Automatic priming of trait inferences was discovered in research by James Uleman and his colleagues.[58]

When people are required to read and remember sentences known to imply traits, they tend to find that the implied traits are better cues in later recall than words semantically similar to the contents of the original sentence. For example, the sentence "The secretary solves the mystery halfway through the book" implies that the secretary is clever. "Clever" turns out to be a better cue for surprise recall tests of the sentence than semantically related words, such as "typewriter" and "detective." Even though people are not asked to make trait inferences, they seem to do so, storing the trait inference as a part of the learning episode, as Tulving and Thompson suggested in their theory of episodic memory.[59] If the trait inferences were not made, it would be difficult to understand how they could be better cues in later, surprise recall than words meaningfully associated with the original sentences.

The likelihood that trait inferences are made depends in part on the task readers are given or the task implied by the kinds of questions asked. In one study passages that invited trait inferences lead to more inferences of this type than comparison passages with similar words but less likely to invite trait inferences.[60] Moreover, the trait inferences increased markedly when the researchers' questions suggested that the readers' tasks were either to form an impression or understand the passage rather than simply recall the facts of the passage. The authors note that thinking "of the traits used in this study as concepts linked together as part of a network of knowledge about dispositions, the present data suggest that the task variable affects how strongly the traits are activated."[61]

Impression formation and comprehension are tasks likely to guide consumers of political information under most circumstances. Trait inferences should follow whenever they are implied, even if reporters do not directly attribute them to the individuals in the news story.

Negative information about people and events has more alerting power than equivalent positive information. It carries more weight in social judgments[62] and is easier to recall.[63] These effects are well established, but they are usually assumed to apply only when the audience is actively attuned to the activity of monitoring what is negative and positive about stories. What happens to negative social information when people are passive consumers or are engaged in other activities? Does negative social information have any special status in these contexts?

When the traits inferred are potentially consequential to the reader's well-being, attention to such traits may be redirected toward them even when the person is engaged in relatively automatic processing of other materials. Felice Pratto and Oliver John asked people to respond to negative (e.g., selfish, intolerant) and positive (e.g., sincere, kind) trait words in the Stroop color test.[64] This test involves a highly automatic task in which people have to name the color of the word appearing on a screen as soon as possible. Their task is to attend to the word's color, not its meaning. The subjects were both accurate in doing so and very quick (about .650 seconds). The authors found that negative words slowed the speed of responding (by about 30 milliseconds), did not change accuracy of color recognition, and increased the accuracy of later (surprise) recall of the words. Common and uncommon negative words produced the same effect.

These data suggest that automatic vigilance regarding negative information is

a default response: ... [monitoring] potentially undesirable information when specific information processing goals are not active. ... Thus, bias toward undesirable information and the influence of such information on judgment seem most pronounced when people do not realize that such influences are occurring.[65]

When readers are processing information about candidates simply to understand and stay informed, they may be most susceptible to the biasing effects of negative trait inferences, attending a bit longer and learning a little more than with positive traits.

Summary

Let us summarize our conclusions so far. Political knowledge is organized as a set of associations among constructs more and less strongly linked. The activation of one or more constructs spreads to constructs linked to the activated ones. This organizational system for knowledge is compatible with explanations of priming and inference-making and minimizes the need for using the concept schema as an organizing vehicle. Narrative knowledge may be especially important in making sense of new information, retrieving old information, and organizing information in personally meaningful structures.

The content of political knowledge is centered on policy and position, and character and personality. The character traits of political actors are in large part the result of inferences from policy positions and spontaneous inferences from stories that imply trait inferences. Character traits are both the shorthand for organizing behavioral information and the organizing inferences in stories, especially stories about people. Negative traits are especially strongly weighted, producing attention and recall even when the audience is not consciously aware of the information's social implications.

The structure and organization of political knowledge set the stage for understanding framing effects in general, and strategic framing in particular. To explain the effects of news frames on learning and judgment requires understanding the processes by which political information stored in memory is used by more and less well-informed citizens who make political judgments.

From Knowledge to Political Judgments

Two processes have been hypothesized to link external messages, political knowledge, and political judgments: memory-based (MB) and on-line (OL). The memory-based approach assumes that political judgments depend on the integration of information retrieved from memory, and that what is retrieved depends on what is accessible. The clearest and most pertinent statement of this position about the framing effects of news is that of Vincent Price and David Tewksbury.[66]

The on-line approach assumes that the key information in a news story is evaluated and stored as an evaluation as it is processed. The basis for the evaluation is assumed to be lost. The strongest statement of this position in the arena of political judgment has been advanced by Milton Lodge.[67]

We examined each of these processes and reached three conclusions. First, both processes — memory-based and on-line — are needed to explain framing effects. What is learned from news, how the learned material is translated into emotion-laden evaluations, and how people understand and explain politics to one another are questions answered by a theory that finds a place for learning, forgetting, and sense-making. Second, we believe that Lodge's theory of on-line processing, which he offers as a position counter to memory-based processing, overstates the role of on-line evaluation and understates the role of retrieval. Third, the effects of news frames on learning, cynicism, and attitudes and lay explanations of politics can be seen as direct consequences of our theory.

Memory-based Judgments

Memory-based models of framing effects are based on the assumption that political judgments are the result of retrieving information that is accessible in memory. Accessibility in turn depends on several factors. These include how recently[68] and frequently[69] the information has been used, how chronically accessible[70] it is, and its current state of activation — either directly by outside stimulation or indirectly through stimulation and spreading activation (cognitive priming). Information that is accessible contributes to the evaluations made of political actors, policies, and events.

Price and Tewksbury's explanations of media priming, framing, and agenda setting are memory-based accounts that offer a careful, detailed examination of the processes by which information in memory is made more or less accessible. They argue that all three media effects are the result of changes in accessibility of stored information. When the news media adopt a relatively consistent approach to what is reported or how what is reported is framed, then the news environment is homogeneous and so are the patterns of activation of knowledge. Under these conditions, changes in the accessibility of knowledge can be attributed to the what and how of news coverage.

The memory-based model reduces media effects to accessibility effects. What is accessible is retrieved and what is retrieved is the basis for judgment, interpretation, and action. The position presented by Price and Tewksbury offers a thorough discussion of the complexities of accessibility. However, the link between what is retrieved and how this information enters into political judgments is given a less detailed explication.

Over thirty years ago, in research on how people were judged, verbal and impression memory were distinguished.[71] Verbal memory was the repository of raw, unadulterated information; impression memory was the summary evaluation based on reception, extraction of evaluative implications, and integration into an overall evaluation. Subsequent work has aimed at providing a theory of how incoming information affects valuation and integration necessary for understanding how judgments are made.[72] The view is *not consistent* with the assumption that the information is stored, then retrieved, then valued, and then integrated. The research shows instead that people remember best recently received information, and their evaluation is determined more by what is presented first. Hence, two different repositories and processes are posited.

In a 1975 monograph on attitude formation, Martin Fishbein and Icek Ajzen reviewed literature on the relationship between beliefs recalled and a person's attitude. They concluded that "there appears to be little evidence for the hypothesis that belief statements consistent with a person's own position are recalled or recognized better than belief statements inconsistent with his position."[73]

Simply put, the attitudes people report do not seem to be related to the beliefs that are supposed to support those attitudes. The link between judgment and what is accessible from memory appears tenuous.[74]

On-line Judgments

Hastie and Park[75] proposed a resolution of this paradox by distinguishing between two types of *tasks*:[76] those in which judgments occur as information is being processed (on-line tasks) and those in which judgment is suspended while information is processed and stored (memory-based tasks). When instructions led people to make judgments on-line, correlations between the overall evaluation and memory measures were low. When judgment was suspended until after the information was processed, correlations between judgment and memory were more substantial. The authors interpret these findings to suggest that under most circumstances people build evaluations as they consume information. Since the basis of the evaluation is not stored with the evaluation, the recall-judgment relationship is weak. When the judgment is a surprise, recall of pertinent information forms the basis of the judgment and the correlation between recalled information and judgment is enhanced. But if most of the tasks of everyday information processing are treated as if they are on-line judgment tasks, then accessibility of memory as the basis for judgment may be over-rated. If Hastie and Park's findings are robust, holding in the context of more realistic political judgments and not just the hypothetical person judgments of the laboratory, then accessibility of information may be a misleading route to political judgment.

Two important studies by Lodge and his colleagues offer the basis for claiming that political judgments are made on-line and that the memory-based models of judgment are misleading.[77] We will argue that Lodge's conclusions offer a necessary balance to the emphasis on memory-based processes of judgment. However, we will also conclude that balance is the key to understanding judgment. A reasonable model of political learning and judgment from news requires both on-line and memory-based components.

Lodge, McGraw, and Stroh conducted a field experiment in which people read position statements by hypothetical Republican and Democratic candidates for office.[78] One group read forty position statements for their grammaticality (the memory-based task). Later, after giving their overall evaluation of the candidates, they evaluated the statements. The other group read the forty statements, rated them in terms of liking and disliking, and were instructed to use the statements to "form an overall impression of the candidate while rating the issues" (p. 404). Evaluations of the issue positions done while reading them were strongly correlated with evaluations of the candidate. Correlations between remembered issues and candidate evaluation were not significant except in the memory-based task. When reading candidate profiles in order to form an impression, issue evaluations were strongly related to individuals' overall evaluation of the candidate but their later recall was not. When distracted from forming an impression, memory for issues is related to candidate evaluation.

The authors seem to dismiss memory for issues as a basis for judgment when they conclude "voters do not typically rely on their memory for specific issues to inform their evaluation but instead call up their tally when asked for an evaluation."[79] This interpretation is too strong, we think. First, the instructions to those in the on-line group were too direct. They were told to use the issue stands to form an impression. They did and these effects were strong. The presence of the on-line effects may be as much the result of strong and unnatural instructions as they are of real on-line processing of candidate profiles. If people treat tasks such as processing news and reading profiles as on-line tasks, then the instructions in this condition are unnecessary and produce experimental demand.

Second, the memory group is given an equally strong and unusual instruction — to evaluate the grammaticality of the statements. The instruction to process superficially would reduce memorability[80] and distract readers from the content of what they are consuming. The experimental instructions afford little opportunity to process information in a manner that reflects the way people ordinarily consume news or politics. Under realistic conditions of news processing, people are not told to form impressions or to evaluate grammar. Rather, they try to understand what they are reading and evaluate it. Under such circumstances, the on-line judgments might have been less strong and the memory-based judgments stronger predictors of outcome.

We do not deny that the absence of correlation between memory-based judgments and candidate evaluation is a solid effect, consistent with many others reported in the research literature. The absence of a correlation between memory and judgment along with the presence of an on-line correlation is consistent with the existence of an on-line evaluation process. But potential problems with experimental demand in the on-line task instructions and the unrealistic instructions in the memory-based task lead us to be hesitant in assuming that memory-based judgments do not occur in real political contexts.

A recent study offered a further test of the role of on-line and memory-based processes in political judgment.[81] This work provided a testing opportunity more realistic than the first study. People first completed attitude and opinion surveys and then read a campaign fact sheet—like those used in local media—about two hypothetical candidates. Half the participants then evaluated the candidate and listed likes and dislikes. This procedure constituted a manipulation of deeper processing of the fact sheets. The other half were dismissed. Everyone was re-contacted at some later time (up to thirty-one days later) and asked to evaluate the candidates and recall what they could remember about their positions. Those dismissed in the first round were asked to evaluate the candidate for the first time.

The authors reach two conclusions with consequences for a theory of political judgment. First, memory for facts and gist from the campaign fact sheet are low overall and drop quickly over time while candidate evaluation remains stable. In their words,

> memory for campaign messages is weak: citizens forget a lot of campaign information rather quickly. By all normative standards — *were we to rely on recall*, the citizen would appear to be rather unaware of what goes on in political campaigns.[82] (emphasis in original)

Second, candidate evaluations are the result of on-line evaluations of candidate messages and not what is recalled from those messages. The researchers conclude:

> [T]he campaign raises issues that mobilize issue opinions that voters successfully integrate, along with other factors . . ., into a running affective tally for each candidate. In this process recollections do not play a decisive role, short of the requisite that the OL tally be recalled.[83]

These conclusions would seem to suggest that memory, learning, and retrieval are unimportant factors in understanding citizens' judgments of political processes. Such a conclusion flies in the face of considerable research in attitude formation,[84] voting,[85] and public opinion.[86]

The conclusion is also too extreme for the data of the studies by Lodge and his colleagues. The second study finds little evidence of memory for gist or detail of the messages studied even under conditions in which participants were required to process the information deeply. But, at the same time, this was a study of hypothetical candidates for whom the participants had no vested interest or history. The absence of previous information structures to which to connect the new information makes retrieval especially difficult. The information was presented in the form of "campaign fact sheets," which are little more than listings of positions. No narrative structures,[87] no emotional

tags,[88] no typical news structures[89] were employed to enhance recalla-
bility of the information. The task was a complex one, requiring a long
initial survey and a dry fact sheet followed by even more questions for
those in the deeper processing conditions. These factors conspire to
reduce the absolute levels of recall across the participants.[90]

The conclusion that memory is not related to candidate evaluation
in the Lodge study is certainly consistent with their analysis. At the
same time, basic correlations between recall and candidate evaluation
and on-line judgment and candidate evaluation are not significantly
different. The differences arise in the more sophisticated regression and
structural equation analyses. Although we do not dispute the conclusion that on-line judgments predict candidate evaluation — they clearly
do — we are reluctant to conclude from this and the previous study
that the on-line judgments supplant or replace memory-based evaluations in accounting for candidate evaluations.[91] Rather, the two processes may be complementary, existing side-by-side as the messages of a
political campaign produce evaluations, activate knowledge, create new
associations, and provide the stock stories for understanding the
specifics and generalities of political events.

On-line and Memory-Based Processes

The bottom line is that on-line evaluations account for overall judgments for on-line tasks such as processing news when evaluating candidates or officeholders. The absence of correlation between judgment
and memory in a variety of studies and a variety of contexts is too
consistent to deny that something else besides simple retrieval is going
on. At the same time, one should not conclude from the few studies
done to separate memory-based from on-line processes that on-line
processes *replace* memory-based ones. In fact, Lodge seems to accept
memory-based processes as a part of the judgment model. "We are not
concluding that issues involving encoding, representation, and retrieval
of political information are unimportant."[92] In a theoretical statement
about the candidate evaluation process, Lodge includes recall as an
input to candidate evaluation, but also argues that the fallibility and
deterioration of memory of campaign issues minimizes the impact of
memory-based evaluations.[93]

> [M]emory traces weaken over time, if not reactivated. Hence, a plausible
> explanation for the failure of citizens to recall many, if any, campaign

events is that most instances and policies are so seldom activated ... that they weaken with disuse and become decreasingly accessible.[94]

We agree that discovering the conditions under which on-line and memory-based processes are activated is a priority. But achieving it does not begin by assuming that all memory-based findings are an artifact of searching memory for supportive beliefs when evaluating candidates or stating attitudes, or expressing public opinions. It is difficult to believe that all the research on voting and attitude and opinion formation in the public opinion context shows no effect for memory, only on-line processing. At the same time, the existing data do indicate the existence of on-line processes, especially perhaps in understanding the effects of media framing.

A Model of Framing Effects

Our goal has not been to lay the groundwork for a general cognitive model for the processing of political information but to make explicit the necessary cognitive assumptions for a model of media-framing effects. A schematic version of that model is presented in Figure 4.1. The model aims to account for the relationship between news frames generally and two categories of outcomes—learning and judgments.

News frames include strategic, conflict, personality, issue, and episodic frames. They are always about a topic and usually carry substantive information within their particular frame. News frames highlight certain aspects of news and downplay others through selection, emphasis, exclusion, and elaboration.[95] News frames activate constructs, invite inferences (trait as well as other types), and cue stories in receivers as a function of the content and style of the news story.

The processes of spreading activation and priming increase the accessibility of nodes associated with those directly activated by the story itself. News frames that describe behavior will tend to activate trait inferences easily and even automatically. Constructs in the associative network that are semantically related to those activated directly will also tend to be made more accessible, allowing them to be more retrievable in the short run. Stories stored as associations among constructs and personal episodes may also be activated by the stories presented in the news (as well as other cues), especially under conditions where stories in the news are similar to those stored in memory.

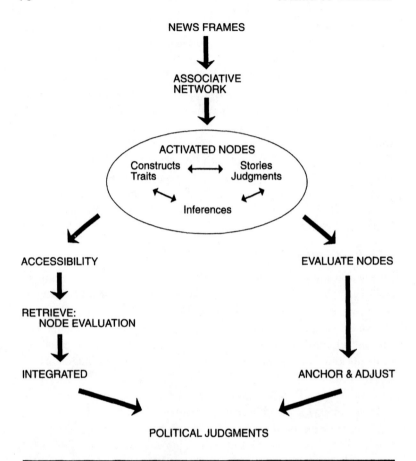

Figure 4.1. Components of a Cognitive Model of Effects of Framing on Political Judgment.

The model of Figure 4.1 hides a great deal of information in the notation that inferences and traits are activated by political news frames. When the texts direct attention to behaviors implying personal characteristics, traits can be inferred automatically from texts. Even political issues have an effect on character evaluations.

Once information has been activated, it becomes available for use. Political judgment in the form of affective evaluation or choice occurs through two processes: memory-based and on-line. The first presumes that information is retrieved from memory along with its affective implications[96] and integrated into a summary judgment.[97] What is retrieved is the basis (or reasons) for the summary judgment. The on-line process presumes that the message is evaluated sequentially. These evaluations are integrated with the existing evaluative node (the anchor) and an adjusted evaluation is made and stored.[98] We think that the currently available evidence supports our assumption that on-line and memory-based components of judgment together account for evaluative outcomes.

Retrieval of information depends on what is accessible; that in turn depends on the recency and frequency of activation and chronic accessibility levels. What is accessible depends in turn on the spread of activation, priming, trait, and other types of inferences drawn within the associative network and cued initially by the message.

Retrieval and evaluative judgments give feedback to the associative network. They strengthen (and weaken) existing association, add new associations, modify existing evaluative tags, and, in general, alter the patterns of association tying the network together.

The basic assumption of our research and of the model of Figure 4.1 is that people learn from news. What they learn is both explicit and implicit, substantive and evaluative. And what they learn depends in large measure on how information about the political world is framed. In these senses, our model is consistent with current cognitive models of political information processing.[99] It differs from other models primarily in emphasis. Price and Tewksbury specifically take up the effects of news, reducing them to changes in accessibility and failing to give serious consideration to rules for integrating information in the judgment process. Lodge's model seems to minimize the role of memory-based judgment, implying that most of what has passed for a correlation between memory and judgment is an artifact. The model of Figure 4.1 finds a place for both memory-based and on-line judgment and assumes that stories play a significant role in the information retrieved about politics and in the judgments people make about political events.

The issue for our model is not whether memory-based and on-line components contribute to judgment but when, how much, and under what conditions. The tasks facing consumers of news determine whether the on-line or memory-based component is given greater weight. When evaluations of political entities are invited, impression formation is the primary task and on-line judgments should predominate. This does not mean that consumers cannot adopt goals that allow both to have strong memory effects on judgment, even while carrying out a judgment of political character.[100] For example, in making up one's mind about two candidates vying in a primary, over-all evaluation is the key judgment. But, if, at the same time, the evaluator knows that talk at the workplace will focus on not only who but why, then attention to the reasons for the judgment may be given some prominence while a judgment is being reached. Personal goals and needs could lead to a balancing between memory-based and on-line bases for judgment.

When the audience is distracted from processing, overloaded by other stimulation, surprised by a subsequent judgment request, or processing information superficially because interest or attention is low, then memory for information in the news will probably be poor and the judgment largely due to memory-based processes.

An interesting problem is posed by the poor memory regularly found when tasks invite memory-based judgment. Numerous studies show that when people are asked to memorize facts, they recall fewer than when the same facts are supposed to be used in deeper psychological processing such as impression formation.[101] This is what Lodge and his colleagues found in one of their studies. Under impression-formation instructions, memory for issues was stronger than when the positions were rated for grammaticality. Yet, memory did not correlate well with judgments. This lack of correlation does not mean that people do not learn when they are processing on-line. Rather, they simply do not seem to be able to unpack the reasons for the evaluation they have built up.

The reason for this paradox is not completely clear. Robert Wyer and Thomas Srull speculate that asking people to recall everything they can about a target of judgment leads to the retrieval of relevant and irrelevant information that together will be only weakly related to overall judgment.[102] Hastie and Park, however, find that in on-line tasks the recall of relevant information is greater than irrelevant while the two are about equal in memory-based tasks.[103] Impression-based tasks, then, do enhance learning (in contrast to tasks instructing memorization) and what is learned is relevant to the judgment requested.

The weakness of memory-based processes in predicting judgments may also depend on the kind of retrieval task employed. The studies by Lodge and Hastie and Park all obtained information through free recall, rather than using cued recall or recognition. Free recall under most conditions produces the lowest levels of retrieval from memory while other forms yield greater retrieval.[104] Social conditions such as group discussion, which are a place for stimulated recall and recognition, may also produce greater recall and stronger memory-based judgments.

Our knowledge about the conditions favoring memory-based versus on-line judgments is incomplete. Processing news for impression formation, candidate or policy evaluation, comparison to opponents and the like would seem to favor on-line processes of judgment. Conditions of information overload, distraction, surprise judgments, and superficial processing of news would seem to favor memory-based judgments. The goals guiding the consumption of news and the conditions surrounding retrieval can also be factors shifting the relative importance of memory-based and on-line processes in accounting for overall judgments. Hastie and Park employed talk-aloud procedures to discover how people were carrying out their judgments:

> Talk-aloud procedures suggest that our spontaneous judgment conditions ... are treated as both on-line and memory-based tasks by the subjects. They both induce an initial impression on-line, spontaneously, and rejudge in a memory-based fashion when the experimenter explicitly requests a judgment at the end of the experiment. Of course, even this complication seems trivial when compared to the duration and complexity of real world legal ... medical ... or diplomatic judgments.[105]

And, we might add, political judgments.

Agenda Setting, Media Priming, and Framing

Our model of processing political news has implications for the three most important media effects: agenda setting, priming, and framing. Agenda setting may be most easily understood as a memory-based process in which accessibility of topics increases with their availability in the news environment. Media priming has also been explained in terms of cognitive accessibility, but may require a version of the on-line tally to make the account satisfactory. Framing effects involve on-line processes of judgment in central ways.

Agenda setting research reports a consistent correlation between topics the news media treat and problems the public identifies as salient.[106] Media priming draws a correlation between the attention the news media give to an issue and the importance the issue has in evaluations of political actors.[107] Evaluations are more heavily biased toward issues receiving a great deal of attention.

Iyengar has described media priming as the result of changes in accessibility.[108] As the media treat the same topic again and again, frequency of activation increases along with the short-term accessibility of the topic. With repeated exposure, long-term (or chronic) accessibility may increase. The longer term changes may evolve through processes analogous to media cultivation of social perceptions[109] that are believed to alter patterns of accessibility.

Cultivation theory holds that people's perceptions of the extent of violence in society are distorted to reflect the unrepresentative amount of violence portrayed in prime time. Recent attempts to explain these effects have prominently featured the principles of cognitive accessibility. One theory holds that people who are heavy television consumers have more accessible examples of violent behavior because television increases accessibility through frequency and recency of activation and availability through vivid and distinctive examples provided by the television experience.[110] Research has shown that heavy television users exhibit the usual distortions in their estimates of violence in society compared to light consumers.[111] Consistent with the accessibility-availability explanation, heavy viewers made these judgments more quickly than light viewers. Just as television entertainment may cultivate distorted beliefs about society by altering patterns of accessibility, so too political news may cultivate beliefs and judgments by altering patterns of what is made available. If so, we would expect heavy consumers of political news to make judgments about the importance of issues that reflect media priorities and to make those judgments quickly in contrast to those who consume less political news.

Media priming may also be the result of changes in accessibility as the news media give more or less coverage to issues relevant to the judgment of political actors and groups. If the issues are then rated as more and less important and accessibility becomes concomitantly easier or more difficult, so media priming results from changes in accessibility. One problem with this explanation is that changing the accessibility of issues may change their retrievability but not their correlation with judgments of performance. The correlation is the heart of the media-priming effect.

Media priming may indeed change accessibility, but it may also lead people to think about the issue more and, according to the principle of self-polarization,[112] develop more polarized attitudes. The polarization effect could manifest itself as a stronger correlation between the issue and an overall evaluation.

Future research will be needed to test whether media priming and agenda setting both result from the same underlying accessibility processes. If the media-priming effect is the by-product of accessibility only, then, *in the absence of any media coverage*, issues that are high in accessibility should exhibit strong issue-judgment correlations while low ones should not. If the accessible items do not show this correlational pattern, then the media-priming effect is simply a result of accessibility. If thinking about some issues and not others increases the correlation between the contemplated issues and overall judgment, then some form of thought polarization stimulated by media coverage may be the causal mechanism. Media-priming studies might then use thought-listing techniques to determine if coverage that focuses on certain issues leads to more thought about those issues than more diffuse or balanced coverage.

Episodic News Frames

Framing effects are more subtle than media priming and agenda setting. Framing is not simply concerned with the presence of the topics but with how topics are treated in the news. The implication is that how the news frames issues will invite certain inferences and suppress others, cognitively priming some information in the network of knowledge while bypassing other nodes. These inferences and associations become a part of what is made accessible by the framed message. Framing may alter the interpretation of the events described through these inferences and associations.

Shanto Iyengar's research examined the effects of episodic and thematic news frames.[113] Episodic frames focus "on specific episodes, individual perpetrators, victims, or other actors at the expense of more general, thematic information" (p. 5) and depict "concrete events that illustrate issues while thematic framing presents collective or general evidence" (p. 14).

Iyengar finds that episodic frames tend to elicit attributions of responsibility for the cause and the treatment of problems that are

directed at individuals rather than society or situations. The reasons
for this effect may be found in what has been called the fundamental
attribution error and actor-observer differences.[114] When viewing the
behavior of others, there is a consistent tendency to explain actions in
terms of a person's characteristics rather than the surrounding situation. This bias is stronger for explaining other's behaviors than
explaining one's own. Creating situational explanations requires more
cognitive energy than person-based explanation does.[115] When television portrays the news in personal terms, psychological biases attributing responsibility to individuals are activated and require the least
cognitive work.

Iyengar explains episodic framing in terms of the accessibility bias,
indicating that "[e]pisodic reporting tends to make particular acts or
characteristics of particular individuals more accessible, while thematic
reporting helps viewers to think about political issues in terms of
societal or political outcomes."[116] Our model suggests an alternative.[117]
Viewers do not perform heavy cognitive work remembering details of
individual events. Instead, viewers exposed to episodic frames make
relatively automatic trait inferences to the individuals portrayed and
in so doing orient their attributions toward persons rather than
situations. These same trait inferences may be made accessible in later
recall or may contribute to an on-line judgment of the situation portrayed through the process of trait evaluation, and anchoring and
adjustment.

In our view, the effects of episodic framing on attributions of
responsibility occur through a process of automatic trait attribution
implying personal rather than situational responsibility and *not* a
process of retrieval of concrete, specific behaviors portrayed in the
news. Whether the inferred traits are retrieved or evaluated on-line in
subsequent judgments depends on the various task, goal, and motivational factors favoring on-line and memory-based judgments. But
what is activated in episodic news is personal trait information rather
than situational considerations.

Strategic News Frames

Like episodic news, strategic news draws the audience's attention to the
motivations of the people depicted. In doing so, personal traits are
automatically activated. With the focus of strategic coverage squarely
on winning and losing and the self-interest implied by this orientation,

the traits activated are likely to be negative ones indicative of artifice, pandering, deceit, staging, and positioning for advantage — in general, mistrustfulness.

Our model suggests that both memory-based and on-line processes will explain the effects of strategic news coverage. People will learn about candidates' strategic activities recalling the basis for their judgments of cynicism and will evaluate candidates and their campaigns in more cynical ways. The stories they tell also will reflect cynicism about political life. In short, strategic news will encourage learning of strategic information, activate cynical attributions, and reinforce cynical political narratives.

Over the long haul, as patterns of association are activated and reactivated and strategic stories told and told again, cynicism about a candidate will be cultivated to become cynicism about candidates and campaigns generally and, perhaps, policy debates and governance as well.

Summary

Our model of how people process news provides an organizational frame for the studies of the effects of news frames on learning and cynicism that follow. We have argued that framing is a way of inducing a particular kind of understanding about events in the news. This understanding comes about through processes of activation, association, and inference. The inferences people make when they read or watch news depend on what the news activates and what patterns of association already exist in the audience's mind. Activation and association will make certain concepts and their semantic neighbors more readily accessible in future encounters and, in this sense, news reception should have a direct effect on learning what is read and watched. It may also have an indirect effect by readying news consumers to learn related ideas because they too are activated, although to a lesser extent, when news is fully received.

Our model recognizes that how the news is covered is as important as what it covers. People are especially sensitive to making inferences about others' personal traits. When strategic news implicates the self-interested motivations of political actors, it invites negative political judgments. It may do so through memory-based learning or automatically through a process of on-line tallying of inferred negative traits or both.

In addition to learning and judging, people are interpreters of political reality, trying to make sense of it. We have argued that personal stories are an important device allowing people to organize, recall, and make sense of the political world they encounter. Strategic news tells a particular kind of story — focusing on winning and losing, positioning for advantage, and implicating self-interested motivation. These news stories may invite a parallel set of personal stories reflecting the cynicism of news.

In the next four chapters, we test some of the effects of news suggested in the previous four.

⫸ 5

DESIGNING THE STUDIES

ALTHOUGH the bridge between the two is commonly asserted in communication scholarship, one cannot divide effects from the simple analysis of media content. Determining the effect of certain forms of news, for example, requires a controlled experiment. Controlled experiments are one of the only ways to establish causality.[1] In this chapter, we describe a series of experiments conducted in 1993 and 1994 to understand the effects of various news frames on the public's learning, cynicism, and attitudes. Here we explain the design, procedures, sample, and the news segments employed.

The research was concerned with two types of news: news about a political campaign, specifically the race for mayor of Philadelphia in 1991, and news about public policy, specifically the health care reform debate of 1993–1994. Early in our broader study of the health care reform debate we had concluded through content analysis that the norms of coverage of campaigns and governance increasingly had come to resemble one another, with each dominated by a focus on strategy and conflict. To determine whether the strategic structure produces effects on readers and viewers, we conducted field experiments of news coverage in the two contexts.

As a method for studying the relationship between news formats and effects, experiments have a variety of strengths. Controlling people's exposure to news allows a researcher to isolate the possible causes that can produce differences in outcome. Randomly assigning people to condition ensures that a priori differences among groups exposed to various types of news formats are minimal. If groups are comparable before exposure, differences in outcome, if any, cannot then be attributed to differences in the groups beforehand. If other sources of influence on the groups are controlled, with groups differing only in the kind of news received, then effects, if any, can be attributed to what is manipulated. Experiments are disarmingly simple ways for establishing the effects of news formats.

At the same time, experiments are subject to a variety of criticisms. These include: unrealistic procedures; unrepresentative samples; and, in the case of news, unnatural messages. To show how we have addressed these issues, we will report our procedures, samples, and messages in some detail.

Our conclusions about the effects of news are based on a variety of evidence — content analyses, laboratory experiments, surveys, secondary analyses, qualitative readings, and field experiments. The field experiments described in this chapter are the cornerstones on which we build our arguments about the effects of news formats. Field experiments in which news is read and watched by individuals at home offer realistic contexts within which to observe effects. Allowing participants to read or view materials in their own homes is preferable to the alternative that assembles individuals or groups in more artificial environments. Most experimental research also suffers from the use of unrepresentative samples of participants. College students are different in education, ideology, political knowledge and experience, and age from the voting public or the population as a whole. The samples used in our studies were not randomly selected, but were chosen to be more representative of the U.S. public than college student populations are. The goal is to make the studies as valid externally as they are internally.

One of our greatest concerns in designing our experiments was news items that contained the framing manipulations. Ours were taken from actual print or broadcast news and, when manipulated in any way, were written or produced by professional news reporters. But there is a further concern that cannot be alleviated simply by making the messages realistic.

News frames are the central manipulation in our research. The theoretical distinction between issue and strategy formats is a sharp one (see Chapter 2), clear enough to describe to coders and for them to evaluate reliably.[2] Nonetheless, this distinction is still theoretical. Researchers and coders may see the distinctions, but do news consumers recognize them? And, more important, do consumers see the distinctions in similar ways?

The question of the similarity between theoreticians' assumptions and a naive audience's perceptions is called *representational validity*.[3] Some would argue that establishing representational validity for messages is unnecessary.[4] So long as the message types are theoretically distinct (i.e., they are said to have construct and face validity) and produce the desired outcomes (i.e., they have predictive validity), then the types identified theoretically are assumed to produce meaningful distinctions for the audience.

The problem with this argument is that it ignores the reasons for the effects produced by a message. Certainly, if two types of news stories (say, issue and strategy) produce differences in outcome for comparable groups, then, aside from explanations due to chance, some difference must exist between the types of messages in the eyes of the readers. But do the readers attribute the same characteristic differences to issue and strategy messages as the researchers do? If they do not, then researchers may find themselves explaining their results in terms they assume to be true of the message types but which readers do not perceive to be the case.

For example, we assume that strategy stories will produce more cynical reactions than issue stories because, among other reasons, strategy stories emphasize winning. If readers do not attribute such a difference to the news segments, but do find the strategy stories more difficult to understand, then their cynicism might be the result of frustration with the strategy stories rather than the story's emphasis on winning. Unless researchers check their assumptions about the messages they are manipulating, they may falsely impute an explanation for an effect. Consequently, all assumptions made about messages by researchers should be questioned. We carefully checked the representational validity of the news items employed in our experiments.

Framing Campaign News: Mayoral Studies
Overview

In March 1993, we conducted three studies to evaluate the effects of issue and strategy frames of news coverage of a political campaign on people's learning, cynicism, and projected voting. The first was a pilot test conducted with a student sample of sixty-nine individuals exposed to broadcast and print materials in a single session (Pre-test). The second was conducted on-site in seven U.S. cities but only included exposure to broadcast news (Broadcast only). The third was also on-site in the same seven cities and included exposure to broadcast and print news (Broadcast-Print). The second and third studies were completed in the same one-week period.

Stimuli and Subjects

Subjects. We recruited 276 participants in Minneapolis, Salt Lake City, Cleveland, Detroit, New York City, Portland, Oregon, and Ft. Lauderdale by posting notices in church newsletters, community centers, and other public locations. Although this sample is not random, we made every effort to ensure that it was representative of the national population of voters. Participants were paid for volunteering; students received extra credit.

Stimuli. Attention centered on the creation of print and broadcast materials. The topic was the Philadelphia mayoral election of 1991. With the cooperation of a local newspaper and a local TV station in Philadelphia, several news stories pertaining to the mayor's race were selected and evaluated for their issue or strategy orientation.

When the segments were clearly of one type or the other, they were left unchanged. Changing them from one style to the other required considerable help from the management of the two major news sources. When necessary, the newspaper stories were rewritten by a national political reporter to the style opposite that of the original; strategy became issue and vice versa. Every effort was made to retain as much continuity in content as possible. Six print news stories were selected for use in the studies (two were given on the second of a five-day sequence). (See Appendix A for an example of a strategy-and-issue version of the same article.)

The broadcast segments retained almost all the original visual material, but the introductions of the news segments and the voice-overs were changed to emphasize issue formats instead of the more typical strategy orientations. The professional staff of the local news program re-recorded news segments for us so that the changed segments would be comparable to the originals. Five broadcast segments were used in the studies, simulating a week's programming. (See Appendix B for an example of the voice-overs for a strategy- and-issue version.)

The print segments were reset in the same font and column layout of the original stories. Only the story itself was given to the participants, not the whole page. We felt that it was important to focus the reader's attention on the stories and not permit distractions from other extraneous materials. The broadcast segments were embedded in a typical 30-minute local newscast, with the story about the mayoral election always the lead.

Stories for the control groups were of equivalent length, complexity, and tone to the election stories they replaced, but their content did not involve the mayoral election.

Finally, one of the televised debates among the four mayoral candidates was edited to 30 minutes. The debate was shown to all participants prior to completion of the final questionnaire.

Design and Procedures

All three experimental tests (which took place in March 1993) employed a post-test-only design with a control group. A pre-test questionnaire was administered that obtained demographic information, reports on political knowledge,[5] and, regarding recall of the presidential election of 1992, measures of political cynicism and personal narratives about the election.

In the Pre-test study, student volunteers in groups of fifteen to twenty first filled out the pre-test questionnaire. Then each read a news story, watched a broadcast segment, read a second story, watched a second broadcast segment, and so on for five repetitions. About one-third received strategic materials only, one-third were given issue materials only, and one-third received control materials. Everyone then watched the 30-minute debate segment and filled out a questionnaire on recall, likelihood of voting, cynicism about the campaign, personal narratives about the mayoral race, and reactions to the manipulations.

In the two field experiments, a researcher was dispatched to each of the seven sites. Participants first filled out the pre-test questionnaire, watched and/or read news materials for five consecutive days in their own homes, and came together as a group to watch the final debate and fill out the post-test forms.

Because most voters get most of their news about politics from television, one study included only broadcast news. The Broadcast-only study simulates this situation. Although we formed the experimental groups by random assignment, we also equalized distribution by race, sex, age, and education across groups. The groups received only broadcast news, one half-hour segment a night for five nights, issue versions (I), strategy versions (S), or control versions (C). All the groups came together on the sixth day to screen the final debate and respond to the final questionnaire.

The broadcast-print experiment exposed participants to print and broadcast materials over a five-day period. Five groups were run: control (BPC); print-issue and broadcast-issue (II); print-issue, broadcast-strategy (IS); strategy-issue (SI); strategy-strategy (SS). Otherwise, this experiment was identical to the Broadcast-only version in procedures. The two-way design allows us to ask whether print or broadcast exposures are more or less effective (or whether they interact) in producing changes in voters' knowledge, behaviors, and attitudes.

Sample Characteristics

Demographics. We worked to select a sample that would parallel the demographic characteristics of the U.S. voting population. Appendix C compares the distribution of people in the Broadcast-only and the Print-Broadcast studies to the U.S. population (1990 census) and to the U.S. voting population (NES sample from the 1992 election). Our groups show acceptable levels of similarity to national norms. The most significant departures are in education. Our sample overrepresents the most highly educated elements in the population (both general and voting) and underrepresents the least educated (high school and less). This discrepancy suggests that generalizations from our sample can probably only be made to the somewhat more highly educated people. However, our sample is similar to the general and voting populations in gender, age, and racial composition.

Random Assignment. Participants were randomly assigned to either the Broadcast-only or Broadcast-Print studies and randomly assigned to condition within each study. Evaluation of random assignment to condition within each study was judged to be successful.[6]

Perceptions of Print and Broadcast Segments. The key to our study is the successful manipulation of issue and strategy components of the print and broadcast stories without altering the comprehensibility, typicality, or other features of the message that might create spurious effects. To test people's perceptions of the messages, we conducted two studies. The first involved a student sample different from the samples in the field experiment. The second included the participants in the field experiment in a series of follow-up questions, after the conclusion of the experiment itself.

The student sample was exposed to five broadcast messages and five print messages in one of two orders:

(PI1)(BS1)(PS2)(BI2)(PI3)(BS3)(PS4)(BI4)(PI5)(BS5)
(PS1)(BI1)(PI2)(BS2)(PS3)(BI3)(PI4)(BS4)(PS5)(BI5)

where PI1 is print story 1 in issue format, BS1 is broadcast story 1 in strategy format, and so on. In this way, each subject was exposed to both strategy and issue stories in both media, received them in the order that subjects in the field experiment did, and had full exposure to print and broadcast materials.

After each news story, evaluators answered eight questions. Four questions assessed whether the messages were comparable on understandability, interestingness, typicality, and personal relevance. Two questions tested strategic information: who's winning and knowledge of campaign strategy; two tested issue information: plans once in office and knowledge of issues in campaign. These results are summarized in Tables 5.1 and 5.2.

If the messages function as they were designed, four of the questions (typicality, comprehensibility, relevance, interest) should show no significant differences on any of the ten comparisons between issue and strategy versions. Of these forty comparisons, thirty-four conform to hypothesis. The others are significantly different, but not in any consistent way.

The two strategy questions (winning, strategy) should exhibit greater agreement in the strategy versions of the messages (e.g., BS2 > BI2). Of twenty such comparisons, seventeen are in the correct direction and, eleven are statistically significant (and the right direction) at $p < .10$. None are statistically significant in the wrong direction.

The two issue questions (plans, issues) should show greater agreement in the issue versions of the message (e.g., BI4 > BS4). Of twenty

Table 5.1. Perceptions of Broadcast Stories During Pretesting: Expected
Direction, Correct Direction, and Incorrect Direction.

Item	Expected Direction	# Correct Direction	#Signif[a] Right Dir.	# Signif[b] Wrong Dir.
Understand	I = S	4	4	1
Know issues	I > S	3	3	0
Know winning	S > I	5	3	0
Personal relevance	I = S	5	5	0
Know strategy	S > I	1	0	1
Know plans	I > S	4	2	0
Interesting	I = S	5	5	0
Typical	I = S	4	4	1
TOTAL	I = S	18 of 20	18	2
	I > S	8 of 10	5	0
	S > I	6 of 10	3	1

Note. [a] Significant and right direction means $p < .10$ for I > S or S > I expected or $p > .10$ for I = S expected. All tests are two-tailed.
[b] Significant and wrong direction means $p < .10$ when I > S or S > I expected but oppo-
site to hypothesis and $p < .10$ when I = S expected.

such comparisons, fourteen are in the correct direction and, nine are
statistically significant (and in the right direction) at $p < .10$. One is
statistically significant in the wrong direction.

Although one could hope for stronger and more uniform differences across all the messages, for the most part the issue versions were
perceived to carry more information about plans once in office and
issues in the campaign while the strategy versions were judged to be
more informative about the horse race and the strategic action during
the campaign. With the exception of interestingness of the print message, the messages were judged to be similar on typicality, comprehensibility, personal relevance, and interest (broadcast only). The
differences in interestingness for the newspaper stories did not favor
the issue version or the strategy version and so we did not view this
difference as jeopardizing our experimental manipulations.

The messages were also evaluated by the participants in the field experiment. Six assessments were made about the news stories: similarity to local news; likelihood of watching (reading) if local news was similar; like normal news; segments like those normally watched (read); especially close attention paid to stories; watching (reading) was done in a normal way. If the messages were functioning as designed, no differences would exist in either study across conditions.

The Broadcast-Print study shows no differences among conditions in how the print messages were perceived and no differences in how the broadcast messages were perceived. The means are not reported because the absence of difference is consistent with our expectations. This suggests that the print, broadcast, and control messages were

Table 5.2 Perceptions of Print Stories During Pretesting: Expected Direction, Correct Direction, and Incorrect Direction.

Item	Expected Direction	# Correct Direction	#Signif[a] Right Dir.	# Signif[b] Wrong Dir.
Understand	I = S	5	5	0
Know Issues	I > S	4	4	0
Know Winning	S > I	4	3	0
Personal Relev	I = S	4	4	1
Know Strategy	S > I	4	3	0
Know Plans	I > S	5	2	0
Interesting[c]	I = S	2	2	3
Typical	I = S	5	5	0
TOTAL	I = S	16 of 20	16	4
	I > S	9 of 10	6	0
	S > I	8 of 10	6	0

[a] Significant and right direction means $p < .10$ for I > S or S > I expected or $p > .10$ for I = S expected. All tests are two-tailed.
[b] Significant and wrong direction means $p < .10$ when I > S or S > I expected but opposite to hypothesis and $p < .10$ when I = S expected.
[c] Two of five issue stories and one of the strategy stories were rated more interesting than their counterparts.

Table 5.3. Means and Probability Values for Significance of Difference on TV News Evaluations in Broadcast-only Study

| Questions | Broadcast-only: TV News Evaluations | | | |
	I	S	C	p
Like local news (4 = very different)	2.55	2.35	1.89	.02
Likely to increase watching (3 = less likely)	1.92	1.76	1.68	.31
like normal TV news (6 = agree)	3.76	3.89	5.00	.01
like typical TV segments (6 = agree)	3.95	4.32	4.96	.03
Paid especially close attn (6 = agree)	4.35	3.97	4.04	.48
Watching was normal (6 = agree)	4.46	4.08	4.53	.39

judged equivalent on normalcy, typicality, and conditions of watching, at least across conditions.

The Broadcast-only study does show some differences, particularly on questions related to normalcy and typicality. Results for the Broadcast-only study are presented in Table 5.3.

The differences observed in the Broadcast-only study are caused by differences between the control and the two experimental groups, not between the two experimental groups. How should we interpret these differences? First, the differences are not present in the Broadcast-Print study, even though the broadcast messages are identical to the ones in the Broadcast-only study. Therefore, the differences are not stable ones. Second, the differences between the issue and strategy versions of the broadcast news segments are not significant. Instead, the control news stories differ from the combined issue and strategy stories. Since differences between issue and strategy conditions will be relative to the control as baseline, the important differences are those between experimental conditions. Third, all the significant differences revolve around typicality judgments. People in the experimental groups of this study thought that the news segments were less typical than they expected — yet the newscasts had actually aired in the Philadelphia market (at least in one of the two versions). So the differences in judgment were most likely the result of regional differences in newscast styles. No differences arose in how attentive people were to the newscasts. The bottom line is that the significant differences do not jeopardize the interpretations that we might make in comparing the effects of the issue and broadcast messages because experimental conditions did not differ from one another and no differences in attention arose across conditions.

One of our central goals was to create messages that were ecologically valid — that is were realistic and were perceived as we intended them to be perceived. Great pains were taken to rewrite the print news stories in a way that would fit the norms of national news. Similarly, the broadcast stories should adhere to the norms of local news in style, content, and format. These primary goals must serve the conditions of the experiment in achieving the desired manipulation and avoiding possible confounds such as differences in comprehensibility or typicality. The data of this section, we believe, indicate success on all these fronts simultaneously for the campaign study.

Effects of Print News During Health Care Reform Debate
Methods

Subjects. Approximately 350 people from six media markets (New York; Philadelphia; Washington, DC; Dallas; Los Angeles, and Chicago) were recruited for pay to participate in the field experiment through notices posted in fraternal, social, and religious groups, work, and other settings. The sample was not random.

Stimuli. The types of news coverage tested were chosen to reflect our reading of the kinds of coverage that journalists had been giving to health care reform from September 1993 through March 1994. These included:

> • *Issue:* articles focusing on problems facing the country's health care system and their solution.
> • *Groups:* articles focusing on which social and institutional groups would be harmed and benefited by various health care reform proposals.[7]
> • *Strategy:* articles focusing on winning and losing the health

care reform debate; strategic maneuvering for advantage in advancing one's own program or undermining that of an opponent.

• *Process*: articles focusing narrowly on specific legislative tactics by various congressional committees as health care reform moves forward.

• *GSP*: a combination of group, strategy, and process articles.

• *IGSP*: a combination of all four types of news articles.

• *Control*: news articles on current affairs other than health care reform.

Fourteen articles were selected for use in the Issue, Groups, Strategy, and Process categories. The GSP and IGSP groups were created from the other four groups of articles. The articles consisted of current contributions from major newspapers and news magazines circulating in each of the six media markets studied. A few op-ed pieces were also included. The articles in each category were chosen to provide a balanced treatment of the various plans for health care reform. When an op-ed piece attacked the need for reform, an article with the opposing position was also included. Since the study did not try to change people's attitudes, balanced treatment was important. The titles of the articles used are provided in Appendix D.

Design and procedures. A research assistant was on-site for a full week in each of the media markets. He or she administered a pre-test questionnaire to each participant before any news articles were read. Everyone received fifteen news articles, three per day, to read. One factual article on the basic issues in health care reform was common to all groups, including the control. The control received fourteen other news articles on current affairs but not on the health care debate.

At the end of the week, all participants in a city met to watch an edited, 20-minute debate on health care that had previously appeared on C-SPAN. They filled out the final questionnaire, and were debriefed.

Seven experimental groups were formed in each location. The groups differed by type of news articles read; the types were chosen to reflect our reading of the kinds of coverage that journalists had been giving to health care.

The final questionnaire was designed to elicit information on learning, attitudes, media consumption, and cynicism as they related to health care reform.

Sample and Stimuli

The demographic characteristics of the sample are depicted in Appendix C. Our participants were more highly educated (58 percent college degree or higher), more female (60 percent), and more Democratic (47 percent) than national samples. With regard to age and race, they were roughly comparable to national norms.

Random assignment to condition was successful for various demographic variables, as well as media consumption, attitude toward the Clinton plan, political sophistication, attention to political issues, civics knowledge, ethnicity, ideology, partisanship, and pre-test cynicism variables. Participants reported following instructions about reading news articles (anyone reporting reading fewer than ten articles was dropped from our analysis). They also found the news articles realistic (73 percent), similar to the ones normally in newspapers (70 percent agreed), but they reported reading them somewhat more closely than they normally would have (62 percent). However, no differences across groups were found on perceived normalcy or typicality of the articles and, while closer attention than normal was the rule, reported attentiveness did not differ across groups.

The news articles themselves were carefully evaluated before taking them into the field. This evaluation took two forms: a structural and syntactic analysis of the stories and a student sample's judgments of the stories.

Structural Analysis. Appendix E presents data on readability of news and control articles. Readability, long sentences, and average word length of the articles do differ between experimental and control conditions, but experimental articles are more readable than the control. Lowered readability of the control occurs because control articles have longer words and more passives. The differences across conditions work against hypotheses about cynicism since the less readable texts in the control group could frustrate the reader and increase the cynical response of those in the control group. The opposite is true of the news stories: those related to health are more readable than the control and so should be less difficult to read than control articles. The experimental messages themselves do not differ from one another on any features of readability, except for longer words in group versus process articles.

Differences in readability between the control and experimental news stories should not confound any learning effects. Learning is tested by recall and recognition scores from the follow-up televised debate that everyone sees and does not depend on what is learned (or not) from the control articles. The only learning questions from the news articles focused on the "backgrounder" article on health care that everyone in all conditions, including control, received.

Perceptions of News Stories. The news stories were evaluated by undergraduate students as a class assignment. One hundred sixty-two students each received four news articles — one issue, one strategy, one group, and one process. After reading an article, the reader rated it on thirteen questions, then read the next article, rated it, and so on. After reading all four articles, they ranked them as a group on five criteria.

Of the thirteen questions asked about the individual articles, two were supposed to assess increases in substantive knowledge, two concerned strategy, two focused on interest groups, two asked about cynical reactions indirectly, and one focused on legislative process. The other four questions concerned comprehensibility, personal relevance, interestingness, and balance (in contrast to supporting or opposing health care reform).

In general, we expected that group, process, and strategy articles would function like strategic frames on questions about winning and positioning as well as on questions about cynical reactions. But they would also be perceived as providing unique information. We assumed that issue articles would be perceived to increase substantive knowledge about health care reform in contrast to the other three types. Strategy, group, and process articles would be seen as more strategic than issue articles. Group articles would be read as focusing more on groups than the other three types. Process articles would be evaluated as contributing knowledge to how legislation would maneuver through Congress. The specific questions and their average ratings are presented in Appendix E.

Table 5.4 shows that our expectations were confirmed except for the question: "How much did this article contribute to your knowledge of the benefits offered by any of the health care plans currently being considered by Congress?" This question was intended to tap into substantive knowledge that we assumed would be highest in the issue articles. Either the second knowledge question was faulty as a measure of substantive knowledge or the issue articles themselves were more strategic than we thought. A good case can be made that the question is faulty.

Table 5.4. Perceptions of Four Types of Articles about Health Care: Expected, Correct, and Incorrect Direction.

Item	Expected	Direction OK	Signif. Right Dir[a]	Signif. Wrong Dir.
Know issues in debate	I > G,S,P	3	3	0
Know benefits of plans	I > G,S,P	0	0	3
Plan w/ most support	G,S,P > I	3	3	0
Which plan will pass Congress?	G,S,P > I	3	3	0
Benefit powerful interests	G,S,P > I	3	3	0
Good for all[b]	G,S,P > I	3	2	0
Know maneuver through Congress	P > G,S,I	3	3	0
Groups support which plan?	G > I,S,P	3	2	0
Which groups win/lose	G > I,S,P	3	3	0
TOTALS		24 of 27	19 of 27	3 of 27

Note. [a] Significant means $p < .05$ or $.01$ by t-test since, with N = 162, power to detect small differences is good.
[b] Reversed wording.

The first knowledge question produced precisely what was expected — perceptions that the article contributed the knowledge of the issues more than articles of the other types. If this question had failed or even faltered, doubts about the issue articles would be raised. Also, the strategy questions that focused on public support and passage in Congress worked as anticipated. Issue articles were viewed as less strategic than the other types on these questions. The second knowledge question may have inadvertently cued readers into strategy thinking by focusing on "benefits." While the question was designed to ask about knowledge of plan benefits provided by the article, it may have instead alerted people to persons and groups who might benefit more generally (e.g., economically) from the passage of various plans. If this interpretation was activated, then strategy would have been cued and people would have evaluated the issue articles as dealing less with who benefited than the other types. This scenario seems to have occurred.

With the exception noted above, the individual articles seem to have been evaluated consistently with our expectations. Issue articles were perceived to provide more substantive information and less strategic information; they also induced weaker cynical responses. The group articles provided more information on which interest groups are advantaged and which disadvantaged. Process articles told more about the tactics of getting through Congress.

The students also ranked the four articles they read on five criteria. The criteria were: "which told you most ... about tactics; about health care reform and plans; about groups affected; which did you read most closely; and which made you feel most cynical about real reform." The results from these rankings are presented in Figures 5.1a to 5.1e and in the tables in Appendix E.

In the ranking task, judges were making comparisons among the four articles by indicating which one most clearly fit the criterion and which fit least well. The ranking results tend to support the findings

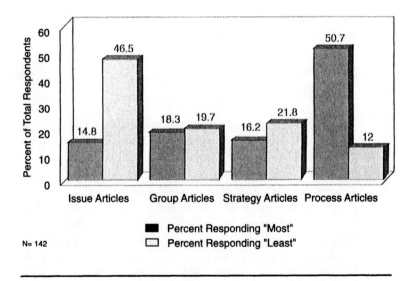

Figure 5.1.a. Articles Carrying Information About Tactics: Percent Responding "Most" and "Least" to Four Types of News Stories.

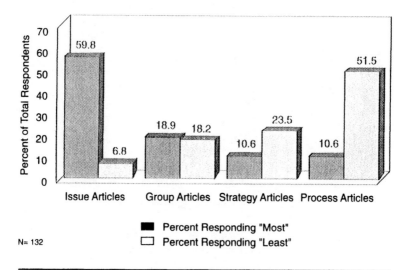

Figure 5.1.b. Articles Carrying Information About Substance of Health Care Reform: Percent Responding "Most" and "Least" to Four Types of News Stories.

from the ratings of individual articles. The issue articles were chosen at a far higher rate than any of the others on the criterion of "information about whether to support health care reform or which plan to support." No other type of article was close to the 60 percent rate of the issue articles. Process articles were seen as meeting the criterion of "told you most about tactics." All others were selected at much lower rates. The types of articles engendering feelings of cynicism tended to be the process, strategy, and groups articles more so than the issue articles. This judgment is consistent with our assumptions that these three types are more strategic in orientation than the issue articles. Group and issue articles were perceived to meet the criterion of how groups would be affected better than either process or strategy articles.

Summary

Ratings and rankings of news stories by judges were generally consistent with what we had assumed about how the articles would be perceived. Theoretically based expectations and perceptions of similarity and difference are not the same as effects on readers. But knowing that

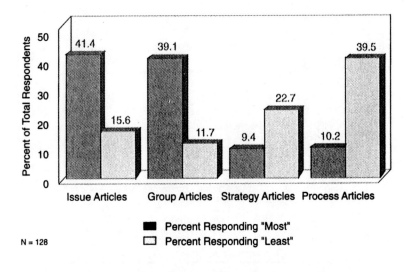

Figure 5.1.c. Articles Carrying Information About Groups: Percent Responding "Most" and "Least" to Four Types of News Stories.

readers see the news articles in ways that are similar to our own assumptions is crucial for interpreting results. If different news frames do have effects on learning, cynicism, attitudes, or involvement, then one can cite underlying characteristics of the articles as explanations, not just because the underlying features are presumed by the explainer, but because readers can also recognize these features implicitly.

Effects of Broadcast Narrative News on Cynicism

Our third major study evaluates the effects of a two-hour program on the health care system and health care reform produced by NBC News and sponsored by the Robert Wood Johnson Foundation. Our evaluation was based on re-contacting those who had participated in our earlier study of health care reform and assigning them to watch the special or not in random fashion.

Methodology

Subjects. Participants were solicited from the pool of participants in the health care reform field study conducted in March and described above. Interviewers attempted to contact all the original participants to request their participation in exchange for pay ($20 to $40 depending on condition). As a result of vacations, relocation, and changed telephone numbers, interviewers could not contact the entire original group. Of the original 350 participants, 248 participated in this study.

Design. Participants were randomly assigned to one of three conditions. Interviewers telephoned participants in the first condition (PWP) the week before the NBC Special (Pre-test), asked them to watch the program (Watch), and then telephoned between two and three days after the program (Post-test). In the second condition (WP), interviewers asked participants to watch the NBC Special (Watch) and then interviewed them between two and three days after the program (Post-test). Participants in the final condition (P) were only telephoned between two and three days after the program. There were 63 participants in the PWP condition, 67 participants in the WP condition, and 118 participants in the P condition.

The NBC Special. "To Your Health" was a two-hour special produced by NBC's news division and aired without commercial interruption. The format was a mix of personal stories, interviews with panels of

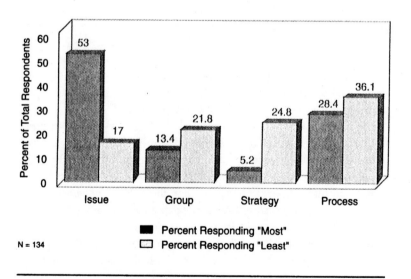

Figure 5.1.d. Articles Read Most Closely: Percent Responding "Most" and "Least" to Four Types of News Stories.

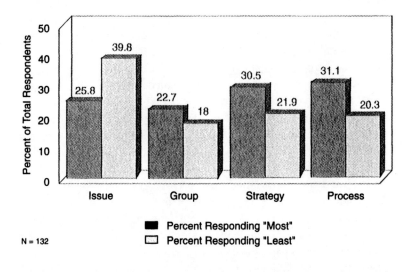

Figure 5.1.e. Articles Leading to Feelings of Cynicism About Real Change: Percent Responding "Most" and "Least" to Four Types of News Stories.

politicians, experts, and business leaders, questions from audience members, and a large dose of Hillary Clinton. The NBC special cannot be considered a standardized news format. It was longer than most other news shows, and it mixed personal stories, talking heads, town meeting, and factual information. It averaged approximately a 5.8 percent rating at 923,000 households per rating point.

"To Your Health" was produced solely by NBC News without input from the Robert Wood Johnson Foundation or from those charged with evaluating the program's effectiveness. Our expectations about the effects of the special were completely dependent on its format and content. In our judgment, the special had the following characteristics. It avoided focusing on political strategizing; it emphasized personal narratives with real people in involving situations; it avoided confrontational debates between health care policy wonks; and the political actors presented themselves as sincere individuals of good intention interested in solving a problem of national concern.

Unlike our previous two studies, these assumptions about the NBC special cannot be easily validated. There is no obvious comparison program on a similar topic. The result is that our perceptions about the format of this particular message must be treated as assumptions, perhaps shared by a general audience but perhaps not.

Sample Characteristics

The participants, as before, were not a random but a recruited sample. They were more educated (60 percent college educated or higher), more female (62 percent), and more Democratic (52 percent) than the population as a whole. Seventy-six percent were Caucasian, 17 percent African American, and 5 percent Hispanic, Asian American, or other. The average age was 36 to 45, ranging from 18 to 26 to over 75. About 48 percent said they had been following the health care debate fairly or very closely; 52 percent said they had been following it not too closely or not at all.

The participants were randomly assigned to the three groups described above (PWP, WP, P). No significant demographic differences across groups in age, gender, political party, race, or education resulted. A marginal difference between watchers and nonwatchers was found in reports of how closely the debate was being followed. Watchers were more likely to say they were following more closely. These reports may have been the result of the watchers being asked to view the special and heightening their sensitivity to following the debate.

Ninety-three percent of those who watched the program (120 recruited to watch and 15 watched on their own) reported that they watched an hour or more, with 76 percent watching the entire program. Of the watchers, 85 percent said that they did not channel surf and of those who did, only 5 percent switched channels more than usual. The vast majority (92 percent) correctly identified the format of the special as a combination of interviews, panels, and personal stories and only a small number (9 percent) incorrectly said that Ross Perot personally had an opportunity to present his views on health care. These two questions were aimed at testing whether those asked to watch in fact did so.

Other Studies

In this chapter, we have focused only on the field experiments central to our conclusions about the effects of news frames on members of the public. Other studies will also be reported. Content analyses, laboratory experiments, secondary analyses of national surveys, and our own surveys are a part of the evidentiary base building the case for the effects of news formats. We will present the particulars of these other studies as needed.

Summary

There has been increasing interest in political science and communication in the use of the controlled field experiment, a method able to tie message, medium, and audience in ways permitting inferences about cause.[8] Good experiments need to be valid both internally and externally. Internal validity is concerned primarily with control, random assignment of people, and careful design. External validity focuses on the representativeness of the participants and procedures. In this chapter, we have described the features of our studies in terms of both internal and external validity. But we have also argued that a third form of validity — representational — is also necessary when studying the effects of sources of news.

In our field experiments, the greatest threat to internal validity is the inability to completely control all the sources of information. This is the price of allowing people to consume news in the comfort of their homes and at their own pace. Realism is traded against control. But the checks of random assignment to condition, exposure to carefully crafted print and video news stories, and the use of control groups are not lost.

We have tried to craft our experiments to be representative and generalizable by maximizing the similarity of our participants to the general population of voters or citizens; by having them carry out tasks parallel to ones in the real world; by reading, watching, and evaluating politics and news in realistic contexts; and by using messages similar to ones encountered in daily news and politics. Experimental reality is not reality but, like a well-done theatrical performance, a carefully staged field experiment can transport the participants to a domain that feels real.

One aspect of this staging that we believe is extremely important is what we have called representational validity. When others have used real news or ads in their research on effects, they have typically established inter-coder reliability — a set of rules confirming that researchers and their coders see distinctions among messages in the same way. But do consumers of news and ads recognize them? And, more important, do consumers see the distinctions in ways that are similar to the researchers?

The problem with failing to evaluate this distinction is that reasons for the effects produced by a message are ignored. Certainly, if issue and strategy news stories produce differences in outcome, then, aside from explanations due to chance, some difference must exist between the types of messages in the eyes of the readers. But do the readers attribute the same characteristic differences to issue and strategy messages that the researchers do? If they do not, then researchers may find themselves explaining their results in terms they assume to be true of the message types but which readers do not perceive to be the case.

For example, in our work we assume that strategy stories will produce more cynical reactions than issue stories because, among other reasons, strategy stories emphasize winning. If the readers do not attribute such a difference to the news segments, but do find the strategy stories more difficult to understand, then their cynicism might be the result of frustration with the strategy stories rather than their emphasis on winning. Unless researchers check their assumptions about the messages they are manipulating, they may falsely impute an explanation for an effect. This is why we have checked audiences' perceptions of the messages so thoroughly.

Representational validity can be seen as a third supportive leg in the content-effects dichotomy. Content analysis represents how experts see news structures. Effects studies indicate the outcomes of news structures on their audiences. Studies of audience representation provide information on how consumers understand news structures. When audiences' representations differ in fundamental ways from experts' representations, an opportunity — and not just a problem in invalidity — exists.

It is as important to evaluate how audiences understand news and its structures as it is to evaluate the accuracy of theorists' representations of news. Audiences' understandings may differ in significant ways from those of content analysts. When they do, such interpretations may serve as mediators of the effects of news. Failing to assess representational validity is both a threat to careful experimental design and a lost theoretical opportunity.

⟫ 6

LEARNING FROM

STRATEGIC AND ISSUE

COVERAGE

IN THIS and the following chapter, our focus is on learning from news. Learning from news can be explicit or implicit. Explicit learning—the focus of this chapter—concerns the acquisition of factual knowledge from news stories about campaigns and public policy debates. Implicit learning—the focus of Chapter 7—concerns the acquisition or activation of attitudes, especially those about the motivations and trustworthiness of political actors.

Here, we raise three questions about learning from news. If strategic news deals primarily with the game of politics—winning and losing, self-interest, and performance and artifice—can people be expected to learn anything of consequence from such coverage? We will argue that strategic coverage typically carries information about both the maneuvers and tactics of political positioning and about problems and solutions. So, it is possible for consumers of strategic news to acquire substantive as well as strategic information from exposure to game-oriented political reporting.

We also raise the possibility that exposure to strategic news will predispose the audience toward learning what is strategic rather than issues, problems, and solutions. If the public is exposed to a steady stream of strategic rather than issue coverage, might they also be primed to acquire political tactics and plans to the detriment of other knowledge?

Although we are concerned with learning both cynical and substantive information directly from news, news may have a more subtle effect on learning. Knowledge may beget knowledge. Learning from one source of news may advantage the consumer in learning from other sources of political information. Direct learning is important, but it is no more important than readiness to learn from subsequent sources. We ask: Does exposure to strategic news ready the consumer for subsequent learning? Does strategic news bias the learning of subsequent material toward the cynical and away from issues?

To answer these questions, we turn first to the relationship between strategic and issue news stories.

Issue and Strategic Coverage

During the health care reform debate, our research team carried out extensive coding of television and print news stories. A large percentage (62 percent of the print stories and 67 percent of the television stories) were identified as strategic.[1] But such figures do not tell the whole story about strategic news. Strategic news often includes significant substantive issue material that has been framed strategically, either because the story headline or lead paragraphs focus the reader on strategic intent or because the issues themselves are discussed in strategic ways. Nevertheless, substantive information is often present and sometimes is freed from what we would otherwise describe as a strategic treatment—even though the story itself is framed strategically.

Our coding procedures tried to take account of this reality by providing primary, secondary, and tertiary codes for print news stories. For example, in print news stories, the primary code reflected the headline, the secondary code, the first few paragraphs, and the tertiary code, the story's other focus, if any (including a continued strategic focus). Of those newspaper articles with a strategic focus at either the first or second level, 24.1 percent actually had an issue focus at the third level. For articles coded as having a strategic focus in the first few paragraphs (our primary criterion for calling an article strategic), 28.6 percent had an issue focus elsewhere in the article.

We believe that this observation is important for understanding what the public learns from news. First, those of us who study news act as if each news piece has a simple, singular, well-defined character. Our coding suggests that this is not true. A story framed strategically may still have a substantive focus at other points in its discussion. Second, it is possible that framing a story strategically invites readers and viewers to transfer the assumption of the strategy frame to the parts of the report that are not characterized by it. Third, the presence of substantive information about policies and positions within strategically framed news provokes the obvious question. What do news consumers learn from strategic news? The equally obvious but equivocal answer is that they could learn substantive information about policies, positions, their champions and opponents; they could learn about the self-interested strategies leaders are using to manipulate their constituents and their opponents; they could learn less explicitly identifiable things such as whom they trust, who is reliable, honest, and direct, and whether "politics as usual" continues. In short, they could learn both more substantive and more cynical information.

By tying strategic news to cynicism as we have in the previous chapters, we do not mean to suggest that the public is not informed by the information carried in these stories. On the contrary, strategic news has the potential to be richly informative, although the public, politicians, and even journalists may not always be happy with what is conveyed.

Previous Research on Learning from News

The question about whether and how much people can learn from mass-mediated news has a long and controversial history. Popular perception suggests that the media should have large effects on learning and attitude change.[2] But, as William McGuire has pointed out, there are many reasons why massive media effects do not materialize even when the topic is important and citizens are uninformed.[3]

John Robinson and Dennis Davis reviewed large-scale, national surveys of public knowledge about candidates and public affairs issues completed in the period 1967 to 1990.[4] Their review concluded that the most important predictor of accurate recall is education followed by political interest. Newspaper reading was a weak but consistent predictor, while viewing television news had a very small to negligible effect on learning.

Jack McLeod and Don McDonald distinguished between general and specific media exposure to public affairs content in both broadcast and print media.[5] They also assessed attention to the media. The authors argue that how people use the media may have important mediating effects on learning. Surveillance and utility are two of the typical gratifications sought from the media. Perhaps learning would be elevated when these needs are activated.

They found that simple, generic measures of exposure are not effective predictors of learning specific content. Rather, when researchers obtain measures of exposure to specific content, they can predict specific types of learning. For example, exposure to news about foreign affairs during a presidential campaign is more likely to predict knowledge about candidates' positions on foreign affairs than is general exposure to news. Also, attention to the media and gratifications sought in processing information are important predictors in achieving even modest amounts of explanation.

Steven Chaffee and Joan Schleuder suggested the need for general and specific measures of attention to various media in addition to exposure measures.[6] They found that media attention added significantly to variance explained in learning.

Chaffee has also challenged the claim that learning from television news is minimal. One study showed that newspaper reading and television news consumption are related to voter's knowledge of issues (candidate and party) and to knowledge about the candidate's personal characteristics.[7] The strongest relationship was to knowledge about the candidate's character where variance explained was 10.5 percent.

The authors conclude that "this study adds to the documentation of television's emergence as a principal medium of campaign communication."[8] Contrary to what detractors say about television news consumption, it "stands out particularly in relation to knowledge about issue differences between the candidates."[9]

The consensus across a range of research is that simple measures of exposure to news on television, in print, and on radio do not account for much variance in the public's knowledge about campaigns or public policy debates.[10] This consensus does not imply that the public does not learn from news. Instead, the what and when of learning from news depends on a complex of factors related to education, prior knowledge, attention to issues and to the media themselves, audience motivations, and specificity and reliability of measurement.

When education is elevated,[11] when prior knowledge is strong,[12] when attention to issues and the news media is high,[13] when the audience is motivated to gather information[14] and when measures of news exposure are reliable,[15] then exposure to print news and to broadcast news elevates learning.[16] Each of these factors is significant in understanding the effects of news on the public's knowledge about campaigns, candidates, and policy debates.

Learning Under the Influence of Different News Frames

Most of the previous research about the power of news to educate assumes that the key issue is whether and under what conditions people learn from news. This question has been taken to mean What do people learn directly from the news stories they read and watch?

Our research tries to answer two related but slightly different questions. The first is: How do news frames, specifically strategic and issue frames, affect the kinds of information people acquire? Here we are concerned with both strategic and substantive knowledge as well as the attitudes formed toward those covered and their policies — specifically whether certain structures actuate cynicism. The second is: Does the reception of news ready receivers for the acquisition of information from other sources? Here the focus is not on what is learned from news stories themselves but rather the effect of news in readying the audience to acquire information — strategic or substantive, cynical or skeptical — in other contexts where political information is available. The role of information in facilitating information acquisition motivates our research on learning.

The first question differs from much of the previous research about learning from news. A complex set of factors works together to account for learning from news. In our experimental studies, some simplifications occur. It is not necessary to be concerned about audience attention, motivation, education, prior knowledge, and so on because these are equalized by random assignment across conditions. The focus also shifts from when people learn from news to when and what people learn from particular news frames.

The second research question focuses on the way that news frames dispose the audience toward learning in contexts beyond the news frames themselves. We ask: Does strategic framing of news bias what is

accessible to consumers of political discourse? How does strategic framing compare to issue framing in what information is made accessible?
How does either type compare to no exposure in what information
is made accessible? In short, we are trying to understand whether and
how news frames can alter what viewers and readers of political materials carry away from their vicarious encounters with politics. If the
forms of coverage of politics have changed over time as those who see
a rise in the amount of strategic coverage argue, it is incumbent on
us to understand how those changes alter the way the public engages
politics.

The Psychology of News Consumers[17]

The term *accessibility* is key to understanding the potential biasing
effects of news frames. Even when attention to a political event — such
as a debate — is high and unwavering, the content that is able to be
retrieved at a later time depends on what is accessible in memory. Accessibility is shorthand for retrievability, which in turn depends on
how recently knowledge has been activated, how deeply information
was processed at first exposure, the information's vividness, its personal salience, novelty, representativeness, and a variety of other factors.[18]

In the psychological literature on recall and learning, two consistent
findings stand out. The first holds that initial learning and later
retrieval are related to the activation of information stored in memory.
This activation in turn depends on external cues semantically related
to stored information as well as how accessible the learned information
is. The second finding concerns the activation of whole structures of
information, usually called schemata, by external stimulation that cues
specific knowledge structures but not others. We will refer to the first
as *semantic* activation and the second as *schematic* activation.

Although the two types are closely related, they can be distinguished. Both assume that learning is the result of the activation of
concepts previously stored in memory and the association between
new and old or between established concepts, previously unconnected.
The more frequently concepts and their associations are activated, the
more well learned and the easier it is to retrieve them later. Activation
is not restricted to the concepts energized by external messages.
Activation spreads to other concepts associated mentally with those
directly activated by external sources. The pattern of associations

among concepts is another name for the mental network commonly called a knowledge system.

Schematic and semantic activation differ in their pattern of associations, with semantic associations referring to the connections among concepts based on what the terms commonly mean. So, for example, "pancake" and "spin" probably do not have a strong semantic association, while pancake and "makeup" and spin and "doctor" have stronger (although uncommon) associations in ordinary usage.

Schematic associations refer to connections among concepts where the linkages are determined by social experiences. So, for example, in the context of a presidential election debate, pancake and spin might be closely associated, given the need to have an attractive physical appearance and with spin the interpretation of the candidate's performance in favorable ways. Both constructs might be activated when a "televised presidential debate" schema is triggered while, on semantic grounds alone, neither would normally prompt the other.

The crucial point distinguishing semantic and schematic activation is what gets activated on the basis of the two types of cuing — common meaningful associates for semantic activation and socially determined connections for schematic activation. And, since activation is presumed to be the basis of learning, semantic and schematic cuing should lead to learning of different material whenever semantic networks differ from schematic ones. Semantic cuing should activate the learning of semantically related content. Schematic cuing should lead to learning content that is present in the cued schema.

If what is accessible from one political context depends on the news frame that surrounds that context, then accessibility will be determined in part by the activation caused by one frame as opposed to another.[19] Activation spreads through semantic and schematic knowledge structures making what has been activated accessible for retrieval. Various news frames may make accessible different types of information available through semantic and schematic activation of information.

Implications for Learning Political News

Strategy and issue formats for presenting political news should have different implications for the storage and retrieval of political information. The implications depend on the two types of activation — semantic and schematic. To illustrate what we mean about learning and activation, consider an example — a news story about the privatization of city services as an issue in a campaign for mayor. In a strategic news story on privatization, the discussion might very well focus on how privatization plays with various groups within the city — wealthy tax payers, union members, liberals, conservatives, city workers, and so on. When treated from the issue frame, the story about privatization might emphasize the city's financial difficulties and the impact of privatization on the city's budget. In both cases privatization is likely to be defined, examples given, the impact on city unionized workers discussed. The two differently framed stories will almost certainly use many of the same concepts and so will cue or activate a core of similar concepts regardless of which frame is used. Both frames should activate knowledge associated with privatization, unions, financial crises, competition, strikes, savings, budgets, and so on. This is what we mean by semantic activation.

If both stories activate in readers similar core concepts and ideas closely related to those core concepts, then the concepts' accessibility and their ease of activation is increased. Later exposure to other materials about this issue and issues semantically related to it will allow easier retrieval of the information on privatization and related concepts than if persons had not read stories like these. In the case of semantic activation, it is less the format of the story — issue or strategy — that matters and more the core content of the story.

This leads to our first expectation about learning. Both strategic and issue frames for a story should produce greater recall of substantive information related to the content of the story *and to related stories* than would be the case for a group reading (or watching) materials unrelated to the topic being tested. Our assumption is that both strategy and issue stories will activate knowledge that is semantically related to the topic of the story. Subsequent recall of information from stories pertinent to the topic should be enhanced because exposure to the topic through strategic and issue coverage reduces the threshold for activation in subsequent recall. This point is important: recall of substantive knowledge on a political topic from related stories should be less for those receiving no coverage than for those receiving either strategy or issue framings of the topic. Exposure to either news frame is expected to yield greater learning than the absence of political news.

The relationship between schema activation and learning is a bit more subtle. Let us return to the example of a news story about privatizing city services written from a strategy or issue frame. The question is: Does the news frame cue in the reader an organized section of knowledge — sometimes called a schema — instead of cuing individual concepts? If a strategic news frame activates a strategy schema in the reader, then the reader is likely to make inferences consistent with the strategy schema and find it easier to learn strategic information consistent with the schema. A story about a candidate's strategic use of the privatization issue might lead a reader to assume that the candidate's appearance before union members who would be unaffected by privatization was an attempt to carry a "divide and conquer" maneuver, even if the tactic was never mentioned in the story. Or it might cement knowledge about how far behind the candidate is with unionized city workers. Strategic news frames could activate structures of strategic knowledge.

A number of scholars have assumed that people organize their political knowledge into various types including issue, personal character, and party.[20] Jamieson[21] and Patterson[22] have speculated that the electorate has also come to develop a strategy-based schema for processing political information. This structure assumes that political actors are focused primarily on winning. Their actions are then understood in terms of the need to appeal to voters (or supporters) or appease those with influence rather than solve problems.

If strategy schemas exist, they should be cued by news stories framed in strategic terms. When such cuing recurs, the subsequent recall of strategic information from the stories *and from related stories* should be enhanced.

If issue schemas exist, they too should be cued through news stories framed in terms of problems and their solution. Subsequent recall of substantive information should be enhanced by issue frames instead of by strategic frames.

When a strategy schema is activated, a bias should exist in the direction of recalling strategic information. When an issue schema is activated, the bias should be in the direction of recalling more substantive than strategic information. But these biases are laid over the process of semantic activation. People receiving strategic and issue news are assumed to be better prepared to process, store, and then recall political information on related topics in comparison to those without news on the topic.

The claim about semantic activation is that the knowledge news provides allows greater access to knowledge from other news contexts.

The claim about schema activation is not so easy to anticipate. Frames for news stories will make certain types of information more accessible than others through the cuing of schemas. We hypothesize further that continued exposure to one frame will bias receivers toward interpreting actions in terms of that frame even when the actions are not so framed by journalists — for example, in free-form debates or town meetings with questions from the audience. If our suppositions are correct, then journalists and politicians must carefully weigh what frames they employ or seek to impose because they will determine what types of knowledge the audience carries away from other, more ambiguously framed political events.

We now turn to the test of some of these ideas.

Election Campaigns

We conducted three separate studies of an election campaign. The materials for the studies were taken from news about the Philadelphia mayoral campaign of 1991 and described fully in the previous chapter. They include a preliminary study with a student group and two field experiments with more representative samples. One field experiment used only broadcast news and the other broadcast and print news.

Learning from exposure to news about the election campaign was assessed by asking participants to watch a debate among the four candidates for mayor and answer questions about their positions on issues and their performance. This procedure for evaluating recall is somewhat unusual and needs a bit of elaboration. Participants were not asked directly about what they read or watched in the news about the campaign; they were questioned about a debate that everyone — including those in the control — watched after completing their exposure to the news materials. Instead of testing people on what they learned from articles read or television news watched, they were tested on what they were able to recall from related materials. So, if there are effects on recall of information from the debate caused by exposure to news materials, these effects are due to enhanced (or depressed) abilities in consuming relevant, but different, content.

After viewing the debate, participants were asked a series of multiple-choice questions for which the correct answer was one of the mayoral candidates (a false fifth alternative was "Jim Gardner," who was not a candidate but the anchor for all the newscasts). We also provided pictures and names of all candidates and Gardner so that the task of remembering names and faces would be eased and the experimental groups would not be as significantly advantaged over the control groups. Since all participants saw the same debate, all were equally able to answer questions about the candidates' verbal and nonverbal cues and positions on issues. No questions were asked that came solely from news accounts.

We used twenty-three recall questions and asked two types: those concerning substantive matters in the campaign (fifteen items) and those concerning more strategic aspects of the campaign and its candidates (eight items). Some questions were factual and some required inference-making by the viewers. Some of the issue questions included:

> Which candidate seeking the mayorship of Philadelphia was the Republican?

> Which candidate proposed selling the Philadelphia airport to raise revenue?

We will call this *substantive recall.* Some of the questions assessing more cynical aspects of the campaign were:

> Which candidate for mayor of Philadelphia was ahead in the polls?

> Which candidate obtained the most endorsements?

We will call this measure *strategy recall.* The questions assessing both types of recall were the same across the three experiments.

The hypotheses being tested centered around what we have called semantic activation and schematic activation. Semantic activation suggests that any group receiving political news about the campaign should have greater recall of debate events (strategic or substantive) than the group receiving no news about the campaign. Schematic activation suggests that substantive recall should be greater for those receiving issue framing than strategy framing and that cynical recall should be greater for those receiving strategy instead of issue news frames.[23]

Preliminary Test

In the pre-test, a student sample was divided into three groups, each receiving both television and print news. The groups were exposed to

Table 6.1. Proportion of Recall and Overall Test of Difference for Pre-test: Substantive and Strategic Information.

	II (N = 28)	SS (N = 23)	Control (N = 18)	$F(2,66)$
Substantive	.90	.87	.46	64.0 $p < .0001$
Strategic	.80	.88	.78	2.79 $p < .07$

Table 6.2. T-test, Significance, and Direction for Comparing News Frame Groups: Substantive and Strategic Recall.

	II vs. C	SS vs. C	II vs. SS
Substantive	10.1 $p < .001$ I > C	9.7 $p < .001$ S > C	.60 $p < .55$ I > S
Strategic	.41 $p < .69$ I > C	1.95 $p < .06$ S > C	2.31 $p < .025$ S > I

five days worth of news coverage in one sitting, watched the candidates debate, and then answered questions about the debate. One group received news in issue frames (the II group for issue broadcast and issue print). A second group received only strategically framed news (SS). The third group was a control that watched and read equal amounts of material unrelated to the election (C for control). The purpose of this pre-test was to simulate the most intense conditions from the two field experiments.

Table 6.1 reports the mean proportion of accurate recall across the three groups for the substantive and strategic questions. Tests of the specific hypotheses are presented in Table 6.2.

First consider the hypothesis about semantic activation. This implies that the issue and the strategy frames should each have higher recall than the control for both substantive and strategic knowledge.

Table 6.3. Proportion Recall and Overall Test of Difference for Three News Frame Groups in Broadcast-only Study: Substantive and Strategic Recall

	I (N = 37)	S (N = 37)	Control (N = 27)	F(2,97)
Substantive	.51	.45	.44	1.43
				p < .24
Strategic	.62	.69	.55	3.53
				p < .03

Table 6.4. T-test, Significance, and Direction for Comparing News Frame Groups in Broadcast-only Study: Substantive and Strategic Recall.

	I vs. C	S vs. C	I vs. S
Substantive	1.73	.26	1.33
	p < .09	p < .79	p < .19
	I > C	S > C	I > S
Strategic	1.57	2.51	1.33
	p < .12	p < .01	p < .19
	I > C	S > C	S > I

All four comparisons among means are in the right direction and three of four are significant. Substantive knowledge is greater in both the issue and strategy news exposures than for those receiving no campaign news. Only the issue-framed news is about equal to the control for strategy recall.

Schematic activation implies that issue framing will yield greater recall accuracy for substantive information than strategy framing and lower recall accuracy for strategy information than strategy framing. The mean levels of recall accuracy are in the correct direction, but only strategy knowledge shows the schema activation effect. Those exposed to the strategy frame have more strategy information activated than those exposed to the issue frame. Issue framing did not significantly advantage substantive recall compared to strategic framing.

Broadcast Only

Three groups were formed in the broadcast-only field experiment. Group one received television news segments about the mayoral race in an issue frame (I group); another got strategically framed news segments (S group); the third group watched news about events unrelated to the mayoral campaign (Control group).

Table 6.3 presents the proportion recall for the various viewing groups and Table 6.4 shows tests of difference among the groups. As in the pre-test, the mean recall across conditions falls into the patterns we expected.

Consistent with the semantic activation hypothesis, the groups getting either issue or strategy news have higher recall of substantive and strategy information than those receiving no campaign news. Three of four comparisons are at or near significance. Consistent with schematic activation, issue framing tends to facilitate issue recall while strategy framing tends to facilitate recall of cynical information. This effect is only a trend, however, since the difference would not ordinarily be considered a reliable one.

We think that these two trends, one for substantive and one for strategic knowledge, in combination with the pre-test findings are reliable. To show this, we created a difference score between substantive and strategic recall accuracy. This index is more negative for those getting strategy-framed news ($\underline{M}$ = -.24) than those getting Issue-framed news ($\underline{M}$ = -.12) and this difference is significant [$\underline{t}$(72)= 2.2, $\underline{p}$ < .035). The index shows that individuals in the strategy condition recall more strategic than substantive information on average than individuals in the issue condition.

Broadcast-Print

In the second of field study, newspaper articles about the mayoral election were added to the television news segments. One group received issue framing in both broadcast and print (II); the second received only strategy framing in broadcast and print (SS); the third and fourth received a mixture of either broadcast-strategy and print-issue (SI) or broadcast-issue and print-strategy (IS). A fifth group received broadcast and print materials unrelated to the election (C for Control).

Table 6.5 presents the mean levels of recall for the five groups for substantive and strategic information. Understanding the patterns is a little tricky. First, notice that the recall level in the four groups that received campaign news is always higher than it is in the control. This is true of both substantive and strategic information. Table 6.6 shows that all these differences are statistically significant. The semantic activation hypothesis continues to be strongly supported in this study.

But how can we evaluate the schema activation hypothesis? For the groups receiving issue frames only (II) or strategy frames only (SS), schema activation should facilitate substantive learning in the II condition and strategic learning in the SS condition, just as in the pre-test. For the groups receiving a mix of issue and strategy framing, no clear hypothesis emerges. Strategy frames in print might dominate issue in broadcast or vice versa.

The last column of Table 6.6 indicates that II framing activates learning of substantive material in comparison to SS and that SS activates strategic material more so than II framing does. But only the first of these is a real difference. When the group received issue frames in both broadcast and print segments, the accuracy of its recall was elevated in contrast to those getting strategy frames in both. Although the means were in the right direction, the schema activation effect was not obtained for strategic recall.

What about simultaneous priming of issue and strategy frames? Which, if any, dominates? To test this, the four experimental conditions (II, IS, SI, and SS) were compared in a two-way analysis of variance for broadcast (issue and strategy) and print (issue and strategy). Only one significant main effect emerged for print ($\underline{F}(1,146) = 11.2$, $\underline{p} < .001$) with substantive recall higher in the issue condition ($\underline{M} = .69$) than the strategy condition ($\underline{M} = .59$). No other effects were found for substantive recall. No effects at all showed up for strategic recall.

In the presence of both print and broadcast coverage, semantic activation was strong, but schematic activation was limited to print news articles. When people read news articles framed in issue terms, their recall of substantive information was elevated in contrast to when they read articles framed in strategic terms. This was true whether they watched issue-oriented or strategy-oriented news from television on the same topic. The effect was due solely to print coverage and evidenced itself only with recall of substantive information.

No schema activation of strategic recall was found in this study, unlike the findings of the two previous studies. Schema activation was

Table 6.5. Proportion Recall for Five News Frame Groups in Broadcast-Print Study: Substantive and Strategic Information

	II ($N = 38$)	IS ($N = 38$)	SI ($N = 36$)	SS ($N = 38$)	C ($N = 18$)
Substantive	.70	.59	.68	.58	.41
Strategic	.73	.72	.77	.74	.54

Table 6.6. T-test, Significance, and Direction for Comparing News Frame Groups in Broadcast-Print Study: Substantive and Strategic Recall

	II vs. C	IS vs. C	SI vs. C	SS vs. C	II vs. SS
Substantive	5.39 $p < .001$ II > C	3.00 $p < .004$ IS > C	4.86 $p < .001$ SI > C	2.95 $p < .005$ SS > C	2.75 $p < .008$ II > SS
Strategic	2.09 $p < .04$ II > C	2.61 $p < .01$ IS > C	3.66 $p < .001$ SI > C	3.20 $p < .002$ SS > C	.17 $p < .86$ SS > II

present, but directly resulted from issue framing within the newspaper articles.

Summary

In the election study, semantic activation as the basis for recall was a strong and consistent finding. Of sixteen possible tests of this hypothesis, all are in the right direction and fourteen are at or approaching accepted levels of statistical difference. People exposed to either strategic or issue-oriented news about the election were better able to recall information from a related election event than those who had not been previously exposed to election information. The effect was present for both print and broadcast news. We think that this effect is the result of activating political knowledge during a week of exposure prior to the debate. This activation would strengthen the availability of information about the election, thereby reducing the difficulty of subsequent retrieval in other contexts.

Schematic activation was a more elusive effect. In six independent tests (I vs. S or II vs. SS), all the recall differences are in the right direction with two statistically significant, two not, and two exhibiting trends toward significance. The pre-test showed a difference for strategic but not substantive knowledge, while the broadcast-print study showed a difference for substantive but not cynical knowledge. The broadcast-only study manifested trends for each effect.

Policy Debates: Health Care Reform

The same ideas about learning from news during a simulated campaign were tested during an active public policy discussion — the health care reform debate of 1993–94. Procedures and design were discussed in detail in the previous chapter.

We assumed that the strategy, groups, process, and GSP articles would function in the same manner as the strategy articles in our campaign studies and that the issue articles would function similar to the issue articles in the previous studies. The IGSP group was unclear. This group of articles combined the four types of coverage that we thought existed during the health reform debate. The coverage in this group was intended to mimic the coverage available in the print news environment.

Recall

After reading news articles for five days, participants came together on the sixth day to view a debate on health care reform that had previously appeared on C-SPAN. The participants included an opponent of the Clinton plan (Representative Newt Gingrich) and a supporter (Communication Director David Gergen). The content of the debate was substantive and its style civil.

After the viewing, everyone answered questions about the debate and filled out the remainder of the questionnaire. Two types of close-ended questions were asked about the debate: substantive recall (seven items) and strategic recall (five items). Some of the substantive questions were:

Who advocated providing vouchers to individuals for health insurance?

Who complained that the Cooper Plan would only help poor people and not the middle class?

Who said that the current system causes the rationing of health care services?

Some of the strategic questions included:

Who wanted to "tone up specifics and tone down rhetoric"?

Who leaned back in his chair and looked overconfident?

A third type of question asked specific factual information about the plans being considered (five items). Information necessary to answer these questions was contained in one of the newspaper articles read by everyone in the study, including those in the control group. It could be described as a background piece. Some of those questions included:

Which of the plans set government limits on national health spending?

When would most of the health reform plans go into effect completely?

Which of the following health reform plans keeps government intervention to a minimum?

These questions differ from the substantive and strategic types in that they can only be answered from participants' background knowledge or from the one article that everyone read.

The hypotheses for this study were similar to those from the campaign study. Accurate recall of information from the debate and from the background news article should be higher for those receiving any type of news than for those receiving none (the control). This is the semantic activation hypothesis. Issue coverage should lead to greater substantive recall accuracy than strategy (or group or process or GSP) coverage; strategy (or group or process or GSP) coverage should lead to greater cynical recall than issue coverage.

Neither hypothesis was supported. The means, standard deviations, and sample sizes are reported in Appendix F, but there is no evidence to support either the semantic or schematic activation hypotheses.[24]

Compared to the relatively consistent and strong findings on recall from the campaign study, these are puzzling. Although the studies differ in many ways, one factor is central. The health care study focused on a complex, ongoing issue of concern to the public and was covered extensively in the news media. Our campaign study was not particularly salient to the participants since it focused on an election for mayor taking place in another city and that election was already over. The upshot may have been that, in the health reform study, exposure to news beyond the articles we provided may have washed out the effects on learning we anticipated.

There is some evidence to support this explanation. Before the week of news exposure people were asked about using various media sources for their political news. At the end of the week, they were asked nine questions about media use *during the week of the experiment.* The questions were of the following type:

Did you read, hear, or see anything else about health care this week in the media beside what you got from us?

Newspapers

_____ NO

_____ YES (How much?) _____ A lot _____ Some _____ A little

Four of the nine questions had enough variation to compare consumers to nonconsumers *during the week's experiment.* As a result, we were able to examine the effects of radio news, newspapers, national television news, and talking with friends.

Two significant findings emerged and are presented in Table 6.7. On factual learning, those who did *not* talk with friends during the week learned more under strategy and issue conditions than in the control condition [$F(2,319) = 4.88$, $p < .008$]. Those who did talk with friends about health reform had high levels of factual learning in the control condition. In the control group, those talking with friends were more accurate about various health plans than those who did not. These discussions with friends, family, and co-workers may have allowed information gathering and rehearsal, thereby elevating factual recall for the talkers.

Moreover, regardless of condition, talking with friends about health reform during the week neither increased nor decreased from previously expressed levels of talk about politics with friends. Our study did not change conversational patterns about politics, but conversation about health reform was linked to the control group's higher recall about facts associated with various plans.

Table 6.7. Proportion Recall of Strategic and Factual Information by Experimental Condition and Media Consumption During the Week of News Exposure

	Strategic Recall			Factual Recall		
	Radio = No	Radio = Yes	Radio Yes & No	Talk = No	Talk = Yes	Talk Yes & No
Issue	.52	.68	.57	.60	.54	.57
Strategy	.57	.59	.58	.55	.57	.56
Control	.50	.66	.57	.45	.65	.52

On strategic learning, those who did *not* use radio for news about health reform showed the expected pattern of recall while those who used radio did not show this pattern [$\underline{F}(2,318) = 3.93$, $\underline{p} < .02$]. Radio users had higher levels of strategic learning in issue and control conditions; nonusers had lower levels. It may be that the information activated by the strategy condition was unaffected by radio coverage while in the other conditions radio news about health reform provided an assist to recalling strategic information. Consumption patterns of radio news also changed, with those in the control reporting higher levels of listening during the week than previously while those in issue and strategy conditions reported no change or less consumption during the week of the study.

One of the problems in trying to conduct a field experiment during an ongoing public debate is that participants are subject to influence not only from experimental materials but also from the continuing contributions by the media and other sources. Two media sources interacted with the news frames we provided our participants: radio news and talking with friends about health care reform. When outside influences were at a minimum, learning from issue and strategy frames was elevated over that of the control, consistent with the semantic activation hypothesis. In the presence of outside sources, learning was altered to include the additional information.

Health Care Reform: Effects of NBC's "To Your Health" on Learning

We found few effects on learning about health care reform in our field experiment. Given the complexity of the issues, it may be that simpler, more user-friendly formats would be more effective in increasing knowledge across the population.

On June 21, 1994, NBC news aired a two-hour special "To Your Health," sponsored by the Robert Wood Johnson Foundation. Ads in the *New York Times, Washington Post, TV Guide, People,* and the news weeklies proclaimed "Whether you're healthy, sick or just sick and tired of being confused about health care, you can't afford to miss this unprecedented television event that's so important we're presenting it with no commercial interruptions." The program received applause and condemnation from commentators.[25]

We evaluated the effectiveness of the special using the same people who had participated in the field experiment. Of the original 350 participants, 248 participated in the NBC study.

The participants were randomly assigned to one of three conditions. In one group (PWP), the participants were interviewed prior (Pre-test) to the NBC special, asked to watch the program (Watch), and interviewed after the program (Post-test) as well.[26] A second group (WP) was asked to watch the NBC Special (Watch) and then interviewed after the program (Post-test). A third group (P) was only interviewed after the program. The participants were randomly assigned to the three groups. No significant demographic differences across groups in age, gender, political party, race, or education resulted.

Two kinds of questions involved learning. One asked people whether they *felt* they had learned anything. Most viewers felt that they learned some or a lot (66 percent) from the special, while the other third said they learned a little or not much.

We assessed actual learning in four ways:[27] questions about the health care system in general (Health Care Knowledge), health care terms (Term Knowledge), questions about the views of various political actors regarding health care reform (Political Knowledge), and questions about specific facts from the show itself (Show Knowledge).[28]

The mean proportions of correct answers across the various groups are tallied in Table 6.8. Analysis requires two steps. First, is there any *change* in knowledge resulting from watching the special? All the knowledge scores increase from before the special to after. The levels of knowledge are higher for watchers than nonwatchers for every type of recall. The increases from before to after are either significant or show a trend toward significance but were small. Watchers have significantly higher levels of recall than nonwatchers for all learning measures.

Table 6.8. Mean Proportion Correct (and standard deviations) for PWP, WP, and P Groups: Four Measures of Recall

| | Panel Watchers | | Independent Post Only | |
	Pre (N = 59)	Post (N = 59)	Watchers (N = 76)	Nonwatchers (N = 109)
Health care knowledge	.59 (.22)	.71 (.24)	.63 (.21)	.59 (.19)
Term knowledge	.69 (.19)	.74 (.22)	.71 (.20)	.66 (.24)
Political knowledge	.61 (.22)	.71 (.22)	.66 (.25)	.56 (.28)
Show knowledge	—	.68 (.29)	.67 (.31)	.42 (.29)

As every teacher knows, asking the same questions twice (even when separated by six to ten days) can lead to increases in correct answers. By having a group that watches the special but is only questioned afterward as well as a group that does not watch and is questioned afterward, it is possible to determine whether the increase in learning can be explained by repetition of the question or whether some of the learning is due solely to watching the special.

Can the differences in knowledge from before to after and from watchers to nonwatchers be attributed to test sensitization and history alone or is it attributable to exposure to the NBC special? The best way to evaluate this claim would be with a four-group design with random assignment to conditions. Since our sample size would not permit such a luxurious design, we used a somewhat more indirect procedure.

The effects of sensitization from pre-testing and history can be ascertained by comparing the post-test scores of independent watchers to the post-test scores of panel watchers. If the differences are significant, at least some of the observed change results from sensitization and history. But if watchers differ from nonwatchers, then some of the original difference may be due to sensitization (as well as watching).

Table 6.9 gives the appropriate statistical comparisons. The second

Table 6.9. T-tests and Significance Levels for Comparisons of Knowledge Across Groups: Four Measures of Recall

	Change Panel: Pre vs. Post	Sensitization Panel: Post vs. Independent Post	Watching Yes vs. No
Health care knowledge	3.78	2.16	2.96
	(.000)	(.03)	(.003)
Term knowledge	1.63	.78	2.15
	(.11)	(.44)	(.032)
Political knowledge	3.44	1.21	3.40
	(.001)	(.23)	(.001)
Show knowledge	—	.13	6.67
		(.89)	(.001)

column yields information about sensitization and/or history effects. The third tells about watching effects. Health Care Knowledge exhibits a sensitization/history effect; the others do not. All four types exhibit effects from watching. Changes in Political Knowledge are clearest since they are the result of exposure rather than sensitization; changes in Health Care Knowledge are caused by both exposure and sensitization. Change in Term Knowledge is borderline, but is due more to exposure than to sensitization/history. Show Knowledge is higher for watchers than nonwatchers, as it should be.

Our results suggest that a good case can be made that the NBC special "To Your Health" produced some, albeit small, learning in our sample of viewers. Some sensitization was present, especially for health care knowledge, but the pre-testing alone cannot account for increases in knowledge. The group studied was not a nationally representative sample and was surely different from any similar group because they had participated in our previous field experiment. However, another study of the NBC special was also done with a national probability sample using measures of learning similar to two of our four.

Harvard Study of "To Your Health"

The NBC special was also evaluated by a research team from the Harvard School of Public Health. As part of the evaluation, we exchanged data sets. The Harvard study used two nationally representative samples. A panel group ($\underline{N}$ = 806) was tested before and after the special, with some of the participants in the panel watching ($\underline{N}$ = 237) and most not ($\underline{N}$ = 569). A second, independent group ($\underline{N}$ = 701) was tested only after the special with one-half watching ($\underline{N}$ = 351) and one-half not ($\underline{N}$ = 350). Participants self-selected into the watching and nonwatching groups and so, while the two samples were randomly chosen, they could not be randomly assigned to watching and nonwatching conditions.

Two measures of learning were employed in the Harvard study that were very close to our own. Five questions assessing factual knowledge about health care were identical to those we used in the Health Care Knowledge measure. Seven items were used to assess knowledge of health care system terms; four of these were identical to the ones we used.

Tables 6.10 and 6.11 are parallel to Tables 6.8 and 6.9. The new tables present the proportion of correct answers for the four groups studied and appropriate tests of difference from before to after and from watchers to nonwatchers.

Since the panel includes both watchers and nonwatchers, the nonwatchers exhibit the effects of sensitization and history without the effects of exposure. The watchers exhibit the effects of sensitization, history, *and* exposure. Comparing the pre- to post-scores for watchers to those of nonwatchers gives an estimate of the effects of exposure alone and provides a precise control score for each person in the sample—namely, the person's previous score.

In column one of Table 6.10, the scores from pre- to post-special

Table 6.10. Means and Standard Deviations for Knowledge Scores: Panel and Independent Groups

	Panel Pre-Test		Panel Post-Test		Independent	
	Watch	Nonwatch	Watch	Nonwatch	Watch	Nonwatch
Health care knowledge	.566	.537	.625	.557	.577	.533
	(.22)	.(.21)	(.22)	(.22)	(.23)	(.22)
Term knowledge	.729	.636	.754	.656	.697	.633
	(.21)	(.24)	(.22)	(.26)	(.24)	(.23)

are compared for watchers and nonwatchers separately. For Health Care Knowledge, the watchers increase from before to after but so do nonwatchers. The watchers, however, increase more than the nonwatchers (see column 3). The same result is *not* found for Term Knowledge. Although both watchers and nonwatchers increase pre- to post-, the difference in their rates of increase is not significant. In the independent sample, the watchers have higher Health Care Knowledge and higher Term Knowledge.

The only difference in findings between the Harvard study and our smaller, less representative, sample is in Term Knowledge. We concluded that knowledge of health care terms increased marginally as a result of the NBC special. The Harvard data suggests a nonsignificant increase from before to after. When comparing the watchers to the nonwatchers, both samples find watchers with greater knowledge.

The only difficulty with the Harvard data is that the watchers who self-selected could be very different from the nonwatchers. Our study permitted random assignment; the Harvard study could not.

When we compared the watchers and nonwatchers in the Harvard study, several differences emerged, including differences in age, education, voter registration, whether they voted in the 1992 elections, the extent that they follow the health care debate, self-report of health care knowledge, whether they have health insurance, newspaper reading,

Table 6.11. T-tests of Difference and Probability Levels for Knowledge Scores Across Groups

| | *Panel Pre vs. Post* | | | *Independent* |
	Watchers	*Nonwatch*	*Watchers vs. Nonwatch* [a]	*Watchers vs. Nonwatch*
Health care knowledge	4.23	2.40	2.42	2.59
	(<.001)	(.02)	(.016)	(.01)
Term knowledge	3.27	3.63	.54	3.62
	(.001)	(<.000)	(.59)	(<.000)

Note. The first entry in each cell is the two-tailed t value and the second is the associated probability of significance. Positive signs indicate (a) increases from pre-test; (b) stronger effect for watchers.

[a]This column tests the pre-post differences from the panel for watchers vs. non-watchers.

TV news consumption, listening to talk radio, and whether they have seen ads relevant to the health reform debate.

These differences were used to construct a model accounting for membership in the group that watched and the one that didn't.[29] Six factors accounted for 64 percent of the watch–no watch categories: age, following health care, self-reported knowledge, TV news, talk radio, and media ad exposure. This set was used as controls for the watching and nonwatching groups and the differences in the panel data and in the independent sample re-analyzed.

Controlling for covariates of watching (and not) does not change the results reported above except for Term Knowledge in the independent sample, which is no longer statistically significant. The increases in Health Care Knowledge are greater for the watchers than nonwatchers in the panel sample and higher for watchers than nonwatchers in the independent sample.

After controlling for the effects of self-selection into the watch and no-watch groups, Term Knowledge must be seen as unaffected by the NBC special. Coupled with our own finding that Term Knowledge increases only marginally, the more conservative conclusion would be to claim increases only for Health Care Knowledge across both studies.[30] We also obtained effects for political knowledge, a set of questions not used in the Harvard study.

Despite substantial differences between samples, methods, and measures, some consistency in results emerges across the studies. Learning effects are present in both samples. Certainly, sensitization exists as well, but that is to be expected when the same questions are asked twice in a relatively short time span. What is also clear is that sensitization is only part of the reason for increases in knowledge. The other reason is exposure to the special itself. The effects are not large but they are consistent.

Summary

In Figure 6.1, we summarize the four field experimental studies of learning reported in this chapter and present the strongest tests of our semantic and schematic activation hypotheses. From the mayoral study, the broadcast-print study displays only the II and SS conditions where frames from television news and from newspaper articles are consistent. From the health-care reform study we portray the data only for those participants who did not listen to radio and did not talk to their

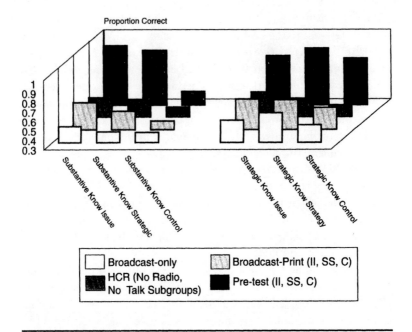

Figure 6.1. Proportion Correct Recall of Strategic and Substantive Knowledge in Response to Issue and Strategic News Frames: Four Studies

friends about health reform during the experiment (see Table 6.7).

With these caveats in mind, we must view the pattern of results across studies as consistent. Substantive knowledge gain is always greater in both issue and strategic news frames than in control. People getting strategic news (or issue news) were better able to derive information from subsequent political events related to the news of the week. A similar pattern is present for strategic knowledge gain. Those exposed to either strategic or issue news frames retained strategic information from subsequent exposures to political news. The sixteen comparisons always show greater recall in the news conditions (issue and strategy) than in the control condition. In short, all comparisons are consistent with the semantic activation hypothesis.

The schematic activation hypothesis is also supported in Figure 6.1, but less definitively. Schematic activation implies a kind of "congruence" effect whereby strategic news encourages recall of strategic information from subsequent political events and issue news biases recall in favor of substantive information. The appropriate comparison is between issue and strategy conditions for each type of knowledge. All eight comparisons in the figure are consistent with the schematic activation hypothesis, even though some are very close.[31]

What have these studies indicated about what and how people learn (and fail to learn) from political news? We think that the lessons are clear. First, political news, regardless of how it is framed, enhances learning of related political information whether cynical or substantive. In the mayoral campaign studies, people exposed to political news about the campaign consistently outperformed those in the control group in recalling both strategic and substantive information from a debate among the candidates. Everyone saw the debate, but those with previous exposure to news about the candidates and their opinions and strategies were able to extract more accurate information from different, but related, events.

Those who watched the NBC special "To Your Health" also had elevated levels of knowledge about health care issues compared to those who did not. This was true of our smaller, selected sample and of a nationally representative sample. The knowledge gained was what we have called substantive knowledge; no questions assessing strategic knowledge were asked.

In contrast to the consistent results in support of what we earlier called semantic activation, the field experiment on health care reform showed no evidence of elevated recall for those exposed to any type of news versus the control group. Because our experiment was conducted during the heart of the public debate on health reform, media coverage was intense and participants could not be kept from consulting other sources. When relevant sources (such as conversation with friends and listening to radio news) were controlled, the pattern of strategic learning and factual learning for those with no outside exposure conformed to the semantic activation hypothesis. That is, those in the control with no additional radio news or discussion with friends recalled less strategic and factual information than those who received issue or strategy news about health reform.

Had we been able to control participants' use of other media during the week of the health reform experiment, we could have obtained a fairer test of the semantic activation hypothesis. However, based on the results from six separate studies, a reasonable conclusion is that people learn substantial and insubstantial information from political news, regardless of how it is framed. Most important, our studies have also tested learning from related events, not directly from the news materials themselves. Political news in a sense readies people to learn more political information. Some of what they learn from issue-based coverage is substantive and some is more strategic. But strategic coverage itself produces learning of both substantive and strategic information.

The more subtle question is whether strategic frames advantage strategic learning while issue frames advantage substantive learning? Our second major conclusion is that strategic framing of political news in the broadcast medium enhances recall of strategic information, while issue framing enhances recall of substantive materials. Four of our studies are relevant here. In the pre-test and broadcast-only studies of the mayoral campaign, there is solid evidence of what we have been calling schematic activation — differential learning of strategic versus substantive materials cued respectively by strategic and issue story frames. However, when print news was coupled with broadcast news, the effects of print dominated. Issue-oriented print news elevated substantive recall but strategically framed print stories did not elevate strategic recall. In the health care reform study (which only used print news articles), the only evidence of strategic learning resulting from strategic coverage was found for those avoiding outside news coverage.

If strategic news frames predispose an audience to attend to and later recall strategic information more so than substantive, our data suggest that this is especially true for television, less so for print news. Our view is that this effect should be seen as an "overlay" on the stronger and more systematic process of semantic activation that seems to occur in both print and television news. Both issue-based and strategic news activate strategic and substantive knowledge but, at least with television news and measures of learning that are fixed, a bias toward strategic knowledge accompanies strategic coverage. In Chapter 8 we will use other windows to look into the way news coverage affects strategic thinking and learning.

Strategic knowledge is a kind of cynicism. Having accurate information about performance and maneuvering is not the same as presupposing that those in public life are corrupt, dishonest, or incompetent. The next chapter deals with this next step to cynicism from the framing of news accounts.

7

ACTIVATING
THE PUBLIC'S CYNICISM
ABOUT POLITICS

OUR CENTRAL arguments, forecast in Chapters 2 and
3 are: (1) strategic frames for political news activate cynical responses to
politicians, politics, governance, campaigns, and policy formation; (2)
issue frames, by contrast, may depress cynical reactions or, at least, fail
to activate them. This chapter provides results testing these hypotheses
across a series of studies in contexts including print and televised news,
a simulated campaign, and a public policy debate. To our knowledge,
these studies are the first to directly evaluate the impact of strategic coverage on audience cynicism.

Conceptualizing and Measuring Political Alienation

Research on the nature and assessment of what we call political cynicism has a long and rich history. That history is occluded in part by
various labels attached to this concept and its kin. Political alienation
(and alienation more generally), mistrust, lack of confidence, powerlessness, political inefficacy, apathy, meaninglessness, normlessness,
as well as other terms and phrases have served as synonyms.[1] This

terminological morass has helped to produce both apparent and real conflict in research findings.[2]

Of the many attempts to clarify the conceptual foundations of this family of concepts,[3] none is more comprehensive than that attempted by Kevin Chen[4] who analyzed the National Election Study (NES) data on political alienation gathered during presidential election years from 1960 to 1988. Chen concludes, as have others,[5] that there are four dimensions of political alienation, two of which have subdimensions as well.

The four dimensions are named (1) normlessness or distrust; (2) powerlessness or inefficacy; (3) meaninglessness; and (4) apathy. Distrust refers to "unfavorable evaluation" of government officials (incumbent-based) or of the entire political system (regime-based).[6] Questions typically focus on trust in government to "do what is right" and whether people in government are crooked. Inefficacy can refer to a person's ability to understand and participate in politics (internal) or to the government's ineffectiveness (external). The external dimension can apply to incumbents (external, incumbent-based) or the government as a whole (external, regime-based) to deal with problems facing the country. The focus of questions reflects person-based efficacy (e.g., "I am well qualified to participate in politics") as well as the efficacy of government or its representatives (e.g., officials lose touch once elected).

Meaninglessness concerns a person's uncertainty about political distinctions or what is desirable in political affairs. For example, those who fail to see much difference among candidates, parties, or policies are said to have higher scores on meaninglessness.

Apathy is precisely that — a lack of interest and involvement in political affairs and a separation from matters political. Questions usually ask people how closely they are following campaigns or issues, what levels of knowledge they perceive they have on political matters, and how much attention they pay to political news.

Chen's conclusions follow from his careful re-analysis of NES data on political alienation.[7] Specifically, he retains a cluster of questions as a cluster measuring a single underlying component of alienation when the questions are coherent within the group and the coherence remains stable over several testings with different samples. His dimensions have conceptual coherence and make important and potentially useful distinctions. For example, the distinction between incumbent-based and regime-based alienation, although introduced almost thirty years ago,[8] is necessary because incumbent-based alienation is likely to be ideological. One's alienation is likely to be less when one's own party is in power, more when the opposition party is. Alienation from government as an institution, however, is more general and less tightly bound to who is in power.

None of these dimensions of political alienation is precisely right conceptually or operationally to guide our own study of political cynicism. Although all four types of political alienation may have some relationship to political cynicism, each has features that make it unacceptable as a measure. To understand why, let's consider what political cynicism means.

Conceptualizing Political Cynicism

First consider the conceptual base of political cynicism.[9] The center of this concept is the absence of trust. The cynic fundamentally believes that people and the groups they represent cannot be trusted, even in the absence of evidence pro or con. That is, the cynic's first response is one of distrust. The issue is not whether the mistrust is deserved or not. Rather, the cynic begins with mistrust and must be persuaded to the opposite view.

Mistrust implies a set of beliefs about the honesty of the actor or group mistrusted, about Machiavellian motives, about things not being what they seem, about venal purposes driving apparently selfless actions, and about advancing one's own self-interests. In short, the cynic's political attributions are fundamentally different from those of his or her more trusting counterpart.

How is cynicism activated? Here we are not considering the cognitive processes of activation of cynical response (see Chapter 4), but the more deliberative mechanisms by which information can activate mistrust.

Trust is a personal feeling that operates in private, interpersonal, and public life. Trust implies connection as a necessary condition. Without connection, trust is not an issue. Connection requires that your actions have some affect on me. In private life, trust or its absence matters only when there is connection between people — whether the connections are ones of business relations or intimate relations.

So too in public life. Trust matters when there is connection. If actions at the highest levels of government are not seen as affecting daily life, no connection exists and trust cannot be an issue. With many elections, connection comes through identification with candidates and their positions. Some public policy debates involve issues where connection to the public is direct (e.g., sending U.S. troops to Bosnia); others are more remote (e.g., policies regarding displaced persons in Bosnia).

Given connection, trust further implies that the leader's actions are undertaken so as to preserve common interests and not simply the leader's interests and the interests of her constituents. So the absence of trust and, worse, the assumption that an actor is untrustworthy is based on the view that her actions are ones that are undertaken with her own interests paramount and "our" interests subsidiary. Alternatively, self-interest and the public interest are seen as antagonistic. In short, cynicism implies that the self-interest of political actors is their primary goal and that the common interest is secondary at best or played out only for its political advantage.

The public's perceptions of the motivations of actors are what determines their trustworthiness. Relationships with public figures are still relationships, even when these relationships are separated in time and space. If Roderick Hart is correct that television is fundamentally an interpersonal medium,[10] then identification with political figures is at heart an interpersonal process in which the attribution of motives determines the success of the relationship. Trust in others must be earned through actions that are not always and only in pursuit of one's own interests.

When reporting about politicians and their policies is repeatedly framed as self-interested and seldom in terms of the common good — whether such characterizations are correct or incorrect — the public's experience of their leaders is biased toward attributions that induce mistrust. Strategy coverage invites precisely such attributions and it is our hypothesis that one result is the activation of political cynicism.

Measuring Political Cynicism

If political cynicism at its center is trust in political actors, why not use one or more of the standard measures of political alienation as the indicator of cynicism? The closest relative is distrust (or normlessness). The reason that this definition does not work for us is that in the NES studies distrust is not correlated with three of the other components — apathy, meaninglessness, and internal efficacy.[11] These factors cannot substitute for normlessness. Conceptually, neither are they indicators of political cynicism as we conceive it. Measures of distrust and political inefficacy (which correlate moderately ranging from about .3 to .4) are possible candidates.[12] We have rejected them because they focus on the wrong targets for our purposes and assess trust in ways that are not suited to our goals.

The targets of these widely used measures are elected officials, based in Washington, engaged in governing the country. For our purposes, a measure of political cynicism must address ongoing political events such as campaigns and policy debates. The object of our concern is really the political processes through which the electorate makes decisions (campaigns) and through which the government, social institutions, and the public make decisions (public policy debates). Consequently, our measures must reflect on the trustworthiness of the process of public deliberation, including especially the motivations of actors in these deliberations.

The most direct measure of distrust of government employs questions about wasting taxes, being crooked, the influence of big interests, and trusting Washington to "do what is right." Such items are too specific or simply inappropriate to distinguish those who are politically cynical about campaigns and policy debates. The consequence is that we must develop measures of political cynicism anew, using the accepted measures of distrust of government and (external) political inefficacy as ways of establishing the construct validity of our new measures but not as a substitute for them.

The details of scale construction and the questions used are reported in Appendix G. and the results are summarized here. We employed a variety of measures to tap political cynicism. These included agree-disagree questions, forced choice questions, questions about actors' motivations for their actions, and a question about what people thought they learned. Three components of political cynicism were obtained.

The central one is derived by using six point agree-disagree questions and forced-choice questions. Both types focused on manipulativeness of advocates (candidates in campaigns and representatives of groups in policy debates), dishonesty, winning and getting ahead, looking good, using fear, the absence of real choice, and the role of big money. The two types of questions could have been kept separate or combined into a single index.[13] Simplicity of presentation and correlations between the forced choice and agree-disagree versions in two samples (.59 in the mayoral election study and .61 in the health care reform debate study) argued for the single index. The combined forced choice and agree-disagree questions are called *Political Cynicism.*

The learning question was designed to force people to choose three of six possible statements about what they believed they learned from the materials they read and watched. Three statements were biased toward information concerned with positioning for winning or appealing to selected constituencies, while the other three are biased toward problems, solutions, and substantive differences. These questions were not intended to measure actual learning; they try to determine what people perceived they had learned. The answers were treated as a single measure of *Cynical Learning.*

A set of four questions attempted to ascertain the attributions that people made about the motivations of advocates. Respondents were asked to choose between two possible motives for an action, one more cynical and the other less so. For example, is the president attacking opponents to maximize his plan's chances and allow him to get re-elected or because his plan will give better care to more people at lower prices? This component is called *Cynical Motivation.*

The three components of political cynicism were found to be reliable and valid across two samples totaling about 600 people (see Appendix G). The measure of Political Cynicism is assumed to assess general distrust of the political process and its participants. Cynical Motivation attempts to measure bias in interpretation of a political actors' motives toward the self-interested or the public good. Cynical Learning is a measure of perceived, rather than actual, learning, asking what kinds of information people thought they carried away from the articles read or broadcast segments viewed. It complements the measurement of strategic recall reported in the previous chapter.

The three components of political cynicism were found to have acceptable reliability and validity, providing some confidence that the questions indeed are associated with the class of concepts commonly called political alienation — specifically, government efficacy and trust. At the same time, our measures are clearly not highly redundant with these other concepts, tapping instead, we believe, a more general construct of cynicism about political processes, including, but not limited to, the political actors involved.

From News Frames to Political Cynicism

People learn about the motives of political actors through the media and their representations of political action. The form of this representation is primarily, but not exclusively, strategic and oppositional. Strategic coverage implies motives that are self-interested and which in turn are interpreted to mean that political actions are both self-interested and not focused on the best interests of the public. This packaging invites an interpretation that is no different from ordinary reasoning about other types of personal relationships — that is, that politicians who focus on their own self-interest are no more to be trusted than others who do the same in daily life. Cognitively, framing actions in the language and structures of strategy invites inferences and interpretations associated with motivations of actors. Framing strategy in terms of self-interest (rather than the common interest) invites interpretation of politicians' motivations as self-interested and hence not worthy of trust.

These speculations are untested. We next describe several studies that offer evidence evaluating the ability of strategic coverage to activate political cynicism, inducing attributions of mistrust.

Election Campaigns

The same three studies described in Chapter 5 also provide information about the audience's political cynicism in response to issue and strategic news frames. The central hypothesis tested is that strategic coverage elevates cynicism over that of the control and of groups receiving issue-based news. Our expectations about issue frames are that the cynicism of those in the issue condition would not be higher than that of the group receiving no campaign news.

Preliminary Study

The student sample was divided into three groups: one receiving strategy coverage for in both print articles and broadcast segments (SS), one receiving issue coverage in both (II), and a control group that received no news about the mayoral campaign.

Across three measures of cynicism, six tests of the strategy-cynicism hypothesis were possible. Four of six comparisons were in the right direction, with the SS condition exhibiting higher cynicism than the control or cynicism in SS greater than II. The two failures were with Cynical Motive, which was opposite in direction to our hypothesis but not significant. Only one significant effect emerged. Political Cynicism was greater in the SS condition ($\underline{M}$ = .37) than in the control ($\underline{M}$ = .34), $\underline{t}(\underline{df}$ = 39) = 2.02, $\underline{p}$ =.05.

Despite the absence of significant effects, the preliminary test was viewed as a success because the direction of effects was as hypothesized for four of six comparisons. No significant differences were found in comparing the issue-based news to the control.

Broadcast-only Study

Three groups were formed in the study of exposure to broadcast news alone: an issue frame, a strategy frame, and a control. At the end of a week's exposure, everyone completed a questionnaire, which obtained information about their cynicism about the campaign.

Table 7.1 presents the mean cynicism scores across condition and Table 7.2 shows the appropriate tests of difference. Two results stand out. All six differences involving the strategic frames are in the correct direction, and five of the six are statistically significant or exhibit trends toward significance.[14] There are no significant differences between issue and control.

The conclusions from the broadcast-only study are clear. There is no evidence that issue coverage either depresses or elevates political

Table 7.1. Mean cynicism (and standard deviation) for three groups in broadcast-only study: Three components of cynicism.

	Issue ($\underline{N}$ = 37)	Strategy ($\underline{N}$ = 37)	Control ($\underline{N}$ = 28)	$\underline{F}(2, 99)$ Prob
Political cynicism	.66 (.14)	.73 (.14)	.67 (.12)	3.07 p = .05
Cynical learning	.47 (.18)	.58 (.20)	.54 (.25)	2.52 p < .09
Cynical Motive	.66 (.15)	.71 (.16)	.65 (.16)	1.69 p < .19

Note. All cynicism scores are scaled to a 0–1 range with 1 equal to highest cynicism.

Table 7.2. T-test (Significance), and Direction for Comparing News Frame Groups in Broadcast-only Study: Three Components of Cynicism

	I vs C (df = 63)	S vs. C (df = 63)	I vs. S (df = 72)
Political Cynicism	.22	1.91	2.22
	(.83)	(.06)	(.03)
	I < C	S > C	S > I
Cynical Learning	1.21	.73	2.41
	(.23)	(.46)	(.02)
	I < C	S > C	S > I
Cynical Motive	.18	1.56	1.56
	(.85)	(.12)	(.12)
	I > C	S > C	S > I

Note. Each cell reports t value, significance of probability (two-tailed), and direction of effect. Hypothesized directions are S > C; S > I; I ≤ C.

cynicism. Those exposed to no news about the campaign had levels of political cynicism no different from those receiving issue-oriented coverage. Strategic coverage on the other hand activated cynicism over that reported by people in the control and those in the issue condition.

Broadcast-Print Study

Both television and print news were employed in this study to determine whether strategic coverage in one medium or the other was a stronger source for activating cynicism. Five groups were formed: one received only issue frames (II), one only strategic frames (SS), one received issue in broadcast and strategy in print (IS), one received strategy in broadcast and issue in print (SI). The fifth group received no news about the campaign, but read and watched other news stories.

We expected strategic news frames to function as before. Specifically, we assumed that the SS group would have greater levels of cynicism than the control and greater levels than the II group. The issue-only group was expected to have cynicism lower than or equal to but not greater than the control group. No expectations about interactions between print and broadcast news frames were formulated but, if anything, both print and broadcast should exhibit main effects such

Table 7.3. Means and (Standard Deviations) for Five Conditions in the Broadcast-Print Study: Three Components of Cynicism

	II (N = 38)	IS (N = 38)	SI (N = 38)	SS (N = 36)	Control (N = 19)
Political cynicism	.74 (.15)	.71 (.14)	.71 (.12)	.78 (.13)	.73 (.12)
Cynical learning	.44 (.19)	.54 (.21)	.61 (.21)	.72 (.21)	.58 (.27)
Cynical motive	.68 (.18)	.68 (.13)	.67 (.16)	.75 (.16)	.70 (.16)

Note. Order of conditions is broadcast-print so that IS means broadcast issue frame and print strategy frame.

that strategic frames would have higher levels of cynicism than issue frames.

Table 7.3 gives mean levels of cynicism across the five groups; Table 7.4 presents specific hypothesis tests. The pattern of means in Table 7.3 is instructive. The II group is always lower than the SS group and the SS group always higher than the control group. These six comparisons are in line with our hypothesis and five of the six are significant or exhibit a trend in the hypothesized direction (see Table 7.4). As before, a strong dose of strategic news activates cynical responses.

What is interesting is the mixed conditions, IS and SI, where exposure involves some strategic and some issue framing. The mere presence of strategic framing does not necessarily elevate cynicism over that reported by the control. The mix of issue framing mitigates the effects of strategic news. But none of these differences is significant individually.

When the four experimental groups and the three measures of cynicism are considered simultaneously, several conclusions result. First, no significant interactions between broadcast and print frames emerged,[15] suggesting that neither print nor broadcast news frames dominated the other. However, multivariate main effects do occur. The multivariate test considers all the cynicism measures at the same time. Both print (Wilks lambda = .914, $F(4,141) = 3.28$, $p = .013$) and broadcast (Wilks lambda = .839, $\underline{F}(4,141)$ = 6.77, $\underline{p}$ < .001) were significant, indicating elevated cynicism when either print or broadcast news is framed strategically rather than in issue terms.[16]

The broadcast-print study presents a somewhat more complicated picture of the effects of strategic news on cynicism. As in our previous studies, exposing the audience to strategically framed news elevates their cynicism in contrast to issue-based or no news exposure. The presence of (multivariate) main effects for print and broadcast separately and the absence of interaction effects are important. These findings mean that exposure to two media, each predominating in one news frame (e.g., strategy), will have additive effects with regard to levels of cynicism. Neither medium overwhelms the other. The presence of an issue or strategy frame will not dominate the alternative frame, it will either subtract or add. In a media environment dominated by the strategy frame, additive effects imply continual re-activation of political cynicism and also mean that small doses of issue-framed news can reduce, but do not have the power to counteract, larger doses of strategic information.

Table 7.4. T-test (Significance), and Direction for Comparing News Frame Groups in Broadcast-Print Study: Three Components of Cynicism

	II vs. C ($\underline{df}$ = 55)	SS vs. C ($\underline{df}$ = 53)	II vs. SS ($\underline{df}$ = 72)
Political cynicism	.35	1.67	1.40
	(.73)	(.10)	(.16)
	II > C	SS > C	SS > II
Cynical learning	2.27	2.12	5.98
	(.03)	(.04)	(.001)
	II < C	SS > C	SS > II
Cynical motive	.58	1.06	1.95
	(.57)	(.29)	(.05)
	II < C	SS > C	SS > II

Notes: Each cell reports $\underline{t}$ value, significance of probability (two-tailed), and direction of effect. Hypothesized directions are SS > C; SS > II; II ≤ C.

Summary

Across three studies of a simulated campaign news environment, we completed eighteen tests of the effects of strategically framed news on cynicism. Sixteen were in the hypothesized direction, with eleven at or near accepted levels of reliable difference. The two means contrary to hypothesis were in the pre-test and most of the nonsignificant effects occurred in that group. Exposure to issue frames did not lower cynicism (except in one case); issue framing of news tended to function as if no news had been received, at least regarding cynical reaction. The absence of effects due to issue frames means that our operationalization of issue-based news was simply unrelated to the cynical reactions of our participants. Strategic news, by contrast, was highly related to cynical response producing elevated levels in comparison to no news and to political news that was based on discussion of the issues.

It is important to keep in mind that our campaign simulation was not particularly salient to the participants and that their level of prior knowledge about the candidates and issues was low. As a consequence, exposure to news about the campaign could produce effects on both learning and cynicism. But could similar effects be produced in an ongoing debate that was both salient to the audience and about which the audience had considerable prior information from both news accounts and personal experience? The health care reform debate permitted us to test our hypotheses about the effects of strategic frames on political cynicism in such an environment.

Policy Debates: Health Care Reform

The same ideas about cynical reactions to strategic news frames were tested during an active public policy debate — the health care reform debate of 1993–94. The procedures and design are discussed in Chapter 5. Briefly, those in the control group read articles about current topics unrelated to health care reform. Six other groups read articles focused on strategy, issue, groups, legislative process, and two combinations, strategy-groups-process (GSP) and issue-strategy-groups-process (IGSP). The same components of cynicism were measured in this study as in the previous ones.

We assumed that the strategy, groups, process, and GSP articles would function similarly to the strategy articles in our campaign studies and that the issue articles would function like the issue ones. That

Table 7.5. Mean Cynicism (and Standard Deviations) for Seven Experimental Groups: Three Components of Cynicism

	Issue $N = 49$	Group $N = 47$	Strategy $N = 46$	Process $N = 47$	GSP $N = 50$	IGSP $N = 47$	Control $N = 49$	F 6,328
Political cynicism (AD)								
	.72***	.67	.70*	.72***	.70**	.69*	.66	1.54
	(.13)	(.14)	(.14)	(.11)	(.12)	(.14)	(.15)	$p = .16$
Cynical learning								
	.63*	.66***	.69***	.68***	.69***	.68***	.59	4.45
	(.14)	(.11)	(.14)	(.11)	(.11)	(.14)	(.10)	$p = .001$
Cynical motive								
	.63	.59	.59	.59	.60	.60	.59	0.47
	(.16)	(.12)	(.13)	(.12)	(.15)	(.13)	(.12)	$p = .83$

Note: *** $p < .05$; ** $p < .10$; * $p < .20$, two-tailed t-test comparing experimental group to control. Expected effects include Group, Strategy, Process, and GSP > Control; Issue ≤ Control.

is, we expected strategically framed news (strategy, group, process, and GSP) to elevate cynicism over that of the control and over that of news framed in issue formats. The IGSP group of articles combined the four types of coverage we think existed during the health reform debate. As before, we expected those exposed to issue frames to report less cynicism about health reform than those getting no health reform coverage.

The data from this study are consistent with our previous findings about strategy frames, but not about issue frames. Table 7.5 presents the means across all seven groups. There are twelve comparisons between strategic news groups and the control; nine of these show the experimental group with higher cynicism than the control. The other three have the experimental group equal to the control (to two significant figures) and all concern Cynical Motive. Cynical Motive shows no signs of the strategy-cynicism effect. Seven comparisons are at or have trends toward significance.

The issue news groups (Issue and IGSP) are a different story. Instead of being less than or equal to the control levels of cynicism, they are higher in all six cases. Four of these reach normal levels of

Table 7.6. Means and (Standard Deviations) for Combined Issue, Strategy, and Issue Plus Strategy Groups: Three Components of Cynicism

	Issue (N = 96)	Strategy (N = 190)	I & S (N = 286)	Control (N = 49)
Political cynicism	.71	.70	.70	.66
	(.14)	(.13)	(.13)	(.15)
Cynical learning	.65	.68	.67	.59
	(.14)	(.12)	(.13)	(.10)
Cynical motive	.61	.59	.60	.59
	(.14)	(.13)	(.14)	(.12)

significance or a trend in that direction. This pattern is clearly contrary to our expectations about how issue coverage would function with regard to cynicism about the health reform debate.

The groups receiving some issue coverage (Issue and ISSP) were combined as were the groups receiving strategic framing (Strategy, Group, Process, and GSP).[17] Table 7.6 gives the means for the combined groups while Table 7.7 presents tests of difference between these combined groups and the control.

Tables 7.6 and 7.7 indicate that Cynical Motive is not affected at all by any of the news story frames. Cynical Learning is elevated in both issue and strategy frames over scores in the control. Similarly, Political Cynicism is also greater in the strategy and issue conditions than in the control.

The combined conditions suggest that strategic news frames activated cynical response for both political cynicism and cynical learning. This finding is consistent with our previous expectations about the effects of strategy coverage but in a new context — that of an ongoing public policy debate. The effects are not large, but in the midst of dense coverage about a topic of some consequence to every citizen the activation of any cynical response from a few news articles, in our opinion, is dramatic testimony to the effects of strategic framing of news.

The combined conditions give a clear but unexpected picture that issue news frames also activate cynical response for both political cynicism and cynical learning. This finding is contrary to our expectations about how issue framing of news should operate. Issue frames do not implicate the motivations of political actors in any obvious way. Rather, they are concerned primarily with problems, solutions, evaluations, and critiques of opposing positions. We explore the possible reasons for the activation of cynicism by issue coverage in the health care debate later.

Health Care Reform: Effects of NBC's "To Your Health" on Cynicism

Cynicism was a concern in our evaluation of the NBC special "To Your Health." Because we had no way of knowing what the format or content of the program would be in advance, it was not possible to set firm hypotheses. The content and format would direct cynical response. For example, if the program emphasized details of the various plans, offering critical reactions from interested parties, it might function as issue coverage but nonetheless might increase cynicism. If the program focused on the politics of positioning and maneuvering one or another plan through Congress, the implications for President Clinton's standing with the public, and projections about what Republicans had to gain and lose from opposition or compromise, the program would have created a strategic frame, elevating cynicism over

Table 7.7. T-test (Significance), and Direction for Comparing News Frame Groups in Health Care Reform: Three Components of Cynicism

	I vs. C ($df = 143$)	S vs. C ($df = 237$)	I & S vs. C ($df = 333$)
Political Cynicism	2.33 (.02) I > C	2.04 (.02) S > C	2.25 (.02) I & S > C
Cynical Learning	2.67 (.008) I > C	4.77 (.001) S > C	4.13 (.001) I & S > C
Cynical Motive	.81 (.42) I > C	.06 (.96) S > C	.35 (.72) I & S > C

Note: Each cell reports t value, significance of probability (two-tailed), and direction of effect. Hypothesized directions are S > C.

that of any control group. To our surprise, the frame and content of the NBC special fell into neither of these categories nor was it a mixture of strategic and conflictual issue coverage. The NBC special cannot be considered a standardized news format. "To Your Health" instead adopted a format that mixed personal stories, interviews with panels of politicians, experts, and business leaders, questions from audience members, and a healthy dose of Hillary Clinton. Our expectations about the effects of this special on cynicism depend in part on the nature of the medium of television and in part on the content of coverage.

We surmised that the special would have the effect of reducing audience cynicism about health care reform, at least in the short run, if the show did certain things. It must avoid focusing on political strategizing; it should emphasize personal narratives with real people in involving situations; it should avoid confrontational debates that impugn the motives of those in the debate;[18] the political actors should present themselves as sincere individuals of good intention (a natural consequence of the television medium if Hart's[19] analysis can be believed). In our judgment, the special, whatever its other weaknesses, did all of these things.

Effects on Cynicism

The details of the study of the NBC special are provided in Chapter 5. Since all questioning was done by telephone, we had to use a more limited set of questions assessing political cynicism. Cynical Motive was dropped because clearly it was an ineffective measure. Cynical Learning was also dropped because it was too difficult to administer by

Table 7.8. Means and Standard Deviations for Cynicism Scores from NBC Special: Three Groups

| | Panel Watchers | | Independent Post Only | |
	Pre (N = 59)	Post (N = 59)	Watchers (N = 76)	Nonwatchers (N = 109)
Political cynicism	.68	.63	.66	.69
	(.22)	(.16)	(.21)	(.21)

Table 7.9. T-tests and Significance Levels for Comparisons of Cynicism Across Groups for NBC Special

	Change Panel: Pre vs. Post (df = 58)	Sensitization Panel: Post vs. Independent Post (df=133)	Watching: Yes vs. No (df = 243)
Political cynicism	-2.91	.73	−1.67
	(.005)	(.46)	(.096)

Note. The first entry in each cell is the two-tailed t value and the second is the associated probability of significance. The conventions for signs are that "positive" indicates (a) increases from pre-test; (b) presence of sensitization; or (c) higher values for watchers.

telephone. Three forced choice and four agree-disagree questions were selected from the set used in the earlier studies.

Table 7.8 presents the mean levels of cynicism for each group. The pattern of the means is clear. Cynicism is lower from before to after the special. Also, those who watched the special had lowered levels of cynicism than those who did not.

Table 7.9 offers tests to establish whether differences are significant or not. The decreases in cynicism for the panel from before to after the special are significant at p =.005. There was a trend for watchers to have lower levels of cynicism than those who did not watch.

But as we noted in Chapter 6 when analyzing the learning data from this study, asking the same questions twice can produce a sensitization effect. In the case of learning, one would expect the sensitization effect to work in the direction of showing more learning at the second testing. Simply asking people questions with correct and incorrect answers might lead them to search out answers to the questions when there is even a hint of possible reassessment. With cynicism questions, the direction of sensitization is not as clear. Would people want to appear socially accepting and trusting and hence less cynical? Or would they want to be seen as fashionably skeptical and thus more cynical? Our point is that sensitization effects are clear when learning is the outcome measure, but less so when cynicism is the outcome.

Nevertheless, column 2 in Table 7.9 treats the difference between the cynicism score after the special for the panel watchers and the independent watchers as if it were a measure of sensitization. No sensitization is present for the index of cynicism.

A reasonable case can be made that the NBC special "To Your Health" lowered our audience's cynicism about health care reform from what it was before the special. The NBC special was condemned by some critics and opponents as simplistic, insufficiently substantive, excessively emotional, and biased. At the same time, it seems to have reduced our participants' levels of cynicism. Perhaps the public needed a personalized and simplified introduction to the issues of the health care debate. After all, one of the recognized functions of television news has been to provide frameworks for later learning and the motivation, through emotional activation, to learn more.[20] By failing to provide an in-depth analysis of the pros and cons of various plans, the NBC special may have had the side benefit of decreasing cynicism.

What is not clear from our study is whether a more representative sample of individuals had the same reaction to the special as our participants did. Those participating in our study of the NBC special differed from a national audience of viewers in many ways. Not only were they demographically more educated, more liberal, and more Democrat but they had been paid to participate in our study, had been members of a previous study reading fifteen news article about health care reform, and for the most part watched the entire two hours of the special.

Harvard Study of NBC Special

This study is described in more detail in Chapter 6. The Harvard study employed two separate samples and four groups. A panel group (N = 806) was tested before and after the special, with some of the participants in the panel watching (N = 237) and most not (N = 569). Another group (N = 701) was tested only after the special with one-half watching (N = 351) and one-half not (N = 350). Participants self-selected into the watching and nonwatching groups. The same three forced-choice questions assessing cynicism about health care reform were asked of the participants in the Harvard study. The agree-disagree questions were not asked.

Table 7.10 depicts the mean levels of cynicism for the four groups. A difference from our study of the NBC special is apparent from this table. In the panel data, both the watchers and the nonwatchers

Table 7.10. Means, Standard Deviations for Cynicism Scores: Four
Groups from Harvard Study

	Panel Pre-Test		Panel Post-Test		Independent	
	Watch.	Nonwatch.	Watch.	Nonwatch.	Watch.	Nonwatch.
Health care	1.18	1.26	1.23	1.41	1.21	1.31
cynicism	(.73)	(.70)	(.76)	(.69)	(.71)	(.71)

increase their reported levels of cynicism from first to second testing.
Watchers increase their scores on cynicism, but this increase is not sig-
nificant [$\underline{t}(\underline{df} = 236) = 1.07$, $\underline{p} = .28$]. The nonwatchers show large and
statistically significant increases [$\underline{t}(\underline{df} = 568) = 5.77$, $\underline{p} < .0001$]. These
two rates differ significantly in that the nonwatchers increase a great
deal while the watchers' increase is the same as no change at all.

Turning to the independent sample, Table 7.10 also presents the differences between watchers and nonwatchers on cynicism scores after
the special. The watchers have lower cynicism than the nonwatchers,
although the difference is marginal [$\underline{t}(\underline{df} = 699) = 1.88$, $\underline{p} < .06$).

Differences in rates of increase in cynicism and between watchers
and nonwatchers seem to indicate that the NBC special may have ame-
liorated the effects of increasing cynicism observed in re-testing the
nonwatchers. However, watchers and nonwatchers were not randomly
assigned to condition, and so the apparent effects may be confounded
with differences in the samples. The group of watchers were different
from the nonwatchers on age, education, whether they are registered to
vote, whether they did vote in 1992, the extent that they follow the
health care reform debate, self-report of health care knowledge,
whether they have health insurance, newspaper reading, TV news consumption, listening to talk radio, and whether they have seen health
care reform ads.

Controlling for factors differentiating the watchers and nonwatchers
did not change the reported results. The increases in cynicism are
larger for the nonwatchers than watchers in the panel and higher for
the nonwatchers in the independent sample. By controlling for the
possible differences between the sample of watchers and nonwatchers,
it is not possible to achieve the same control that random assignment
provides. However, the controls for sample differences do provide a

correction, albeit an imperfect one, for the inability to randomly assign.

Summary

The bottom line is that the Harvard study confirms that the NBC special had an ameliorating effect on the audience's cynicism. The non-watchers showed substantial increases in cynicism; the watchers did not. This conclusion holds even after corrections for political and social differences between the two groups have been made. Across the two studies, there is evidence that exposure to the NBC special "To Your Health," when analyzed in terms of change from before to after the special, led, at least, to a temporary amelioration of the public's increasing cynicism about health care, if not an actual decrease.

Conclusions

This chapter has presented results on the effects of various styles of news coverage of election campaigns and policy debates on the audience's cynicism. These data are, to our knowledge, the first direct attempts to experimentally test the link between strategic news frames and cynical response. Some of our expectations have been borne out in the patterns of findings and some have not.

In Figure 7.1, we summarize the findings from the four experiments on three types of cynicism. From the broadcast-print study, only the II, SS, and control conditions are displayed since they represent the strongest test of the effects of issue and strategy frames consistent across media. The results from health care reform are displayed for the aggregated issue, strategy, and control groups.

The pattern of results consistently shows that those exposed to strategic news have stronger cynical reactions than those in control conditions. Of twelve comparisons, the cynicism reported by those receiving strategy news is higher than control in ten cases, with one opposite and one equal. The comparison that is opposite to hypothesis is found in the pre-test campaign study with a student sample.

The effects of issue frames on cynical reactions are not consistent across studies. We had hoped to see that emphasizing problems and solutions would depress cynical responses at least in comparison to the strategic news frames and have absolute levels no greater than those in control conditions. Putting aside the health care reform study, the cyn-

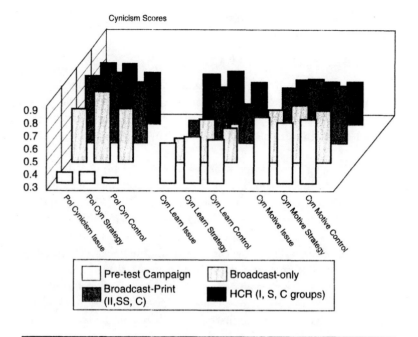

Figure 7.1. Three Types of Cynical Responses to Strategic and Issue News: Four Studies.

icism activated in issue news was less than that for strategic news in seven of nine comparisons with one equal and one opposite. The two deviations were both from the pre-test study with college students. The health care study, however, completely upset these trends as issue coverage activated cynical response in the same way that strategy frames did.

Strategy Frames and Cynicism

If any conclusion is supported by the pattern of findings, it is that strategy frames for news activate cynicism. This conclusion holds in the campaign study and in the study of health care reform. The effect is not large; sometimes it is only marginally significant. But the pattern of differences is consistent.

The effect occurs for broadcast as well as print news, and when the two are combined, the combination is additive. Other forms of coverage do not overcome strategic coverage's effects on cynicism; they simply reduce them somewhat.

Issue Frames and Cynicism

Issue frames did not function quite as clearly. In the campaign studies, they neither elevated nor lowered cynicism. Although issue frames had less cynicism than strategy frames as a rule, the pattern was typically: control equals issue frame, which is less than or equal to the strategy frame.

Issue framing of news about health care reform produced the surprising result, directly contrary to our expectations, that cynicism was activated in this coverage frame as much as in the various strategy conditions. All the news coverage conditions activated cynicism.

The results on issue coverage present two challenges to our current and future research. First, how can we explain the unexpected negative consequence of presenting a steady diet of issue-oriented analysis and news on people's attributions of cynicism? Second, what formats for the presentation of news can we expect to lower or at least to cap cynical response? We take up the first question here and the second in the final chapter.

One might be led to conclude that providing any coverage at all of the health care reform debate activated the audience's deep-seated cynicism about large-scale government programs. However, the NBC special offers contrary evidence. The special provided extensive coverage from all sides of the debate, yet in our study the cynicism of watchers was reduced. In the larger random sample, cynicism was curtailed for those who watched. The notion that any mention of the health care reform debate activated cynicism does not square with the effects of the NBC special.

One explanation of the reason for the effects of issue coverage on cynicism takes into consideration its "oppositional" character in print news articles. Health care reform was a complex issue, testing the understanding of most citizens, who after almost a year of intense media coverage, still showed low levels of accuracy about the president's plan and those of his competitors. Even when knowledge about health care reform was fairly good, people did not feel comfortable reaching a decision about what approach would be best. Many were confused about this important issue. At the same time, much ordinary news coverage and the kinds of articles we gave our participants were oppositional in the sense that every position taken on some solution to health care coverage was countered by a critical rejoinder. Even the issue-based op-ed pieces we provided were balanced by contrary op-eds.

This oppositional commentary may have confused or, worse, frustrated readers. Just as strategic coverage paints the motives of each actor in negative colors, and leads to the rejection of all alternatives, so issue coverage of health care from an oppositional point of view may involve the rejection of all alternatives in the debate. Just as cynicism may be the result of the rejection of all candidates as self-interested manipulators in campaigns, it may also be the result of the criticism and apparent rejection of all solutions to the problem of health care.

Campaigns are usually about people rather than policies. The electorate may feel comfortable in making up its mind about the personal leadership qualities of a candidate. Strategy coverage undermines judgments of persons, impugning their motives as continually self-interested. Public policy debates involve people and groups, but fundamentally deal with issues. Strategy coverage in public policy debates may increase cynicism by undermining the public's evaluations of the motives of the various political actors. But issue coverage when it undermines all available solutions, may do the same leaving the public frustrated, confused, and ultimately cynical about the debate itself, no matter how substantive it may appear to be.

The finding that issue coverage in the health care reform debate increased reader's cynical responses is certainly puzzling. One possible explanation holds that coverage in a complex policy debate like that of health care reform is conflict based, as is the coverage in many political campaigns. But political campaign coverage is more likely to be accompanied by advocacy, while reporting on the health care debate was not.

Our hypothesis stems from the differences between the two campaigns. In an election, the campaigners (and their staffs and representatives), although ready to attack the opponents' substantive plans, must not be seen solely as naysayers. If they acknowledge the existence of a problem,[21] they may attack but must also be ready with their own response. Failure to offer solutions produces the perception that the candidate is incapable of governing.

In the health care reform debate, interested parties often had strong reasons to retain the status quo, so the necessity of offering solutions was absent. The parties were often not politicians but businesses, insurance conglomerates, pharmaceutical companies, and other groups whose interests were affected. They had no need to provide solutions, compromises, and alternatives; they could simply point to the risks that would result from alternatives. Negativism without alternatives had little consequence for the naysayers.

If this explanation is plausible, we should find that campaign coverage is about as negative as coverage in the health care reform debate, but has more advocacy and compromise.

This hypothesis was tested in a limited way on samples of the news coverage in the health care reform debate and the presidential election of 1992.[22] We focused on issue-based coverage, not strategy, because we were trying to account for increases in cynical response to issue coverage in the health care debate.

Advocacy in Health Care. A sample of the issue articles dealing with health care debate was selected for coding. The sample came from four newspapers (*New York Times, Washington Post, Dallas Morning News,* and *Los Angeles Times*) at three different time periods. The time periods (1/24 to 2/27/94, 6/16 to 6/29/94, and 8/1/94 to 8/25/94) were the periods of peak coverage of health care reform news dating from January 15 to October 15, 1994. The duration of the periods around the peaks is bounded by increases from the average value of coverage of health care reform climbing toward the peak and then decreasing back to the average.

Coding focused on the positivity and negativity and compromise and advocacy of the coverage. As units of analysis we used not articles but parts of text that attribute, paraphrase, or quote an individual, institution, poll, unnamed source, or report and refer to a specific health care plan rather than health care reform in general. Each unit was graded for evaluative tone from strongly negative to strongly positive in seven steps.

Each unit was also graded for advocacy, compromise, or the absence of either. Advocacy is present when an alternative to a plan or a candidate's position is explicitly proposed or suggested. For example,

"The American people don't want a government-takeover of the health-care system and they don't support the Democratic bills," Senate minority leader Bob Dole said. "Republicans will work to give America what it wants: affordable health care that will always be there without a hundred new government agencies running the show."

was coded as advocating a position while attacking plans like Clinton's. When an alternative was not explicitly advocated but the stated position sought compromise or common ground with the critiqued alternative, the attribution was coded as a compromise. For example, this passage was treated as a compromise rather than an advocacy of another position.

> President Clinton hinted yesterday that although he is "less than pleased" with certain parts of the Mitchell plan, the two Democrats might be able to come to agreement over the Senate leader's universal coverage provisions.

The absence of either advocacy or compromise was coded as attack. For example, the following was treated as attack:

> "The Clinton plan is an unnecessary government bureaucracy," said Bill Kristol, a Republican analyst. "The Clinton welfare-state must not be allowed to take away individual choice."

Advocacy in the Presidential Campaign. Some modifications for coding coverage of the presidential campaign were necessary. The same newspapers were analyzed and the articles included all issue coverage from September 15 through November 2, 1992. In order to be included, an article had to have a headline pertaining to economic, foreign, or social policy issues or the candidate's character and capacity to govern.[23]

Comparisons

Table 7.11 presents the frequency differences in coverage between the presidential campaign of 1992 and the health care reform debate of 1994 for print stories. The comparisons are telling and suggest that the reported health care reform debate was more negative and more adversarial than even the presidential campaign of 1992. In the health care debate about half (49.8 percent) of the attributions were negative (230/462) while about 42 percent were negative (877/2064) in the presidential campaign; the number of advocacy or compromise statements per article was less than one in the health debate (68/81 = 0.84) and greater than one in the election campaign (348/283 = 1.23). The number of comments seeking to describe some common ground was about one in seven in the health care coverage (68/462 = 0.147) and about one in six in the presidential campaign (348/2064 = 0.169). None of these differences is huge, but they all point toward a more negative, more adversarial, and conflict-centered debate in the print media's

Table 7.11. Frequency of Advocacy and Compromise, and Evaluative Tone of a sample of news articles from the Presidential Campaign of 1992 and the Health Care Reform Debate of 1994.

	Health Care Debate	Presidential Campaign
No. of Articles	81	283
No. of Attributions	462	2064
No. Positive	178	413
No. Self-promoting	—	658
No. Neutral	54	116
No. Negative	230	877
No. Advocacy or compromise statements	68	348

Source: *New York Times, Washington Post, Dallas Morning News, Los Angeles Times.*

coverage of health care reform even in contrast to the mother of all political conflicts, a three way presidential battle.

Perceived Media Negativity and Cynicism. Content differences are not effects. To get some idea of the effects of media coverage during the health care reform debate, we surveyed our participants at the end of the debate but before the November 1994 elections. We tried to test the relationship between cynicism and people's perceptions of the negativity and advocacy of the media. What did people perceive the media debate on health care to be like? And, more important, were these perceptions tied to their cynicism about the health care debate?

Our expectation was that when issue coverage focuses on consensus and solutions (and not just problems and criticisms), cynicism would be reduced. Concentrating primarily on the points of conflict or avoiding the common ground or compromises among interested parties primes the audience for cynical response even when the coverage is substantive. Wouldn't an audience — even one drawn to substantive news coverage — be led to believe that the serious problem of health care reform could not be solved because all avenues to resolution were blocked and proposed resolutions lacked significant areas of consensus?

To test our expectations, we asked participants in our health care reform studies a series of questions about their perceptions of the media during the health care reform debate. These questions were designed to obtain two aspects of peoples' perceptions: (1) how focused on conflict as opposed to agreement the media were and (2) how much the media favored or were opposed to a given plan.[24]

We polled them in October 1994 after health reform had died as an issue but before the fall mid-term elections.

Three patterns emerged from analyzing the relationship between perceptions of the media and cynicism about the health care reform debate. First, those perceiving that the media tended to focus on conflict and ignore areas of agreement were more cynical about health care reform (four of four cases were each highly significant).[25] Second, those perceiving that media were more balanced in their coverage, rather than opposed or favorable, tended to have lower cynicism (three of four at or near significant).[26]

Our participants' cynicism about the health care reform debate was related to two perceptions about the media: its absence of balance and its overemphasis on conflict. When these perceptions were present, so was cynicism about the process. The lowest levels of cynicism were always associated with the perception of balanced coverage and less emphasis on conflict. What is especially interesting is that the same results hold for the Clinton plan, Republican alternatives, single payer, and health care in general. Our respondents associated unbalanced coverage and adversarial coverage with cynicism about the debate, *regardless of which plan they perceived the bias and conflict to be focused on.* This suggests that bias and excessive conflict themselves aggravate cynical reactions. The means are presented in Table 7.12.

An important caveat must be registered. Unlike our experiments, where formats of coverage can be traced as the cause of changes in cynicism, the survey results reported above only show that associations exist between perceptions of the media coverage and cynical reactions to the debate. Although these associations are suggestive, they are not conclusive. It is impossible from our data to know whether cynicism about the debate affected reaction to media coverage or vice versa or whether some external factor was influencing both.

The reason for asking our respondents their views of specific aspects of media coverage of health care reform was to test the idea that either too much conflict, too much negativity, or both were sources of cynicism. The results indicate that perceived conflict is

Table 7.12. Cynicism About the Health Care Debate as a Function of Perceptions of Media Coverage: Conflict-Oriented (High and Low) and Perceived Bias in Favorability

Plan Bias- >	Unfavorable		Balanced		Favorable	
Conflict- >	High	Low	High	Low	High	Low
Health care general	.88	.81	.79	.74	.87	.83
Clinton plan	.87	.80	.84	.77	.83	.77
Republican alternative	.85	.84	.85	.75	.86	.82
Single payer	.87	.81	.84	.76	.81	.81

strongly related to cynical response. Unfavorable coverage of a particular plan is not a source of cynical reaction; instead, the perception that coverage is unbalanced, either too favorable or too unfavorable, is linked to cynical reactions. Our results imply that people are especially concerned about journalists' emphasis on conflict, their failure to recognize and report agreement, and unbalanced negative or positive coverage. Our earlier speculations about conflict-oriented coverage being part of the basis for cynical reactions, even in issue-based stories, are supported in these data, although in fairness we must caution against overinterpretation.

Summary

Political cynicism is a kind of political judgment. Most of the research and theory on political judgment is aimed at understanding how citizens develop attitudes toward particular candidates and leaders as the basis for their choice in elections and their decision to support or distance themselves from given leaders. Political cynicism is mistrust generalized from particular leaders or political groups to the political process as a whole — a process perceived to corrupt the persons who participate in it and that draws corrupt persons as participants.

How does strategic framing activate such judgments? Strategically framed news accounts make salient the motivations of political actors. By doing so, they invite attributions to character traits and goals. These attributions may be relatively automatic and not in our immediate awareness. Strategic news frames do not merely draw attention to motivations; they imply or even state explicitly that political motives are directed at giving the actor or her constituents an advantage with voters. In short, the motives are self-interested and they thereby imply attributions that are negative — manipulative, dishonest, self-centered, deceitful, pandering — rather than positive. The negative traits carry evaluative implications that may be integrated with a previous evaluation in an on-line fashion or the traits stored along with the events producing the trait inference for later recall and judgment. If a single central trait attribution, such as mistrust, organizes other, more specific traits, then subsequent information is interpreted in the framework of the central trait dislodging its influence only after much disconfirming evidence.

Consider an example. Suppose that the information that Clinton supports tax relief for the middle class is stored as substantive policy information. What happens when the press frames that stance strategically as a maneuver to win needed middle-class votes of Reagan Democrats? In our account, the news reader or viewer who might otherwise store the information as a positive evaluation of Clinton because the respondent identifies with that position instead stores it as a negative evaluative trait — an instance of self-interested political action — akin to the category "tries to please everybody." This move would undercut two of the typical dimensions of candidate evaluation: the perception of Clinton's integrity and reliability.

And if the respondent is focused on impression formation about the nature of the political process, the campaign itself, or the individual candidates, she might also tally this datum into a conclusion that candidates in general are self-interested partisans unconcerned about the public good, and her ongoing tally would result in her report of increasing cynicism about the political process and its institutions.

The strategy structure and conflict/assertion mode of journalism invite ongoing on-line tallying of political markers of cynicism. Press reports in this structure do not create the cynicism — they activate the judgment operator that tallies indicators of it. In other words, they create a pathway from the attribute schema (policy versus personal) to the negatively evaluative, and invite on-line processing through a judgment set to tally impressions of cynicism. The substantive, explicit learning that strategy frames make possible is undermined by the implicit learning that judges political actors cynically.

Over time, for some, cynicism about people (they're all crooks) and positions (poll-driven pandering) becomes not simply a node but a superordinate node with all other political information subordinated to it. The node is highly accessible, frequently and recently activated, and carries a negative affective tag.

Confronted with a week of strategic news about the Philadelphia mayoral election, subjects tally a large amount of information framed to suggest that candidates are acting not in the public interest but in self-interest. The on-line tally registers increased cynicism. The information on which the tally is based is stored apart from the tally so that the reasons for cynical summary are no longer connected to the summary itself.

Confronted with a week of strategy-driven press coverage of the health care reform debate, the same occurs. Faced with issue coverage saturated with conflict among parties interested in the health care debate, news consumers saw not compromises, advocacy for new solutions, or common ground, they read instead of difference, conflict, and disagreement. Resolution did not seem possible. The continued confrontation of self-interested positions constituted issue coverage. The same negative, self-interested trait inferences may have arisen in response to conflict-centered coverage of health care issues.

Confronted with the NBC special, respondents whose impressions of health care reform coverage activated their cynicism in the first panel of study did not activate that judgment operator because the advocates affirmed and assumed each others' good will and integrity, conflict was framed as philosophical disagreement not partisan efforts at advantage taking, and a collective willingness to address the problems of the country was affirmed. Information stored as position and as person would be valenced negatively or positively depending on the ideological preferences of respondent but not tallied as evidence of a political world unworthy of trust. The judgment operator tallying the usual negative traits as evidence of cynicism is not activated. The special in fact mitigates the rising tide of cynicism about health care reform.

Strategy and conflict coverage activate the judgment operator that tallies evidence about the self-interested nature of the political process and its players. Those consuming a lot of news that is structured this way are as a result more cynical. But it is not necessary to consume a lot of strategic news to see its effects on how the actions of politicians are interpreted.

The findings of this and the previous chapter on learning and cynical reaction have helped us understand how news frames function, but they have also raised related questions. Do people who are primed to receive news learn both strategic and substantive information? Do they carry away knowledge in any more useful forms than those less receptive? Do they attribute greater cynicism to policy debates when the surrounding news environment is itself heavily strategic? Do strategic and issue frames for news prompt audiences to describe and make sense of political events in different ways? Can a single news article activate strategic attributions or does it take a larger dose? We address these questions next.

THE WORKINGS OF

THE CYNICAL PUBLIC MIND

Extending Media Framing

THE RESEARCH we presented in Chapters 6 and 7 focused on learning from news in the broadest sense — learning explicit information, both substantive and strategic, and acquiring implicit, unintended information in the form of cynical judgments of mistrust. The model we proposed in Chapter 4 provides a framework for understanding these effects through processes such as priming, spreading activation, and changes in accessibility (for learning) and automatic trait activation and on-line tallying (for cynical attributions). In this chapter, we provide additional data on learning and cynicism following leads suggested by the framing model of Chapter 4.

In the field experiments of the previous chapters, people were exposed to five days of news — print, broadcast, or a combination over a week's duration. The effects on learning and on cynicism seem to depend on exposure to a large dose of strategically framed news. The theory set forth in Chapter 4, however, does not assume that dosage is important. It operates from assumptions that even one strategically framed story can activate an audience's cynical attributions. We will test that idea first in this chapter.

In testing the effects of news frames on cynicism and learning in the two prior chapters, we used responses that were closed — that is, determined by the experimenters. Here we analyze the open-ended stories we invited people to write. These may indicate other aspects of what people learned during our experiments because writers are less constrained than with the more standard, fixed response alternatives. As we argued in Chapter 4, the stories people use to make sense of politics may reflect a kind of narrative knowledge of potential significance in understanding how people interpret their political worlds.

In a third set of analyses, we study those with more developed systems of political knowledge and ask if they are more ready to receive the information news provides — whether substantive or strategic. Those with more richly connected, accurate beliefs about politics may be capable of acquiring more and more accurate information from the news they consume. They may also acquire more implicit information, information that implies cynical evaluation, especially in the face of a news environment heavily loaded with strategic coverage.

We ask: "Are those higher in political knowledge more likely to learn from news?" If so, will they learn both strategic and substantive information? Will they be more likely to acquire the cynical attitudes represented implicitly in strategic news frames? Based on the model proposed in Chapter 4, we expect the answers to each of these questions to be affirmative. The more complex a person is cognitively about a topic, the more likely he or she will absorb new information about that topic. In turn, the more the information is soaked with implicit valuation, the more likely the hidden valence of the information will accepted along with the explicit content. In short, we expect those ready to receive the media's messages to learn from exposure and become more cynical.

Finally, cynical response to the process of deliberating about policy is linked to attitudes toward the topic of deliberation — in the present case cynicism about the health care reform debate and attitudes toward the Clinton plan. Does cynicism about the health care reform debate and its players explain attitudes toward the substance of President Clinton's plan?

Strategic News Stories Activate Cynicism
Interpretation of and Response Time to Strategic News

One assumption that guided our explanation of the effects of strategically framed news is that the mere presence of a strategic news frames can activate cynical attributions through priming and automatic inferences to traits. If our explanation is correct, two effects should then follow. First, the attributions invited by a strategy frame should be biased toward the cynical and self-interested, emphasizing the advantage to the actors involved. Thus, interpretations of actors' motives when there is some ambiguity in their description should be slanted toward the cynical. Further, if a news story cues a cynical frame of reference, then these cynical attributions ought to be able to be made more quickly than if the story cues some other frame.

We conducted an experiment to test these hypotheses. The basic idea was to have people read a series of news stories in issue or strategy form and then respond to questions about the stories, some of which would assess a cynical attributional bias.

About 120 people were recruited to participate for pay in a study on perceptions of news media. Except for the group's higher education level, the demographics of the sample are consistent with the population of the Philadelphia area.[1]

People came to our laboratory at the Annenberg School individually or in small groups. They were told that they would be reading a series of news stories from a computer screen and then responding to some questions at the end of each story. The stories appeared a segment at a time and participants could advance them by clicking on a mouse button. Questions were answered by moving the mouse arrow to the correct option and clicking. The computer kept track of the reading times for each segment of each story, the responses to the questions, and how quickly the answers were given (called reaction time). Those in the study practiced reading and answering questions using the mouse until they felt comfortable. Participants were randomly assigned to four conditions.[2] In each condition, five stories were read. The stories were the same newspaper articles used in the field study of the mayoral campaign (see Appendix A for an example), five issue and five companion strategy stories. The issue and strategy articles alternated so that in one condition — Issue-first, Order-1 — the order was Issue article #1 followed by Strategy article #2, Issue #3, Strategy #4, and Issue #5. The other three conditions were

Strategy-first, Order-1
| S1 | I2 | S3 | I4 | S5 |

Issue-first, Order-2
| I5 | S4 | I3 | S2 | I1 |

Strategy-first, Order-2
| S5 | I4 | S3 | I2 | S1 |

Everyone read issue and strategy articles, but no one read the same article more than once.

This design was chosen because it produces a conservative test of the hypothesis about cynical attribution and reaction time. Instead of giving one group all strategy and another group all issue news, the news frames were alternated. If the hypothesis is successful, it would be because strategy gets activated and de-activated and then re-activated and so on.

At the end of each article, eight true-false questions were asked. Five were aimed at cynical attributions. One of the five was the same across all the stories and was about positioning with the voters:

This article helps you figure out who is ahead and behind in the polls.

The other four were particular to the content of each article, with two directly implicating cynical self-interest on the part of the politicians involved. For example,

Rendell pushed privatization to appeal to the city's wealthier voters.

The other two questions implied public interest as the motive for various stands. For example,

Rendell pushed privatization to solve the city's financial problems.

The other three questions were more factual and could be answered correctly from the content of the story alone. For example,

Rendell praised Egan's answer regarding the new trash dumping law.

Table 8.1. Adjusted Means for Cynical Attributions and Reaction Times:
News Study

	Cynical Attributions (Adjusted [a])		Reaction Times (Adjusted)	
	Issue—1st	Strategy—1st	Issue—1st	Strategy—1st
Story 1	I1	S1	I1	S1
	2.03**	2.43**	27.50**	22.41**
Story 2	S2	I2	S2	I2
	2.36**	2.76**	31.44**	26.63**
Story 3	I3	S3	I3	S3
	3.33	3.25	23.63	21.08
Story 4	S4	I4	S4	I4
	2.51**	2.18**	28.87	25.68
Story 5	I5	S5	I5	S5
	2.54***	3.15***	27.51	27.26

[a] The higher scores are more cynical attributions. Means are adjusted means from
MANCOVA with three covariates: age, education, and reading time for stories.
** $p < .05$ and *** $p < .01$ by t-test where comparison is issue versus strategy version
of same story.

The three questions that suggested cynical attributions to the campaigners and to the article (who's ahead and behind) were treated as a group. The two implying public interest were treated as a group. We also grouped the three recall questions.

The results partially supported the hypothesis that strategic framing would bias interpretation toward the cynical.[3] Table 8.1 presents the adjusted means for bias in questions with a cynical orientation and reaction time in answering these questions. No clear patterns of significance emerged for the recall questions, the questions implying a public interest on the part of the candidates, or the reaction times to answer either set of questions. Therefore, the means for these questions are not presented here.

Each cell in the table gives a mean score for a strategy or issue version of the same story. Because the story frames changed from the strategy to issue frame or vice versa, each cell is labeled as an issue or strategy story. Columns 2 and 3 are mean cynicism scores and columns 4 and 5 are the (total) reaction times to the three cynicism questions in seconds.

The cynical attributions are significant $F(5, 110) = 10.0$, $p < .0001$, Wilks Lambda $= .687$ across experimental condition. But the key tests are the tests by story across the I and S versions. Four of these differences are significant ones, all but story three. Three of the four are in the correct direction while story 2 goes in the opposite direction.

The reaction times are marginally significant with $F(5,110) = 2.05$, $p = .077$, Wilks Lambda $= .915$. Two of the five stories have significantly different reaction times, but only one is in the direction of faster reaction times with the strategy story, namely, story 1. Story 2, which shows the wrong direction in cynical attributions, also shows that the attributions in the issue version are made more quickly than in the strategy version. In effect, the issue version of story 2 is behaving as if it were a strategy story.

Stories 1 though 5 were evaluated on a variety of criteria prior to using them in the simulated campaign studies. Overall, the set of stories was perceived as we had supposed (see Chapter 5 for a summary of these findings). Specific reactions to story 2 seem to indicate that those judging this story read the issue and strategy versions differently from how they read the comparable frames for the other four stories. Three specific differences emerged. First, unlike the other four story pairs, the strategy version of story 2 was seen as "contributing more to knowledge about candidates' stands on the issues" ($p = .075$). None of the other strategy stories got this response. Also, the issue version of story 2 was seen as "contributing more to knowledge of which candidate has the greater chance of winning" than the strategy version. This difference was not significant, but the other four stories showed the opposite pattern and the differences were significant. Thus, on these two questions, story 2 received judgments that were contrary to the typical issue-strategy distinctions. This suggested that readers may have interpreted the issue version as having strategic elements and the strategy version as having issue elements.[4]

Because of the very real problems with strategy-issue distinctions in story 2, conclusions from this study must be stated tentatively. Story 2 aside, three of the other four strategy stories tended to lead readers to evaluate political actors more cynically than issue-oriented stories did.

Interestingly, this effect only occurred with questions that invited a cynical response (i.e., the "true" response was the cynical interpretation).[5] It did not occur with questions for which the "false" response was associated with the cynical interpretation. The strategic story, along with the priming by the cynically oriented question, that led respondents to their more cynical attributions.

Only story 1 produced the reaction time differences that we expected. If people organize their political knowledge in strategic schemas, then news stories that cue such schemas should produce faster cynical reactions than those that do not.[6] With only one of five stories exhibiting this effect, we cannot be confident that strategy schemas are the basis for organizing political knowledge. At the same time, the presence of the effect in at least one story (story 1) should encourage other research.

This study does show a fairly consistent interpretation bias activated by strategic news. Its design is especially sensitive to the possibility that cynical interpretations might require a series of strategic stories to have any effect on cynical interpretations. That is not possible here since the story frames alternate. A single story can activate cynical attributions — a cumulative effect across many stories is not necessary. This finding highlights the sensitivity of the news consuming public to the way that motivations of political actors are portrayed.

Narratives and News
Narrative News Formats

One of the formats of news we evaluated in Chapters 6 and 7 was represented by the NBC special "To Your Health." In our evaluation and that of the Harvard School of Public Health, the special was seen to enhance people's knowledge about health care and, at a minimum, to counteract rising cynicism about health care reform. One explanation is that the NBC special was not a typical news format — rather it fit what might be called narrative news. It used a variety of techniques, including expert panels and an interview with Hillary Clinton, and it emphasized the personal stories of people who had to deal with the health care system — highlighting their fears, concerns, and very real human dilemmas.

The NBC special did not afford a direct test of narrative versus non-narrative news. Yet the use of personal narratives as a means of carrying information to the public suggests that the role of narrative may be important in stimulating interest, activating knowledge, and taking advantage of the easy accessibility of narrative information.

The NBC special was not strategically framed. But strategically framed news tells a story in its own way. The story is the same again and again—of appearances being deceptive; of the game of competing for votes and advantage over one's opponents; of hidden motives unearthed by exposing the interests of political entities. Indeed, one of the potential attractions of the strategic frame for news is that it can be a good story with protagonists, antagonists, competition, and conspiracy.

In our studies of the mayoral campaign and the health reform debate, we tried to tap into people's stories about these events to understand how they attempted to make sense of them.

Narratives About the Mayoral Campaign

In the research on the simulated mayoral race, participants in all three studies were asked to write an essay about the campaign. They were directed to

> pretend that later on today a good friend of yours writes you a letter asking what you know about the Philadelphia mayoral campaign and its candidates, Egan, Rendell, Lawler, and Wesley. Write a letter to your friend telling him or her the story of the campaign, the candidates, and the election as revealed in the debate you have just seen and the other materials you got from us.

We hoped that the essays would reveal some of the ways people organized their own thoughts about political campaigns.

Word Analyses. The essays were analyzed in terms of the occurrence of word classes. Four classes were identified: strategy, issue, and positive and negative trait. Strategy words included the language of war, games, competition, fighting, attacking, winning and losing, artifice, maneuvering, and mistrust. Examples included bash, battle, bomb, defeat, discredit, front, hit, image, lie, mudslinging, runner, slam, slant, suspicion, tricks, twist, withdrawal, wound.

Issue words identified the topics of problems facing the city, solutions proposed, groups affected, leadership potential, and promises and delivery. Examples included abortion, airport, budget, choice, civil rights, corruption, dollar, education, expenses, gays, gridlock, Haitians, ideas, industry, insurance, knowledge, liberal, management, mistakes, MOVE (a radical group that had a violent confrontation with city police), philosophy, platform, privatize, qualifications, stance, tax, values, and so on.

Trait words identified personal characteristics of the candidates. These were divided into positive, negative, and neutral on the basis of evaluating a series of adjective opposites (e.g., good–bad) by a small group of evaluators. On average, the internal reliability across evaluators was very high (internal reliability .97). Positive trait words included bright, concerned, confident, fair, impressive, kind, polished, savvy, strong, trustworthy, wise, and youthful among a total of more than 150 such terms. Negative trait words suggest considerable dislike: anxious, boring, confused, dirty, hostile, indecisive, liar, nasty, pandering, puppet, sleazy, slick, smug, uncomfortable, unqualified, waffling, and wishy-washy.[7]

We expected that strategically framed news would increase the use of strategy words in comparison to no mayoral news and in comparison to issue-framed news. Because strategic news also indicts the trustworthiness and motivations of political actors, negative traits should occur with greater frequency under strategic framing. By contrast, issue words and positive trait words should be elevated in issue news at least in comparison to strategically framed news.

Identifying words is not the same thing as identifying story structures. Words are isolated and out of context. They do not reveal organization, tension among competing interests, or even the propositions advanced by writers. To check that the word count was a reasonable surrogate for more contextual renderings, we undertook another analysis of a subset of the essays that identified three categories of conceptual units: strategy, issue, and trait, with the latter now divided into campaign and candidate traits. The subset studied was the groups receiving only issue and only strategy news coverage in the broadcast-print experiment.

Conceptual units were sentences and phrases conveying single, distinct thoughts.[8] Positive and negative traits were not coded in the conceptual analysis. Correlations between word analyses and conceptual analyses were strong with issue words and conceptual units at $r = .93$, and strategy at $r = .82$ (significant at $p < .001$). The conceptual coding shows that the context surrounding words does not appreciably alter the *ranking* of essays in terms of how much strategy, issue, or trait lan-

Table 8.2. Strategic Word Counts in Essays Across News Frames: Three Studies of a Simulated Campaign

	II			SS	Control	$F_{(2,63)}$
Preliminary study[a]	.246*			.344*	.137	4.91 $p = .01$
	I			S	Control	$F_{(2,97)}$
Broadcast only[b]	1.70*			1.61*	.78	3.58 $p = .03$
	II	IS	SI	SS	Control	$F_{(4,155)}$
Broadcast-print[c]	1.78	2.63*	1.80	2.34*	.89	2.14 $p = .07$

Note. * Indicates significant difference from control $p < .02$ at least.
[a] The values are proportions of words for this study since no pre-test words available.
[b] Unadjusted means since pre-test strategy words were not a significant covariate.
[c] Adjusted means for pre-test strategy words.

guage is present. Word counts are thus reasonable measures of more context-sensitive, conceptual ratings of writers' strategic and substantive evaluations of candidates.

Neither issue nor trait words produced any clear patterns of results consistent (or inconsistent) with our expectations across the three studies about political campaigns.[9] Strategy words exhibited consistent effects. In the preliminary test, a proportion was created of the number of strategy words divided by the number of words summed across the four types. Table 8.2 displays the means and tests of significance. Strategy words were more numerous in the SS condition, next in the II, and lowest in the no news condition. Strategy coverage elevated strategic language use more so than issue coverage, which in turn was significantly greater than the control condition.

In the broadcast-only study, strategy words were more numerous in the strategy and issue conditions than the control, but strategy news did not differentially increase the likelihood of strategic essays over that of issue news.[10] In the broadcast-print study, two conclusions about the essays follow (see Table 8.2). All the news conditions have more strategic essays than the control condition does — $F_{(4,155)}$ = 2.14, $p = .078$ — and the two print strategy conditions (IS and SS) are significantly different from the control at $p < .025$ and $p < .009$. When the experimental conditions alone undergo an analysis of covariance, a nearly significant main effect for print is discovered — $F(1,134) = 3.35$, $p < .07$ — with the strategy frame (adjusted $M = 2.44$) greater than the issue frame (adjusted $M = 1.84$).

Results across the three studies are consistent. The way television frames news does not seem to alter the kind of essays that people write to make sense of political campaigns. The only effect was for negative traits that increased in response to strategic frames when broadcast news was presented alone. At the same time, strategically framed broadcast news was not associated with more strategic essays than issue oriented broadcast news. Perhaps the interpersonal character of television activates attributions about a person's character,[11] especially negative attributions in strategic news frames.

Print news does have consequences for the essays people write to understand politicians and their campaigns. Strategic print news frames activate strategic language and stories and these stories become the basis for describing, evaluating, and, we believe, understanding political processes. In the preliminary study, the SS condition elevated strategy language in the students' essays while it remained lower in the issue and lowest in the control conditions. On the basis of this study alone we could not know whether the activation was due to print or broadcast framing.

The broadcast-print study shows that it was print and not broadcast coverage that gave the essays their strategic tones. Strategic print coverage was associated with strategic essays; strategic broadcast coverage was not.[12] We believe that the differences in strategic word counts represent more than differences in word choices. The strong correlations between the richer, more context dependent conceptual coding suggests this.[13] So does the content of the essays.

Two explanations of these modality effects are possible. One is that reading and writing are more closely related processes because they are propositionally based, focusing on the words themselves, while listening and writing are more remote. Hearing a few words in a television news story may be insufficient to activate synonyms and semantic associates while the more frequent strategic words in the print news stories may be stronger cues and in the same modality as the outcome — written words. A second possibility is that written texts can be processed more deeply (or centrally, in the language of Petty and

Cacioppo[14]) while orally presented words pass quickly, cannot be re-heard by listeners (unlike printed words), and compete for attention with more attractive visual cues.

Essays. Most of the essays offered negative evaluations of the mayoral race and its candidates. A few were substantive, dealing with the issues and leadership potential of the candidates. One writer evaluated Philadelphia's major problems, what needed to be done, and who seemed to have the ideas necessary to successfully deal with the problems:

> Philadelphia is faced with many entrenched problems: the unions wield too much power over decisions made in city hall: white flight to the suburbs has sapped the city's resource base; old line Democrats have been in power too long.
>
> Philadelphia must increase its revenues and concurrently cut its spending. A mayor strong enough to take on the unions is desperately needed.
>
> Only one candidate — Rendell — appears prepared to take the tough steps needed to resolve the fiscal crises. The others appear long on rhetoric but far short of providing specific solutions. (#56, I)

Essays like this were very infrequent.

More typical were the cynical essays that did little to disguise their mistrust and disdain of political processes. One wrote of falsehoods and misrepresentation as characteristic of campaigns:

> The R[epublican] and D[emocratic] candidates left me feeling that either one would say whatever they thought the most people wanted to here. That lying was alright because it was just a campaign. (#135, SS)

Others focused on the lack of substance and the necessity of attack as a modus operandi:

> The campaign was pretty traditional with the front runner who (Rendell) avoids controversy and the other candidate who has a prayer (Egan) attacks the front runner. In short, little of substance gets communicated to voters and people vote on general principals or party line. (#140, SS)
>
> In my opinion, the candidates talked about nothing, they covered the same things one would find in any election in the country. Everyone said they would not raise taxes or lay anybody off. (#151, SS)

Campaigns and candidates were seen as wallowing in the lowest forms
of behavior as a part of the typical tactics of politics:

> There are four candidates running for mayor: one democrat, one republi-
> can and two "independent" candidates. There is nothing new regarding
> their campaign tactics, they are all somewhat sleazy.... The other two can-
> didates are up to the same old mud slinging that has characterized so many
> other campaigns. (#261, IS)

The results of the constant conflict and attack are a resignation over
the failure of politics and fatigue resulting from its consumption.

> I am so tired of going into the voting booth and trying to pick the lesser of
> the evils before us ... anymore you are not voting for a real person but a
> conglomerate of what a highly paid professional political strategist has put
> together. (#242, IS)

Some simply dismiss the whole process: "Same issues — same pandering as in all elections" (# 149, SS).

The picture of politics seen through these essays is a cynical one
indeed, paralleling almost point for point and term for term the adversarial, tactical, and artificial character of the strategic frame.

Indeed, some essayists adopted the posture of reporters and described campaigning from a third-person perspective.

> The candidates in the Philadelphia campaign face very difficult issues
> because the city has so many problems: high crime, budget deficit, poor
> city services, homelessness. All of the candidates are "slamming" the incum-
> bent, Rendell, for the problems. Rendell is a Democrat who is trying to
> solve the problems without raising taxes. His primary solution is to priva-
> tize services in order to "run them more efficiently." He claims — contrary
> to popular opinion — that this would not involve massive layoffs. Rendell is
> the front-runner with a 42% lead in the polls over Egan, the #2 in the polls.
> Egan is a Republican who is against privatization (although he's waffled a
> bit on this) and seems to have defined his platform as being against every-
> thing that Egan supports. He studies what the public wants to hear and
> reacts accordingly by supporting whatever idea seems to have the most
> popular appeal.
>
> Wesley is a black independent candidate who considering that he hasn't
> held office is realistic about what can and cannot be done to solve the city's
> problems. He knows a tax increase or major layoff would be necessary.

Lawler is a woman who seems to have genuine understanding and insight into some of the city problems and why they occur — but has no solutions, no plan. (#136, SS)

Narratives About the Health Care Reform Debate

Participants in our studies of health care reform were asked to write essays to a friend at two different points during the debate. The first request coincided with the field experiment during March 1994 (see Chapter 5) and the second with a third-wave telephone survey during October 1994, after the legislative effort ended. The first set of essays asked people to "tell him or her as much as you can about the alternative health proposals, the persons sponsoring them, and their likely effect on you if they are passed." Responses were substantive, for the most part, with very little of what we would identify as cynical or strategic stories. Asking people to tell what they know about various plans produced precisely that — knowledge about health reform proposals. The absence of cynical reaction in these essays is not to be construed as the absence of cynicism about the debate, but is more likely the result of instructions.

Those participating in the third wave of our study on health care reform were invited to write an essay on the health care debate and how it turned out. They were asked to assume that a friend had been out of the country and knows that there was a debate and how it turned out. The friend asks, "Fill me in on what happened on this health care debate in the last 15 months." These essays were completed before we conducted the telephone interviews.

Melinda Schwenk conducted a qualitative analysis of the 153 essays written in October. In these essays, people recounted their versions of what had transpired during the health reform debate, why reform failed in their opinion, and whether this was the right decision or not.[15] The 153 essays yielded 431 primary reasons for the demise of health care reform.

These data require one conclusion: people attribute the failure of health care reform to the political processes involved. About 40 percent of the 431 reasons cited for failure fell into categories of "opposing interests which could not or would not be compromised" or "specific special interests which were opposed." Other reasons identified by Schwenk included political party opposition, specific leaders, big government, cost, complexity, too much change too quickly, and satisfaction with the present system (these totaled about 50 percent of the remaining reasons).

A reading of the essays indicates that opposing interests and special interests were seen as defending their own self-centered concerns or those of their constituent groups. For example:

> You see, the insurance and drug companies were really going to lose out if there was reform.

> ... in the end it seemed to boil down to ... "I certainly don't want to pay a penny more to help anyone else get coverage."

> A group of small insurance companies bought air time trashing the Clinton plan, as it would benefit only the largest insurers so they were trying to save themselves.

> I think it all comes down to simple greed — greed of the special interest lobbyists in making sure things went their way, greed of doctors and other health professionals, greed of insurance companies ... but most of all greed of politicians who saw it in their own best interest to decline support for the President's plan while inventing all sorts of other alternative plans that chiefly seemed to have little difference from Clinton's ... to have the advantage of having their own name on it.

Such self-interest is the central component of what we have been calling cynicism and what we have identified as the most common motivation attributed explicitly or implicitly to political actors and groups in strategically framed news. Since people do not cite strategic frames as a characteristic problem of news coverage — instead they list such factors as bias, inaccuracy, sensationalism, and the like — excessive self-interest is not viewed as a problem associated with one-dimensional news coverage but with the political actors and groups in hot pursuit of their self-interests.

A more systematic evaluation of the essays was undertaken to determine how many attributed self-interested motives to the actors in the health care reform debate.[16] Approximately 38 percent were identified as ascribing at least some cynical motives to the actors in health care reform. About the same percentage (36 percent) rated the government as ineffective for failing on health care reform. About 54 percent made clear their mistrust of the process of reform.[17] The three ratings intercorrelated from .32 to .45, $p < .001$ and correlated with our standard measures of cynicism (both media and health care) from .17 to .29, p < .04 at least.

Our own content analyses of television and print news during the health reform debate[18] found that about two-thirds of the print and broadcast news employed strategically framed stories. These framings were six times more likely to have an accompanying photo — thereby making them more salient — than the issue-framed stories. The content of issue-based stories tended to be adversarial and confrontative. We estimated that one in ten comments on television newscasts and one in seven attributions in the print media advocated an alternative or a compromise position. Obviously, the vast majority of comments either advanced the speaker's position or criticized that of an opponent. Most of the print and broadcast ads about health care reform argued against an alternative (60 percent).[19]

If the environment characterizing the health care reform debate is fundamentally strategic, emphasizing self-interest, and is predominantly adversarial, is it any wonder that the audience would say that health care reform failed because of the self-interest of the parties involved? Rightly or wrongly, the parties are seen as naysayers or as problem solvers whose solutions, if any, only advance their self-interest. The media frames these portraits strategically and in adversarial terms. The mixture of complexity, failure, confrontation, and strategic framing is volatile and reinforces, we believe, a public cynicism that adopts the frameworks of blame the media have perpetuated.

Implicit in their understanding of the health care reform debate is an acceptance of the way the debate was characterized in the mainstream news media. Also implicit in their understanding is a clear sense that the reform efforts failed in large part because of the uncompromising conflicts engendered by the self-interested motivations of the political and social groups engaged in dispute. These characterizations of the advocates in health care reform are precisely the ones implied by the predominantly strategic and adversarial coverage of print and broadcast news and advertising revealed by content analyses.

We are not suggesting that these characterizations are either accurate or inaccurate. Rather, we are claiming that the news structures make sense of political events by suggesting that government officials, advocates of public policies, and candidates have motives that, even when seemingly aimed at the public good, are directed at advancing their own self-interest and the narrow interests of their constituents.

In summary, strategic framing of news makes substantive and strategic information more accessible to news consumers. These frames take the form of stories peppered with strategy language that convey cynical characterizations of political campaigns and policy disputes. Strategic framing also produces a kind of implicit learning — what would be described as a judgment in the previous chapter.

Four Tests of Learning and Media Reception

In the simulated mayoral campaign, participants' knowledge of both substantive and strategic information was greater in the experimental than in the control conditions. Some evidence also suggested that strategic frames per se yielded higher learning for strategic information than other news formats. These two findings can be explained by changes in accessibility. The control conditions did not activate information about the mayoral candidates or their campaigns but the experimental conditions did. Specifically, the strategic news conditions may have activated strategic concepts more than other news frames did (what we had called issue in this experiment). Just as agenda-setting findings can be explained by appealing to long-term changes in the accessibility of "most important problems," so the learning in the mayor's study can be explained by the short-term changes in accessibility of the semantically related concepts.

Learning effects were mostly absent in the field study of health care reform. Possible reasons include the fact that too many participants were actively consuming other sources of news about health care reform during the week. Instead of a controlled exposure to news consistent within experimental condition, various news formats contaminated the conditions, activating and increasing the accessibility of constructs that otherwise would have remained quiescent. In effect, patterns of activation were not sufficiently controlled.

To evaluate whether people learned from other sources of news during the health care reform debate, we tested the acquisition of both cynical and substantive information from media exposure to news.

The consensus across a range of research is that simple measures of exposure to news on television, in print, and on radio do not account for much variance in the public's knowledge about campaigns or public policy debates.[20] This consensus cannot be interpreted to mean that the public does not learn from news at all. Rather, the what and when of learning from news depends on a complex of factors related to education, prior knowledge, attention to issues and to the media themselves, audience motivations, and specificity and reliability of measurement.

One alternative has been proposed by John Zaller.[21] Media exposure, attention, and gratifications are at best surrogates for the measure that would be ideal — a direct measure of reception of information. Reception of information assumes that a person has been exposed to the information, attended to it, comprehended it, and can use it effectively in making political judgments. Consider an analogy. Teachers evaluate students in terms of their ability to comprehend, recall, and use the information supplied in lecture and reading. They do not evaluate students' performance solely in terms of attendance, attentiveness, and attitude toward the subject matter. Although these factors are undoubtedly correlated with more direct measures of performance, the direct measures of mastery of course materials are certainly more valid indicators than the indirect measures.

This is precisely what Zaller has proposed at both the theoretical and measurement levels. Reception is measured by asking fairly general questions about the positions of various political actors and groups on different issues. For example, one question might ask: On the issue of abortion, some people are primarily pro-choice and some are primarily pro-life. Where does Ross Perot stand on this issue? To correctly answer this question, a person must have *received* information about Perot and his position on the choice-life issue; that is, there had to be exposure, attention, comprehension, and recall. What Zaller has proposed is that the family of measures of domain-general political knowledge will be better predictors of specific forms of political learning and attitude change than will measures of media exposure to political information (and its surrogates).[22]

Vincent Price and John Zaller specifically tested the relative efficacy of political sophistication versus newspaper and television exposure, along with interpersonal discussion in predicting people's knowledge of specific news stories in the national news agenda.[23] Across sixteen news items (spanning the spectrum from the sublime to the ridiculous), political sophistication was a strong, significant predictor of learning even when education is controlled, while newspaper exposure was insignificant and television news exposure had small effects, significant in about half the cases. The authors avoid concluding that television, print news exposure, and education have no predictive power but do conclude that

> their incremental predictive power is relatively weak, and preexisting levels of general political knowledge clearly offer us the most reliable and parsimonious way of predicting individual differences in likelihood of news reception.[24]

Although the authors do not imply that media exposure measures are useless in studies of learning and opinion change, they do invite students of political communication to "abandon their normal reliance on self-reported levels of news media exposure and look instead to prior political knowledge [political sophistication] as a preferred general indicator of news reception" (p. 160).

The correlations between political sophistication and learning substantive, strategic, and other information from news will allow us to evaluate whether those high in political sophistication (and therefore in news reception) learned from the heavily strategic news coverage during the health care reform debate.

Health Care Reform

Data from people participating in the field experiment about health care reform were analyzed to test the relationship between political sophistication and various measures of political knowledge including breadth (construct differentiation), coherence (indicated by argument quality), and accuracy (indexed by three measures of learning).

Political Sophistication. Political sophistication was measured by means of a series of questions on general political knowledge. Specifically, participants were asked to place Bill Clinton, most conservatives, and most liberals on a continuum that most closely described their positions on various issues. For example,

> Some people say that abortion should not be permitted because it is taking the life of an unborn child. Others say that abortion should be permitted in the first three months of pregnancy as a matter of personal choice.

> What does Bill Clinton say about life and choice issues?

> Pro-life:——:——:——:——:——:——:——:Pro-choice

Other issues included preference in hiring for minorities, NAFTA and jobs, environment and job loss, health reform and price controls, and health reform and government involvement.

We scored the answers by comparing a person's positioning of Clinton, most liberals, and most conservatives relative to one another. For example, if a person indicated that the position of most liberals on NAFTA was more toward the "lose jobs" end of the continuum while that of most conservatives was toward the "gain jobs" end, they would be given one point correct, but not if the order was reversed. Thus, the positioning of Clinton to conservatives, Clinton to liberals, and liberals to conservatives was compared for correct location relative to one another. Being on the "correct" side of the scale was not evaluated, only the relative positions were.[25]

This measure of political sophistication provides a number of advantages. First, it allows people to use the scales in their own way and only makes comparisons within persons rather than evaluating the person's score in relation to some external standard. Second, the measure allows both knowledge and ideology to be factored in simultaneously.

The scale consisted of eleven comparisons with a range of 0 to 11, a mean of 8.50, standard deviation of 2.4, and an internal reliability of .79.[26]

If this is a good measure of political sophistication, then it should reflect knowledge about politics that is more extensive, more richly elaborated, and more accurate. It should not simply measure accuracy of recall but should be associated with indicators of the breadth and organization of political knowledge.

Construct Differentiation. Construct differentiation has been widely used to measure the complexity of a person's knowledge about a topic. In its various guises, construct differentiation has been employed in studies of interpersonal communication,[27] information processing,[28] and political reasoning.[29] Presumably, the greater the construct differentiation, the more different ways a person has to categorize and differentiate issues on the topic. Construct differentiation uncovers the dimensionality of a person's knowledge.

In order to assess the level of complexity of people's knowledge about the health care debate, participants were asked to answer the following open-ended question at the conclusion of the field experiment:

Pretend that a good friend writes you a letter asking what you know about the health care debate in the United States. Your friend has been out of the country and knows nothing except that a health care policy is currently being debated. Write a letter to your friend, telling him or her as much as you can about the alternative health proposals, the persons sponsoring them, and their likely effect on you if they are passed. In responding to your friend, draw on everything you know about the debate including information gotten from other sources and from what you read and watched in the past week as a part of this study.

To evaluate the complexity of these essays, we developed a coding system based on the methodologies of Tetlock and of Burleson[30] that evaluated the number of unique constructs related to the health care debate. Fifty-seven of 340 essays were coded for construct differentiation. The reliability of the coding was very high — in the range of .90 correlation.

However, the correlation between construct differentiation and simple word counts was so high ($r = .95$) that coding was abandoned in favor of word counts. The two measures share 90 percent of their variance. The number of words averaged 161 ranging from 0 to 685, with a standard deviation of 109.

Argument Quality. Construct differentiation shows neither the organization of knowledge nor the person's ability to use the knowledge in that most important of political activities — reasoned argument.

To get more open-ended measures of a person's knowledge about the health care reform debate, we asked our participants the following sequence of questions:

In the debate about health care, almost everyone agrees that between 35 and 45 million Americans have no health coverage.

Why do you think these people do not have health care coverage?

What other reasons come to mind as to why people don't have health care coverage?

If someone were to disagree with your reasons about why people don't have coverage what might that person say to try to convince you that your reasons were wrong?

What reasons could you give to convince your friend that you were right in the first place?

This sequence is based on a method of assessing the quality of a person's arguments developed by Deanna Kuhn.[31] She maintains that the quality of argument depends on (1) making explicit, relevant claims, (2) providing relevant evidence for those claims, (3) conceiving of potential counterarguments, and (4) rebutting the counterarguments.

The first two levels of judging the quality of an argument are almost definitional. The other two are less obvious. Kuhn defends them this way:[32]

> An assertion with accompanying justification — a course of reasoning aimed at demonstrating its truth — is an empty, indeed superfluous, argument unless one can conceive of the possibility of being wrong — in other words conceive of an opposing assertion. Once two assertions are in place, cognitively speaking, the further challenge poses itself of relating available evidence to the two. Presumably, it is a weighting of positive and negative evidence that has led one to espouse one of the assertions over the other. Indeed, it is just such a weighting process that is implicit when we speak of a reasoned argument. When new evidence is introduced to the holder of a reasoned argument, he or she is able to integrate such evidence into this implicit weighting process.[33]

We assumed that the quality of arguments generated would be an indicator of the depth of knowledge that people had acquired about at least one aspect of the health reform debate. As before, the principle of semantic activation guided our expectations: issue and strategy news stories should produce higher quality arguments (that is, deeper knowledge) than news mostly unrelated to health care reform.

Conceptualizing argument quality is quite different from coding it reliably. A valid and reliable coding system based on the number of claims, the coherence of the reasons in support of the claims, the presence of relevant counterarguments, and successful rebuttal of the counterargument was developed.[34]

Recall Accuracy. Construct differentiation and argument quality do not calculate accuracy of knowledge. People could have many constructs that are only peripherally relevant to the issue of health reform or inaccurately linked together. An argument could be rated as high in quality, even if it made invalid claims or offered false rebuttals.

Knowledge should be evaluated for accuracy and the ability to infer correct conclusions from political events. The three measures of recall

Table 8.3.

Regression Analyses of Recall, Argument Quality, and Construct Differentiation by Political Sophistication: Health Care Reform Sample

	Outcome Measures				
	Factual Recall ($\underline{N}$ = 332)	Issue Recall ($\underline{N}$ = 332)	Strategy Recall ($\underline{N}$ = 332)	Argument Quality ($\underline{N}$ = 328)	No. of Words ($\underline{N}$ = 332)
Education	.140*	.061	.020	.101*	.238***
Experimental Condition	.051	.007	-.001	.056	.003
Political Sophistication	.235***	.260***	.167**	.192**	.238***
Civics	-.013	.077	.021	.116+	.021
Involvement	-.012	.129*	.004	-.055	.100
Attention	.122+	.055	.022	.095	.041
Print	-.023	-.073	-.036	.000	-.089
Television	-.033	-.148**	-.041	-.034	-.137*
Radio	-.041	.073	.104+	-.043	-.062
Talk	.005	.033	.067	.077	.050
$\underline{R}$-squared	.154	.197	.054	.143	.243
$\underline{F}$	5.860***	7.879***	1.823+	5.281**	10.305***

Note: Cell entries are beta weights from standard multiple regression.
+$\underline{p}$ < .10; *$\underline{p}$ < .05; **$\underline{p}$ < .01; ***$\underline{p}$ < .001.

accuracy used in the health care reform field study (Chapter 6) were employed as surrogates for accuracy of political knowledge: factual, substantive, and strategic recall.

Results. Table 8.3 presents the results from a regression analysis on all five indicators of political knowledge development from the field experiment on health care reform. Several alternative predictors of knowledge structure besides political sophistication were used as competing predictors or controls. These included education, civics knowledge, political involvement, attention to political issues, experimental condition, and various measures of exposure to media news. The clear and consistent predictor is political sophistication significant at $p < .01$ in all cases. Those who have greater political sophistication also have more constructs, higher quality arguments, and more accurate recall of substantive, factual, and cynical information.

Mayoral Campaign

To assess whether the findings from health care reform were replicable, the same hypotheses about political sophistication were tested on the data from the mayoral campaign. We used very similar measures, and the chief differences were in construct differentiation and argument quality.

Construct differentiation included a word count but also explicitly separated substantive from cynical words on the basis of a list established at the outset of the research. The word counts came from an open-ended essay written by participants in response to the following instructions:

> Write a letter to your friend telling him or her the story of the campaign, the candidates, and the election as revealed in the debate you have just seen and the other materials you got from us.

Participants were not invited to write arguments but to "write the three most important things that come to mind from the materials you saw and read about the Philadelphia mayoral candidates." These were coded into events that included sources, topics, and claims. An event could link a source and topic with or without a claim. For example, if someone said that "Clinton harped on the economy," he or she would receive a +1 score for the event but 0 for claim since no information about Clinton's position on economic matters is provided. However, if someone said, "Clinton wanted to provide tax relief for the middle class," then this response would be coded as +1 for event and +1 for claim.

An "elaboration index" was created to reflect the number of events and claims people made in recalling important things from the mayoral campaign. The index ranged from 0 to 1 with a mean of .17 and standard deviation of .21.[35]

Table 8.4. Regression Analyses of Recall, Elaboration, and Construct
Differentiation by Political Sophistication: Mayoral Campaign Sample

	Outcome Measures				
	Issue Recall	*Strategy Recall*	*Elaboration Index*	*Issue Word Counts*	*Total Word Counts*
	(N = 256)	*(N = 255)*	*(N = 262)*	*(N = 247)*	*(N = 262)*
Education	.130*	.077	-.105	.290***	.288***
Experimental Condition	.276***	.300***	.065	.080	.167**
Political Sophistication	.120+	.151*	.125+	.140*	.125*
Civics	.049	.006	.056	.033	.116+
Involvement	-.026	.046	.127	-.071	-.131*
Attention	.063	.047	.116+	.039	.137*
Print	.041	.019	-.045	-.082	-.053
Television	-.091	-.042	-.042	.085	-.045
Radio	-.043	-.050	.035	-.011	-.041
R-squared	.144	.143	.073	.136	.200
F	4.580***	4.550***	2.216*	4.147**	6.999***

Note: Cell entries are beta weights from standard multiple regression.
+ p <.07; *p < .05; **p < .01; ***p < .001

Results of Table 8.4 indicate that political sophistication is once
again a significant and consistent predictor of recall, construct differentiation, and elaboration. The magnitude of the effects of political
sophistication is somewhat smaller and the statistical significance is
less pronounced. But, given the differences in the sample size and the
context, the parallel results are striking. Political sophistication is positively associated with accuracy of recall, the organization of informa-

tion (as revealed by the elaboration index), and the breadth of knowledge as indicated by differentiation of constructs.

Health Care Reform: Learning at Three and Seven Months

The association between media reception and learning observed in the previous two studies is based on measures separated by at most one week. Political sophistication scores were obtained and then, just a week later, scores from essays or recall from debates or other materials. What about longer delays?

The participants from the March 1994 field experiment were studied in June 1994 as part of the evaluation of the NBC special on health care and interviewed in October just before the mid-term elections and after health care had died. We obtained the measures of news reception including both attention to public affairs and political sophistication in March. The nature of news coverage during the period from January 1, 1994, to October 15, 1994, was primarily strategic. Were people high in news reception (i.e., political sophisticates) learning from the predominately strategic news coverage of health reform?

Two tests were possible: one predicting learning after the NBC special from news reception scores obtained in March and a second predicting overall learning during the debate, measured in October, and based on the same news reception scores from March. Both tests were conducted conservatively, using learning scores from March as covariates. In other words, they were predicting learning in June and October from media reception controlled for baseline levels of learning in March. Media reception effects, if any, would be over and above individual predilections to learn.[36]

Tables 8.5 and 8.6 present the results from the two analyses. Table 8.5 shows regression coefficients from a multivariate analysis of covariance with attention to public affairs, political sophistication, substantive learning (in March), and education as predictors.[37] Four learning measures are evaluated: knowledge of political actors, general knowledge of health care issues and terms, knowledge from the NBC special itself, and knowledge of the health plans.[38] The multivariate test was significant — $F(16, 770.24) = 8.28$, $p < .001$ — as were each of the overall univariate tests ($p < .001$ at least). Attention to public affairs was a significant predictor of learning in two of four outcome measures and

Table 8.5. Multivariate Regressions of Four Measures of Health Care Knowledge Taken in June 1994 Based on Indicators of Media Reception, Education, and Health Care Knowledge in March 1994

	Political Knowledge		Health Care Knowledge		Show Knowledge		Plan Knowledge	
	B SE(B)	Prob	B SE(B)	Prob	B SE(B)	Prob	B SE(B)	Prob
Attention to Public Affairs	.053 (.023)	.020	.044 (.015)	.003	-.005 (.026)	.834	.014 (.025)	.57
Political Sophistication	.024 (.007)	.001	.016 (.005)	.001	.031 (.008)	.000	.013 (.008)	.11
Prior Learning	.168 (.073)	.021	.134 (.047)	.005	.234 (.084)	.006	.107 (.080)	.18
Education	.020 (.012)	.097	.014 (.008)	.078	.028 (.014)	.051	.045 (.013)	.001

Note: B is the unstandardized regression coefficient and SE(B) is its standard error.

political sophistication was significant in three of four. Both were significant on the key measures of knowledge of political actors and general health care knowledge.

Table 8.5 displays the regression of learning in October based on the four predictors: two measures of the uptake of news and two controls — one for education and the other for prior levels of learning. The October learning measure taps into knowledge about the health care system in the United States (such as the number of doctor visits each year compared to other countries) as well as knowledge about the strategic and substantive aspects of the Clinton health plan (e.g., who pays and how was the plan generated — in secret meetings). About 15 percent of the variance is explained with the two media measures showing mixed results but in the direction of the hypothesis. Attention to public affairs predicts learning over and above previous learning levels and political sophistication is positively but not significantly related to learning.

The analyses presented in Tables 8.3 through 8.6 are consistent. They provide further support for the claim that strategic news can enhance explicit, substantive learning perhaps through the cognitive process of activation and accessibility. The nonexperimental results must be evaluated in the context of the time lags involved (three months and seven months) and baseline learning levels. The media effects (through the surrogate measure of reception, political sophistication) that are present suggest that people are learning from strategic media news beyond their initial predispositions. Coupled with findings from our content analysis of the news media during the health reform debate showing that nearly two of three news stories were strategically framed, we have the conclusion that those successfully consuming news during the debate were consuming strategic news and learning from it.

Summary

The fundamental explanation of learning effects in Chapters 4 and 6 is that news activates existing knowledge, either reinforcing it or adding new linkages through the process of spreading activation. How activation spreads depends in part on how knowledge is organized. Semantic and schematic structures are two such organizations. But even within these types, knowledge can be more and less extensive, more and less richly connected, more and less organized, and more and less accurate.

Table 8.6. Regression of Learning About Health Care in October 1994 Based on Indicators of Media Reception, Previous Knowledge of Health Care in March, and Education

	B	SE(B)	Beta	T	Prob
Prior Learning	1.120	.490	.159	2.29	.023
Education	.181	.076	.160	2.34	.017
Attention	.408	.148	.178	2.76	.006
Political Sophistication	.058	.047	.088	1.23	.221
Constant	1.680	.534		3.15	.002
R^2 Adjust	.134				
$F(5,205)$	9.650				

In short, people differ in the quality of the knowledge they have and these differences should affect the amount and quality of learning within the processes of semantic and schematic activation.

Political sophistication is assumed to capture a complex of processes from exposure and attention through comprehension and retrievability. Previous research has shown versions of this measure (e.g., civics knowledge) to be more effective than simple news exposure in predicting learning. The studies presented here demonstrate similar effects for the measure incorporating both knowledge and ideology.

Explaining the effects of political sophistication is based on one fundamental assumption: political sophisticates process news differently than their more innocent counterparts. In the experimental tests conducted both in a policy-debate context and an election campaign context, learning effects were predicted by sophistication, but were not predicted by simple exposure to news. Learning was the result of what participants brought with them to the experimental settings in addition to the information received once there. Most important, what they brought with them was not a ready set of answers to the questions about the C-SPAN debate they watched there — in fact, they could not have done so — but the necessary knowledge structures, motivations, and cognitive skills to acquire even insubstantial strategic information.

Our studies do not provide direct evidence that political sophisticates process news differently, but indirect evidence supports our interpretations. Political sophisticates have more organized, integrated, and utilitarian knowledge structures. Information available from news sources is filtered through attention as a motivational construct and through sophistication as an indicator of the ability to store, retrieve, and use information. The availability of information is only a necessary condition for learning; motivation and ability to process what is available are required for deep processing and stable learning. This position parallels the arguments made by William McGuire[39] regarding persuasion and Richard Petty and John Cacioppo[40] regarding central route attitude change.

The fact that political sophisticates have greater levels of recall from news is consistent with the claim that the measure of sophistication is symptomatic of more developed knowledge structures. Further evidence of the nature of sophisticates' political knowledge is found in the open-ended responses that people gave to questions about the health care debate and election campaigns. These questions were asked to obtain more detailed evidence about the way our participants thought about the health care reform debate and the Philadelphia mayoral campaign. In both cases, political sophisticates generated essays with more differentiated constructs and arguments that were more complex than those who were unsophisticated.

Our interpretation of these results is that political sophisticates have more developed political schemata. Evidence for the existence of schemata is always indirect. However, the techniques of obtaining open-ended essay responses and measures of construct differentiation and argumentative and elaborative depth provide more direct evidence of schema development than is usually available. This evidence can be interpreted to imply that part of the reason political sophisticates learn more and have more anchored beliefs and attitudes is that their systems of political knowledge are more complex, integrated, and available for use.[41]

We are certainly aware that detailed cognitive mechanisms cannot be studied with any precision in field experimental (or survey) contexts. However, our data can be interpreted as being consistent with the claims that political sophisticates are not simply more intense consumers of news but rather deeper processors of it. They bring different motivations to news consumption and carry away knowledge that is more readily integrated into an already elaborated knowledge store.

News Reception and Cynical Response

We used survey data from three waves of our health care reform panel study to determine if those reporting greater news consumption were also more cynical about the debate. As with the tests of learning, news reception was assessed with a measure of attention to public affairs and a measure of political sophistication obtained in March. Three tests were carried out: March to June, June to October, and March to October. In each case, political cynicism was the outcome being predicted and the predictors included a baseline measure of political cynicism (from the previous period), education, and the two news reception measures.[42]

The reasoning for our hypotheses is straightforward. The news environment employed strategic frames extensively. When the strategic frame was not employed, conflict often was. Would those who consumed more news have greater cynicism than that accounted for by their earlier reports of cynicism?

Table 8.7. Regression Coefficients (and Standard Errors) for Cynicism About Health Care Reform Debate Based on Indicators of Media Reception (Political Sophistication), Previous Cynicism, and Education

	Cynicism (June)[a]	Cynicism (October)[b]	Cynicism (October)[c]
Education	—	.011*	.007
		(.006)	(.006)
Prior	.772***	.240***	.308***
Cynicism	(.093)	(.034)	(.054)
Attention to	-.018	.024**	.020*
Public Affairs	(.018)	(.034)	(.011)
Political	.003	.007**	.008**
Sophistication	(.005)	(.003)	(.003)
Watch vs. Not	-.049**	—	—
(0=no;1=yes)	(.026)		
Constant	.218**	.470***	.444***
	(.091)	(.051)	(.053)
Adjust R^2	.226	.247	.184
<u>N</u>, <u>F</u>	238, 18.3	194, 16.9	225, 13.6

Note. *** $p < .01$; ** $p < .05$; * $p < .10$.
[a]Predictions from March.
[b]Predictions from June.
[c]Predictions from March.

Table 8.7 shows the results from three regressions. News reception was associated with cynical reactions in predicting October levels from June and October levels from March but not in predicting June levels from March. The variance explained was a solid 20 to 25 percent and the direction of effects from March to October and from June to October is as predicted.

The nonsignificant effects from March to June are puzzling, but may be due to the statistical problem of correcting the post-test scores for those who watched the special. Recall that the June panel evaluated the NBC special. While everyone was tested after the special, only 60 participants were pre-tested. For us to use all the participants, it was necessary to correct the post-test scores to approximate pre-test levels. Such a correction is statistical and never a replacement for having an actual pre-test measure. In fact, when the sixty people who were pre-tested were used alone, political sophistication was a (near) significant predictor of cynicism — $\underline{B}$ = .021, SE($\underline{B}$) = .011 — with an adjusted variance explained of 27 percent. Attention to public affairs was not significant in this subsample.

Those high in news reception presumably consume more and understand better what they are reading and watching than those low in news reception. In the news environment of the health care reform debate where strategy and conflict dominated the field, cynicism continued to be activated. While previous levels of cynicism were strongly correlated with current levels, political sophistication as a surrogate for news reception still accounted for part of the cynicism expressed.

Political Cynicism and Judgments of Politicians

In March 1994 a *Wall Street Journal* poll showed substantial support for the elements of the Clinton plan when each were described as plan features, but not identified with the President. At the same time the public was much less favorable toward the "Clinton Health Plan" when so identified.

The plan was the subject in two kinds of coverage: strategic and conflict-oriented issue coverage. Each may have had an impact on the public's opinion of the President's plan but in very different ways. Conflict-oriented issue coverage would focus on the substance of the Clinton plan offering critical response, disagreement, and dismissal but seldom compromise, common ground, or solution. The plan may have lost public support because of such criticisms, right or wrong, but the results of the *Wall Street Journal* poll do not support this interpretation. Rather, the poll suggests that the plan's sponsors, not its substantive elements, were in disfavor.

When the Clinton plan is covered strategically, readers may view the substance of the plan favorably or unfavorably, depending on their ideology. Regardless, the structure will impugn the motives of the plan maker as self-interested. The result could be that evaluations of Clinton (and indirectly his plan, when identified as his plan), would be rejected not for reasons of substance but for reasons associated with judgments about the person. This is precisely the claim that the theory of on-line judgment formation would make — judgments of persons activated through evaluative trait inferences and the basis of the evaluative inferences lost. Over time, Clinton comes to be perceived as inevitably manipulative and his positions tagged with cynical markers.

Although we cannot evaluate our hypothesis over the course of the health care reform debate, the claim that conflict-oriented issue coverage and cynically oriented strategy coverage will affect people's attitudes toward the Clinton health reform plan was tested in the March panel of our study on health reform. During the pre-test, people were asked the following question about the President's health plan:

> If you were to draft your own health care plan, would it be close to or far from the plan proposed by President Clinton?

They responded on a seven-point scale from very close (= 1) to very far (= 7). The same question was asked after a week's exposure to news stories.

Those exposed to conflict-oriented issue frames or to strategy frames considered themselves farther away from the Clinton plan ($\underline{M}$ = 4.04 and 3.94, respectively) than did those in the control who received only one background article about health care plans ($\underline{M}$ = 3.78). These differences are significant — $\underline{F}(2,322)$ = 5.51, $\underline{p}$ < .03.[43] The patterns in means indicate that issue and strategy frames were closer to one another than to the control; consequently, these frames are functioning equivalently in increasing distance from the Clinton plan. Issue frames increase distance as much as strategy frames do.[44]

A second consequence of our theory about the impact of strategic and conflict-based issue coverage is that cynicism should mediate the effect these types of news have on attitudes toward Clinton's plan. If strategic- and conflict-oriented news elevate negative personal characteristics of the actors in the health care debate — in particular, their manipulativeness — then, as cynicism is factored out, the differences between experimental and control groups should disappear. This characterization of how the effects of news frames are carried through to attitudes toward the Clinton plan are sketched in Figure 8.1.

To test this characterization of the effects of news on attitudes toward the Clinton plan, the same analysis was run as before, except this time measures of political cynicism were allowed to explain the effect on distance *first* and then news sources explained the effect. If cynicism mediates the relationship between news frames and distance

Figure 8.1. Trait Attributions and Cynicism as Mediators of the Link Between Strategic and Conflict-oriented News Frames to Attitude on an Issue.

from the Clinton plan, then differences across news conditions should be reduced after cynicism measures are entered.

Results show that the effects of news frames on distance from the Clinton plan are lowered when cynicism about government is allowed to explain the distancing effect. However, other measures of political cynicism reduce but do not completely account for differences in distancing on the basis of news frames.[45]

Cynicism does seem to mediate the effect of news frames on distancing since both types of cynicism work in the same way, reducing differences between exposed and control groups. News exposure may also have a small direct effect on distancing from the Clinton plan. Government cynicism is a strong mediator, perhaps because the monitoring is directed at the government specifically as an entity, whose most visible member in the health care reform debate was President Clinton. The questions about political cynicism include representatives of the government through the catch-all term "advocates" in the health care debate. But this term also includes representatives of advocacy groups and the health industry. In the context of our experiment — although certainly not in general — the questions about government cynicism may capture much of people's cynicism specifically about President Clinton and his plan.

The news frames we employed were specifically chosen to be balanced within stories or at least across the set, for an experimental condition, favoring neither the Clinton plan nor its alternatives. As a result, no change in attitudes was expected. Change occurred nonetheless and it was a result of both the news framed in issue and strategic terms. This unexpected occurrence cannot be explained definitively. It is consistent with the suggestion that strategic frames and conflict-oriented issue frames lead readers to infer that the motives of public

Table 8.8. Regression of Closeness to Clinton Plan on Media Reception, Cynicism, Party Identification, and Prior Distance

	B	SE(B)	Beta	T	Prob
Cynicism	-1.130	.390	-.166	-2.93	.004
Distance from Clinton plan	-.255	.033	-.487	-7.74	.000
Party identification (Demo = 3)	.176	.059	.189	3.00	.000
Attention	.015	.071	.012	.22	.830
Political Sophistication	.009	.059	.025	.43	.670
Constant	3.880	.405		9.59	.000
R^2 Adjust	.406				
$F(5,205)$	29.700				

figures are fundamentally self-interested and their public stands are therefore not to be trusted. The result could well be the unintended effect of strategic and conflict coverage increasing the public's distance from policy positions.

We were able to re-test the effect of news reception and political cynicism during the health care reform debate on distancing from the Clinton plan by considering distancing measures in March and again in October 1994. No measure of distancing from the plan was available in the June wave. Predictors included distance from the Clinton plan, and media reception (political sophistication and attention to public affairs) assessed in March along with cynicism about the health care reform process obtained in October. The outcome was distance from the Clinton plan measured in October.

Table 8.8 shows the results. Media reception is not a significant predictor of distancing from the Clinton plan, but cynicism about the health care reform process, party identification, and previous distance all are significant. Democrats are closer to the Clinton plan but cynics are more distant from it.[46] Neither of the media reception variables accounts for any variation in distance from the Clinton plan, either with cynicism in the equation or not. This model, like the experimental test of this hypothesis, suggests that cynicism is a factor in negative attitudes toward policies labeled with their sponsors' names.

Summary

Our data on the relationship between strategic- and conflict-oriented news frames and attitudes toward politicians' policies can only be considered suggestive. The experimental evidence is only one demonstration. Others are needed. The mediating role of cynicism and mistrust on attitudes toward politician's policies cannot be unequivocally placed in a position causally prior to attitudes. With all these caveats, the data and the theory behind them imply that when the news media treat issues in strategic and conflict-oriented frames, attitudes toward the framers of policy and the policy itself will be undermined, but not necessarily for substantive reasons associated with problems with the policy. If the processing of strategic and conflict-oriented news is on-line, negative attitudes toward policy may develop for reasons associated with attributions implied by the strategic frame, not reasons associated with the substance of the policy, and the basis for the attitudes will not be retrieved.

Conclusions and Implications

This chapter has tried to extend the evidence about learning from strategic news compiled in the two previous chapters. We use a variety of data and methods — experiments, qualitative descriptions from essays, cross-sectional survey data on learning and cynical response, and learning over time. The intent is to add to what is inevitably a circumstantial case about the effects of news, building confidence in its final conclusion bit by bit.

What have we added? The studies reported in Chapter 7 supported the activating effects of strategic news formats on cynical response after a week's exposure. The experiment reported in this chapter indicates that cynical judgments can be activated by individual strategic news stories in comparison to more issue-oriented versions. Lengthy exposures to news are not necessary; cynical reactions can be turned on and off depending on how the events are framed. Especially important in this study, the news articles used were not the "stripped bare," telegraphic versions typical of laboratory experiments but rather realistic newspaper stories that sacrificed some control for authenticity.

We also added results from open-ended essays written by our

participants to help us detect learning that might have occurred in forms revealed by methods less constrained than multiple choice tests. The kinds of words used in the essays were more strategic when people read strategically framed news articles than when they read equivalent issue articles. In Chapter 6, learning strategic information was no greater when strategy than issue-framed news was digested, but here the essays revealed a significant bias in language choice toward the strategic in the same conditions. The essays may have revealed a subtle cognitive bias toward strategic formulations of the news — a bias not revealed by the simpler multiple-choice questions.

The essays might also reflect a tendency to organize strategically framed political events in terms of the narratives of self-interest, personal gain and loss, and artifice and performance. A few essays were substantive, describing the problems of the city of Philadelphia, while most were concerned with conflict and games, sometimes dripping with the cynicism the writers saw in the simulated election campaign. The essays written on the demise of health care reform also commonly told the story of colliding institutions and interests and the writer's despair over the absence of serious public policy debates. The unconstrained descriptions we elicited in both studies give some insight to the stock stories people have learned to organize their thoughts about and evaluation of policy debates and campaigns.

The studies of the effects of news about the mayoral campaign were most supportive of our expectations about semantic and schematic learning. These same expectations were not supported in health care reform study — perhaps because our participants were consuming other news during the week's experiment. But in this chapter we asked whether those ready and able to receive news about health care reform learned from it and we asked what they learned. We used political sophistication as a surrogate for "ready and able to receive," testing its ability to predict learning one week later (during the post-experimental questionnaire), three months later after the NBC special, and seven months later after health care reform had failed. The overall pattern of findings confirms our expectation about political sophisticates and their ability to receive information from news. After a week, they wrote essays about health care reform that were more nuanced and had more elaborated arguments. They recalled more information from the C-SPAN discussion — both issue and strategic — and from the news articles themselves. Three months later their learning from the NBC special was greater than that of the less sophisticated, while seven months later accuracy of knowledge was greater for the sophisticates (but not significantly so). In short, those ready and able to learn from news coverage during the health care reform debate did so, acquiring substantive and strategic information, the constructs necessary for comparison and contrast, and the arguments necessary for informed discourse.

But just as strategic news often carries substantive information, it carries implicit information about trust. The political sophisticates "ready and able to receive" news are as ready and able to be influenced by the strategic framing endemic in coverage of health care reform. Indeed, political sophisticates "learned" the cynical responses that strategic coverage implied.

This chapter has presented additional data on learning and judgment from strategic and issue-based news frames. The results corroborate and flesh out the findings of the two previous chapters even though much of our account is speculative and in need of test, replication, and extension to other contexts and frames. Perhaps, the single more important insight that our model has generated is the idea that strategic frames can induce subtle effects unanticipated by those who frame the news as well as those who consume it. When a politician's policies are covered in strategic ways, the negative implications for the politician's character can carry over to the policies lowering the public's favorability toward the policy without attacking it directly. When such judgments are carried out on-line, reasons and evaluations become separated, making the evaluation of policy and evaluation of the policy's author indistinguishable.

Samuel Popkin has argued that judging candidates in terms of likability is a good shortcut for voters.[47] The on-line model makes candidate evaluation an efficient place to store policy evaluations, leadership judgments, and character evaluations in one easy-to-remember slot. But lost to this summary evaluation are the reasons for it, those derived from ideological agreements and disagreements with substantive positions, those resulting from attractive and disliked traits as a leader, and perhaps those inferred from news frames tarring the target with distrust.

Media scholars often attribute relatively small effects to the media.[48] How can the news be asked to shoulder some of the blame for activating or reinforcing cynism when its other effects seem so minuscule?

One answer is found in the typical responses to why persuasion is successful. The answer in part is the simple idea that successful persuasion occurs when the message takes advantage of pre-existing beliefs in the audience. A public that has accepted the belief that officials are acting in their own self-interest rather than in the interests of the common weil can be easily primed to see self-promotion in every political act. When journalists frame political events strategically, they activate existing beliefs and understandings; they do not need to create them.

》9

CONTAGIOUS CYNICISM

THE THESIS of our research has been that the structures of news about politics have direct effects on the public's cynicism about politics, government, policy debates, and campaigns. But there may also be an indirect effect on the press itself. The public's trust in this institution is falling; in part, this may be due to the media's own sowing of the seeds of public distrust. In other words, the elevation of public distrust of political institutions and processes may have attached itself to the bearers of information about those institutions — the news media themselves.

Trends in Media Cynicism

Recent data suggest that the public agrees that the press is part of the problem. The October 1994 *Times Mirror* survey on "The People, The Press and Politics" showed that seven in ten surveyed believe that the media make it more difficult for society to solve its problems. This conclusion was corroborated in the *New York Times*/CBS pre-election survey in 1994 that reported most saying that the media get in the way of solving the country's problems.[1] That poll found no relationship between the medium from which voters got their news and their cynicism.

The evidence for the public's disaffection with the news media is well known. But the decrease in the public's confidence has been especially strong in recent years. The National Opinion Research Center (NORC) is one of several opinion research groups tracking the public's attitudes toward the news media. In the past twenty years, "confidence in the people running the press" changed from a high of 28 percent having a "great deal" of confidence in 1976 to a low of 11 percent in 1993; those having hardly any confidence has grown from a low of 15 percent in 1973 to a high of 39 percent in 1993. Although other social institutions have seen a similar erosion of confidence, aside from Congress, none has been so severe as that of the press.[2] From 1991 to 1993, the number indicating hardly any confidence in the press had increased from 28 percent to 39 percent, the largest change in any adjacent two-year period in the past twenty of NORC surveys about the press.

Almost two in three believe that the news media tend to favor one side in presenting social and political issues. Forty-nine percent think that political preferences of reporters often influence the way they report the news and 64 percent feel that the media emphasize the negative in reporting (in contrast to the 32 percent who believe that the balance is about right).[3] In open-ended questions about what is disturbing about the news media, people cited sensationalism (28 percent), bias versus balance (22 percent), and inaccuracy (15 percent) as the three most common complaints. Whether accurate or not, the public's perceptions of the press affect its credibility and the information it provides about social and political issues.

Who are the media cynics? To answer this question, we analyzed four studies composed of five separate samples. Two were conducted by us: fall 1993 Markle News Study ($\underline{N}$ = 120) and the fall 1994 third wave of our health care reform research ($\underline{N}$ = 240). Although neither of our studies used a nationally representative sample, both employed questions about media cynicism that were sound measures of the concept, more extensive than the usual one or two items.[4]

A third investigation, undertaken by the Times Mirror Corporation in July 1994, was an extensive study of media use and public opinion ($\underline{N}$ = 3800 for some of the questions, $\underline{N}$ = 1900 for others). This study used three questions comparable to ours as measures of cynicism about and unhappiness with the media. They were:

Would you say your opinion of *network TV news* is very favorable, mostly favorable, mostly unfavorable, very unfavorable?

Would you say your opinion of *the daily newspaper you are most familiar with* is very favorable, mostly favorable, mostly unfavorable, very unfavorable?

Which of the following two statements about the news media do you agree with more ...

The news media helps society to solve its problems.

or

The news media gets in the way of society solving its problems.

In general, we believe that respondents to surveys are answering questions about the news media as if the questions are about the mainstream broadcast and print news.[5]

A fourth study was conducted by the Harvard School of Public Health for the Robert Wood Johnson Foundation during June 1994. This study was an evaluation of the NBC special on health care reform "To Your Health," which aired June 21, 1994. That study included two questions on people's cynicism about the media.[6]

Our conclusions about media cynicism are based on trends across the five samples (totaling about 6000 cases) and across the different measures of media cynicism. The only media and demographic characteristics considered were those that were measured in at least three of the five studies.

Among the demographic and social factors associated with cynicism about the media are party, ideology, education, and possibly race. Those more cynical about the media are more likely to be Republican, better educated, ideologically conservative, have higher income, and Caucasian. These conclusions are true of the Times Mirror sample which asked about media in general and the Harvard sample about media in the health care debate. Our own data from the health care reform debate show trends consistent with these larger, more representative national samples. (Tables summarizing these findings are included in Appendix H.)

Clearly, the demographic profile of the media cynics represents a well-defined, almost stereotypical, social-political group — white, educated conservatives. It would be incorrect to conclude that these are the media cynics while others are not. As other data have shown, media cynicism (and government cynicism) have reached very high levels across the spectrum of social and political groups. But among those directing their animus toward the media, white, educated conservatives are the most intense. It would also be incorrect to conclude that these results are tied to the health care reform debate. The Times Mirror data focus on media in general, and not the media's treatment of any particular issue.

The patterns in age, gender, and Hispanic identity are less clear and should not be interpreted as consistent trends. The age effects and those for Hispanic identity are only found in the Harvard sample. They are probably due as much to the issue of health care reform as anything else. No clear patterns on gender and media cynicism obtain across the samples.

If white, educated conservatives are the most cynical group about the media, what are these individuals doing to satisfy their needs for information about politics, news, and government? Our analyses show only a few clear trends in the association between use of media and cynicism about them. Media cynics consume more call-in talk radio (including specifically Rush Limbaugh in two of the samples), use lower amounts of or no television news, and tend to follow social and political issues more closely than their less cynical counterparts. No other clear patterns emerge for newspaper exposure or other news sources (see Table H in Appendix H).

Media cynics clearly do not extend their cynicism about media to radio call-in programs. Nor do they avoid following political news; to the contrary they identify themselves as closer followers than their less cynical counterparts. This description would seem to be paradoxical at least, if not downright contradictory, unless one assumes that part of the reason cynics are so mistrustful of the mainstream media is that they are getting political information elsewhere and that these other sources are critical of their competitors.

What emerges as a description of those most cynical about how the media handle news is that these individuals are not on the political fringes of society. The media cynics are not the uneducated, nor have they divorced themselves from political policy issues. If they have given up on anything, it is television news. If they have accepted any media source as credible and outside the mainstream, it is talk radio. Talk radio may provide what is perceived as a significantly different source of information about political and social issues that allows otherwise cynical consumers to maintain their interest in the issues of public life. Whether talk radio fosters or mitigates other forms of cynicism, whether it produces any more distortion than any other medium, whether it activates political involvement or merely encourages emotional agitation must be answered in other forums and with other data.

In the context of our studies, talk radio can be seen as serving the public's need for different forms of news. What forms will meet what needs of which segments of the public is unclear. Is the capacity to be heard as a caller-contributor a necessary requirement? Does involvement in the discourse about the news give the audience a sense of participating rather than being detached from public life? Is partisan treatment of issues what attracts, holds, and educates the public? Have we so blurred the distinction between reality and fiction, between entertainment and information, that political discourse only attracts when the entertainment and information functions are simultaneously served? We do not know the answers to these questions at this time.

We do know that people do not trust the mainstream media and that those who trust it least are also those most interested in public policy. And we know that they are seeking alternative formats for news and political discussion and consuming the content voraciously. The public is open to alternatives, even primed to test them. The form of these alternatives is less clear.

Beliefs about Media Practices

One of the ways we have sought to understand the media cynics is in terms of their other beliefs about government, politics, and the behavior of the press and broadcasters. Media cynics are also cynical about the government and about politicians and politics. Perhaps their cynicism extends to these arenas in a causal way, perhaps not. What can be said is that cynics in one domain tend to be cynics in the other.

In this section, we report two studies focused on people's beliefs about the practices of the news media. The first is based on a sample of 120 people described above as the Markle News Study. The second focuses on a portion of the group studied during the health care reform debate, after the debate's end, and before the fall 1994 elections.

In the Markle news study, we felt that it was important to get indirect measures of people's beliefs about the media. To do so, questions about what kinds of stories people might be inclined to read, what stories they believed editors would choose to cover, and what "slant" a given story might receive were asked.

About 130 people were recruited initially through newspaper ads and notices posted at various locations in the Philadelphia metropolitan area. All were paid to participate. The study was conducted at the Annenberg School for Communication.

The sample was well educated, with 33 percent having some graduate education or a graduate degree and 32 percent having a college degree; 32 percent were African American and 66 percent were Caucasian. The high number of African Americans is representative of the Philadelphia metropolitan area. About one in six were not currently employed; the remainder were employed, homemakers, students, or retirees. Females made up 48 percent of the group. The median age was 36. People identifying themselves as more Democrat outnumbered Republicans 71 percent to 12 percent with the remainder independents. Self-identified liberals (41 percent) and moderates (43 percent) outnumbered conservatives (16 percent). Overall, the sample was representative of the electorate in age, gender, and employment status, but was more educated, less conservative, and less Republican than the population at large. The high proportion of African Americans and Democrats in the Philadelphia area is reflected in our sample as well.

Are Media Cynics Cynical About Politics?

What general beliefs about government and politics do those most cynical about the media hold? Media cynics are also cynical about the government ($r = .49$, $p < .001$) and about politicians and politics ($r = .50$, $p < .001$). Their cynicism extends into these arenas, perhaps causing or being caused by deeper social forces responsible for cynicism. This particular study does not allow us to say whether cynicism about the news media affects mistrustful attitudes about government and politics or vice versa. What can be said is that cynics in one domain tend to be cynics in the other.[7] This correlation between distrust of media and other forms of cynicism is found in larger, nationally representative samples as well.[8]

Do Readers Select Strategy Over Issue Headlines?

What about the consumption habits of media cynics? Do they tend to consume more strategic materials than their less cynical counterparts? Are people disposed toward articles with headlines inviting them to more strategic versus issue-based coverage? If readers are biased toward more strategic headlines, and if cynical readers are biased even more so, then journalistic norms favoring strategic over more substantive coverage are appealing to the audience's prevailing tastes.

To test this idea, we created six headlines (with subheads) that supposedly came from local newspaper stories about political races. Three headlines were worded in strategy language and three in issue-oriented wordings. Participants were asked to read all the headlines and choose the three they would be mostly likely to read. Later in the same questionnaire, the exercise was repeated with the same six topics, but now the headline wording was altered. A topic first presented using strategic wording was next presented with issue wording. For example, the strategy version of the first topic was

OPPONENTS SPAR OVER ABORTION, TAXES IN BITTER FIRST DEBATE
Winners and Losers Crowned; Rematch Promised

The issue version of the same topic took the form

FIRST DEBATE REVEALS BASIC DIFFERENCE ON ABORTION, TAXES
Voters Split on Candidates' Stands

The question was whether people would choose the stories whose headlines implied that strategy coverage would follow.

What about media cynics? Would they tend to gravitate toward strategy coverage more than their less cynical counterparts? The answer is a resounding no. There is no evidence that media cynics were any more likely to choose headlines implying that strategy coverage would follow than headlines that implied issue coverage.[9] The major conclusion was actually that everyone, cynics and not, tended to stick with the same topics from the first set of headlines to the second, regardless of strategy and issue language. Our sample was not at all drawn into selecting on the basis of packaging of story headlines.

Beliefs About Journalistic Conventions

The same was not true of their beliefs about what kinds of stories news organizations would choose to run or their beliefs about how stories would be slanted. Instead, our group was inclined to believe that news organizations would tend to pick more strategic stories and, once chosen, slant the story toward a strategic frame. To get at these beliefs, we employed some indirect techniques. We did not want to telegraph answers, but we did want them to emerge if they were present as latent beliefs.

To test for story selection, we gave the following instructions:

> News organizations have to make difficult decisions about what to air or print when several stories are breaking at the same time. In this section, we want you to choose which of several stories you think news organizations would typically choose to air or print when they don't have the time or resources to cover them all.

People were then asked to choose two summaries (out of three) most likely to be covered by the press even if all three should be (or none should be). Each person received three groups of three to evaluate. Here is an example of one of the groups:

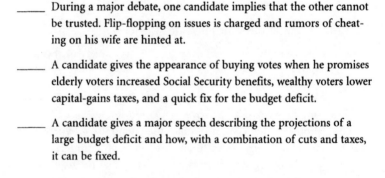

_____ During a major debate, one candidate implies that the other cannot be trusted. Flip-flopping on issues is charged and rumors of cheating on his wife are hinted at.

_____ A candidate gives the appearance of buying votes when he promises elderly voters increased Social Security benefits, wealthy voters lower capital-gains taxes, and a quick fix for the budget deficit.

_____ A candidate gives a major speech describing the projections of a large budget deficit and how, with a combination of cuts and taxes, it can be fixed.

In each group of summaries, two were more strategic (the first two above) and one less so. Our assumption was that this procedure would reveal people's latent beliefs about what kinds of events news organizations choose to cover.

Once an event is selected for coverage, journalists have some discretion over how the story is handled. To uncover people's beliefs about the slant that stories would receive, we gave them nine events[10] (the same nine as in the previous set) and the following instructions:

> Even after the news media choose to cover one story and not another, the
> WAY THEY COVER the story is important. In your experience with broadcast
> and print news, what kind of COVERAGE do you expect the stories above to
> get when they are covered by the print and broadcast media?
>
> CHOOSE THE ALTERNATIVE THAT COMES CLOSEST TO WHAT YOU THINK
> REPORTERS DO.

Each event was followed by two versions of how the story of the event might be written and people were asked to choose among the versions. Here is one example:

> The Democratic and Republican candidates for office decide to release their
> detailed plans about the budget deficit. The plans have a lot of similarity
> but differ in where services are cut and who pays more.
>
> Check which way you think this story will be reported by the press:
>
> _____ They will report where there is agreement and where there is differ-
> ence in the two plans. They will also report on what the experts say is rea-
> sonable.
>
> _____ They will report which voters will suffer most and which will bene-
> fit most in each plan. They will also report which candidate gains votes and
> which candidate loses votes with parts of their plans.

Our assumption was that this procedure would reveal peoples' implicit beliefs about how stories were slanted.

People overwhelmingly said that news organizations would pick the more strategic events to report (the percentage differences were 82 vs. 18, 75 vs. 25, and 78 vs. 22).[11] People reported that stories would be slanted toward the more strategic in seven of nine examples, with percentages sometimes overwhelmingly toward the more strategic choice. On average, 62 percent indicated that an event would be covered from a strategic point of view.[12] The people in our sample tended to share the belief that news organizations give precedence to events that lend themselves to strategic coverage and believed that coverage will be slanted so that stories would emphasize the strategic.

Although people higher in news cynicism were no more likely to select strategy headlines to read, they did believe more strongly that journalists pick and slant stories toward the strategic ($r = .27$,

$p < .002$). People who are cynical about the media's handling of political news also hold that news organizations select events that are biased toward the strategic and, regardless of the events chosen, tend to cover them in a way that is slanted toward the strategic ($r = .33$, $p < .001$). Both effects remain even when government cynicism and political cynicism are controlled out, suggesting that the result is unique to cynicism about the news and not confounded by other forms of cynicism.

Commenting on the Way Media Cover Politics

Participants in our study were also invited to tell newspaper editors and television and radio producers what they "thought was right and wrong with how the media cover politics." Many wrote thoughtful, lengthy essays; some wrote little or nothing. Others were barely able to contain their venom. Selections follow.

Several broad categories of response appeared with sufficient regularity across the essays to say that they were representative of negative evaluations of the media's coverage of politics. These were: lack of objectivity, sensationalism, distortion, inaccuracy, and self-interest.

Lack of objectivity focused on the biases of the news. Statements included criticisms that coverage of an issue was unbalanced because only one side was reported or because the media favored one point of view or one candidate over another.

> Remarkably little effort was made to get the Koreshian point of view [in the Waco debacle] or to inquire why threats and acts of force ... were called for. (#412)

> ... the Lani Guiner debacle. ... the portrayal of this brilliant American as "loony Lani" and "quota queen" was as reprehensible as the failure to discuss her views on proportional representation. (#438)

> Perspectives from participants have not been comprehensive, but have been unbalanced in favor of PLO elements. There is a bias in the continuing failure to recognize PLO/Hamas complicity in the continuing murder of civilians. (#631)

Distortion was primarily concerned with the media's misrepresenting the seriousness of an issue. This criticism can take the form of downplaying the importance of an issue or blowing an issue out of proportion.

You over report crime, and therefore, people fear it. (#430)

Now everyday they still report minor incidents that help to stroke the flames of dissent between Arabs and Jews in America. (#432)

Coverage on Anti-Abortion activities — remember the days when it was peaceful demonstration? Now due to media coverage — they've blown it out of proportion and have become media monsters — their message is lost. DON'T assist the monster. (#422)

The *inaccuracy* category is a set of statements reflecting a lack of trust in the information that comes from the media. Key phrases include "incomplete information," "not thorough," "following hunches," "unconfirmed," and so on.

Much of the information is superficial. I find factual mistakes owed [sic] to the lack of broad cross-cultural background of reporters. (#440)

If you want to report politics get the facts straight first. (#524)

Your coverage of certain foreign political events seemed to be tainted with ignorance of causes of the events and tendencies to follow words and facts and guesses of the different government agencies involved. (#722)

Sensationalism represents statements disapproving the media's focus on scandalous stories, unnecessary grisly details, and excessive coverage of people's private lives.

The constant harping on politicians' sexual shenanigans has turned me off to much of the so-called "objectivity." (#636)

It was irresponsible of you to have former POWs' discuss their tortures — that sort of emotional manipulation sells. (#621)

[regarding Genifer Flowers and Bush's 'mystery mistress'] Voters and non-voters alike were captivated and had their attention diverted from more serious concerns by this tawdry display of "bedroom" politics. (#436)

Criticisms of the media's news coverage as biased, sensational, and inaccurate are not new. They have appeared in other research as well[13] and have almost reached the status of cultural stereotype. Our results were no different from those of previous studies about media credibility. But some categories were surprising.

Self-interest is a component of what we have been calling media cynicism. This category included comments suggesting that media coverage is driven by financial interests; this in turn erodes the quality of news coverage because of an overemphasis on ratings, advertising, and sales.

> You serve the interests of your rich corporate owners. (#430)

> You are always seeking ratings, beautiful newscasters, and you spend tons of money on billboards and commercials to sell your news program and station. (#528)

> All reporters are biased, care about profits first, winning a Pulitzer. Never willing to offend sponsors. (#444)

Our critics chastised news institutions and reporters for allowing their own interests to overwhelm their responsibilities to the public. These comments suggest that people sometimes attribute motivations to the media that are similar to the motivations that political cynics attribute to distrusted candidates.

Two criticisms of the way the media cover politics occurred so infrequently as to be negligible. Since our research has focused on strategic coverage and conflict and negativity in issue coverage, we looked carefully for examples of these in the essays. A few examples were present but they were too infrequent to be cited as regular categories. One critic noted, "I hope some day I can turn on a TV ... and enjoy news that ... reflects a world where not only do we live as one, but in harmony with good news instead of what you spew out — bad news" (#528). Some good examples of concern about strategic coverage were offered.

> One political event in which you did a poor job is ... the absolute reliance on polls. How does the president's new hair cut affect his standing in the polls? Who cares! (#535)

> Headlines like "Showdown in the Gulf" made war a game. (#513)

> P]eople become not individuals but stock characters, acting out their parts in stories whose plots are familiar to readers and listeners. ... the public understands it and it probably sells better than stories that really tried to describe something from reality. (#612)

Except for a few cases, the absence of concern about negativity and strategy is interesting because it suggests that even the reflective consumer of news does not readily employ conflict and game frames that we have emphasized in our research. Low awareness does not imply that these news frames have no effects on their audience. It may simply reflect the fact that these categories for discussing the news have not reached the status of cultural categories for news the way that bias and sensationalism have.

Our two final observations on these essays focus on what is positive. Although many people could not think of a single instance that was well handled by the media, others did. The instances were not as important as what lay behind them. There was a strong, positive preference for uninterpreted political events such as the presidential debates, the Gore-Perot debate over NAFTA, the Hill-Thomas hearings, Clinton's early address on health care, and similar events. Our essayists did not describe these news events as uninterpreted by reporters but that is exactly what they are — unmediated events. Also surprising was a refrain to provide historical background and deeper coverage of political events, particularly those in the international arena and complex policy issues. Several writers insisted that such depth of coverage was the only route to understanding. They acknowledged and lamented its absence.

Conclusions

We are not suggesting that our study implies the media actually choose events on the basis of issue and strategy factors, or they actively slant coverage of events, even substantive events, toward the strategic. Rather, our data show that people hold these beliefs as if they were true and especially when they harbor a mistrust of news institutions. Despite these beliefs, we do not find people reporting that they are disposed to choose news articles to read on the basis of strategic headlines — they show no evidence of that in this study. But they believe reporters and editors make selections in these ways, even though as consumers they are not inclined to do so.

This study is not aimed at unearthing problems in the way news organizations select newsworthy events or present those events in their articles. What it does show is a pervasive set of cynical beliefs by the public about how the news media function.

Beliefs about Media Coverage of Health Care Reform

In October 1994, participants in our health care reform study were surveyed a third time about their reactions to the health care reform debate. This time we obtained information about their cynicism toward the media's handling of the debate.[14]

As in our previous study, those cynical about the media tended to be cynical about the health care reform debate as well (r = .48, p < .0001), to feel more like spectators and distanced from the process (r = .20, p < .002), while also feeling angrier (r = .30, p < .0001) and marginally more anxious and fearful (r = .12, p < .08) about the way the health care reform debate had moved forward. They were also marginally more knowledgeable about government (typically called civics knowledge) (r = .11, p < .10) and more politically involved (r = .15, p < .03). However, those with stronger levels of cynicism about the media were not any more or less politically sophisticated, did not claim to follow the debate any more closely, and were not any more knowledgeable about specific issues in health care reform.

The more cynical our respondents were about the media, the more they believed that the media focused on conflict and ignored agreement among parties (r = .21, p < .002); the more they felt that the media's attention to the Clinton plan, Republican alternatives, and to health care in general was either too much or not enough (as opposed to "about right") (all effects significant at p < .0001 at least). The more cynical, the more likely they were to believe that coverage was unbalanced, either opposed or favorable, to the Clinton plan, health care reform in general, and Republican alternatives. No relationship to cynicism was found for coverage of the single payer plan. All significant effects were very strong at p < .0001. Cynicism about the media went up when people thought coverage was too intense or insufficient and when it was too favorable or too opposed.

Media reporting of health care reform was also seen as more biased by those rating the media as less trustworthy. Perceptions of biased reporting were linked with cynicism for the Clinton plan (r = .55), the Republican alternatives (r =.43), health care reform in general (r= .55), and the single payer plan (r = .16) (all significant at p < .02 at least).

In sum, those who mistrusted the media's handling of the health care reform debate believed that: the coverage was focused on conflict, there was too much or too little coverage, it was biased rather than accurate, and unbalanced in how favorable or unfavorable the treatment. These beliefs cannot be explained by ideology or party since they apply to reform plans both left and right of center.

What do these media cynics believe about the way the press covered the health care reform debate? The more cynical participants reported that their confidence in television news ($r = -.31$, $p < .001$) and newspapers ($r = -.25$, $p < .001$) had declined in the past year rather than increased or remained the same. Media cynics also held the view that coverage of lobbyists' activities, the president's policies, and Congress was inaccurate and more negative or more positive than it should be. These effects were strong ($p < .0001$ in all cases), showing that people who believe that coverage is too positive are about as cynical as those who believe it is too negative. The failure to hit the right tone fostered the cynical responses to the media; it was not simply the presence of negative coverage that was associated with cynical reactions.

The pattern of beliefs about media coverage and its relation to cynicism about media coverage of health care reform seems to plow old ground. But two aspects of our findings are especially interesting. The first is that cynicism tends to be elevated for people who think coverage is too negative *and* too positive, too unfavorable *and* too favorable. It is not the case that cynicism is simply linked with the perception that coverage is too negative; it is instead associated with the perception that coverage is biased, in one direction or the other. The second conclusion is that media cynics believe that the media focus too often on conflict, emphasizing what is adversarial in policy debates, and not attending enough to reporting on agreement among competing parties.

If our reasoning and pattern detection antennae are not malfunctioning, then two conclusions should follow. Ideology and party should not be factors in the correlation between media cynicism and perceptions of balance in the health care reform debate or perceived accuracy in general. And the lack of balance (not the direction of imbalance), inaccuracy (not its direction), and perceived focus on conflict should account for much of the media cynicism about health care reform.

To test these ideas, we evaluated the interactions between perceived media favorability toward health care plans and ideology (liberal, independent or other, and conservative) on media cynicism. None of the four measures of perceived favorability interacted significantly with ideology in accounting for media cynicism scores. Similarly, perceived accuracy of coverage of Congress, the president, and lobbyists (too positive, accurate, too negative) did not interact with ideology in predicting cynicism.[15] These findings show that the pattern of cynical

Table 9.1. Regression of Recoded Media Balance, Recoded Media Accuracy, and Media Conflict on Cynicism About Health Care Coverage: B's, Standard Errors, and Level of Significance

	B (SE)	p
Ideology		
(1=lib, 3=conserv)	.031 (.010)	.002
Conflict-based Coverage	.090 (.016)	.0001
Imbalance on health care Republican Alternatives (= 1)	.056 (.019)	.003
Inaccurate cover Congress (= 1)	.040 (.019)	.040
Inaccurate cover President (= 1)	.082 (.019)	.0001
Imbalance on health care General (= 1)	.058 (.019)	.003
Constant	.321 (.054)	.0001

response to the media across levels of perceived favorability and perceived accuracy are approximately the same for liberals, independents, and conservatives. Although liberals may think the coverage of the Clinton plan was too negative and conservatives believe it was too positive, liberals who thought the plan was too positive are as cynical about the media as those who thought it was too negative; similarly for conservatives and independents.

To test the second idea, we tested the simultaneous relationship between media cynicism, on the one hand, and perceptions of media imbalance, inaccuracy, and conflict orientation, on the other. Imbalance and inaccuracy reflected deviations from accurate or from balanced coverage *in either direction*. Table 9.1 displays a stepwise regression analysis. Ideology was constrained to remain in the equation while seven recoded variables indicating deviation from balanced coverage of health care plans or from accurate reporting of Congress, the president, and lobbyists were entered with the four-item scale for perceived conflict in coverage. In the final model,[16] six variables accounted for 51.2 percent of the variance in media cynicism, $F(6,152) = 30.5$, $p < .001$.

A substantial amount of media cynicism about health care reform is based on perceptions that the media are inaccurate, imbalanced, and concerned too much with the conflict and disagreement between parties. These findings do not depend on conservatives seeing a liberal bias or liberals a conservative one. Instead, people perceive bias and the overemphasis on conflict as linked to their distrust of media.

The public's perceptions may or may not be accurate, but they do exist. Our content analysis of the reporting of advocacy and compromise (see Chapter 7) does indicate low levels of use in both the presidential campaign in 1992 and the health care reform debate — a conclusion consistent with people's perceptions of the media's reporting of conflict to the near exclusion of agreement between competing parties.

Commenting on the Media's Coverage of Health Reform

Those participating in the third wave of our study on health care reform were invited to write an essay on the health care debate. These essays were discussed in the previous chapter as a part of how people made sense of this debate.

These essays indicate that our writers were more likely to single out sources other than media coverage for the death of health reform. In the telephone survey conducted with a larger sample of 230 (including the 153 essay writers), only one person mentioned "negative media" as the primary reason for the failure of health care reform. In national surveys on health reform done during the period before the November 1994 mid-term elections and after health reform was no longer on the congressional agenda, less than one percent[17] identified media as the primary reason for the legislative failure of health care reform.

These data invite one conclusion: People attribute the failure of health care reform to the political events involved and not to how those events were represented in the media. Implicit in this statement is the assumption that the representation of the health reform debate in the media was a fair depiction of the debate's reality.

A reading of the essays indicates that opposing groups and special interests were seen as defending their own self-centered concerns and those of their constituents (see Chapter 8). Self-interest is the central concept of what we have been calling cynicism and what we have identified as the most common motivation attributed explicitly or implicitly to political actors and groups in strategically framed news. Since people do not cite strategic frames as a characteristic problem of news coverage—they instead cite factors such as bias, inaccuracy, sensationalism, and the like—excessive attribution of self-interest is not viewed as a problem associated with news coverage but with the political actors and groups in hot pursuit of their own advantage.

If the environment characterizing the health care reform debate is fundamentally strategic, emphasizing actor's self-interests as well as being predominantly adversarial, is it any wonder that the audience would say that health care reform failed because of the self-interest of the involved parties? The public, in our samples, does not blame the media for the demise of health care, but adopts the frameworks of blame the media have conveyed. In turn, blame, mistrust, dissatisfaction, and accusations of self- interest have been turned on the framers of political action—news organizations themselves.

Summary

We cannot say that cynicism about the news media is a consequence of the way the media have framed their messages about social institutions, particularly political institutions. Such a conclusion would extend far beyond the available data. At the same time, polling shows a downward trend in the public's confidence in the news media, especially in the past two years. There is also a modest association among political alienation, what we have called political cynicism, and cynicism about the news media. In a study completed in 1972,[18] Paul Sniderman found that those most likely to be disaffected with and disenchanted with the government were also most likely to choose newspapers and television as a truthful source about public affairs (about 90 percent) than the government (10 percent). Those most committed to the government were less likely to believe the press. If the same options were placed before the public today, it is doubtful that mistrust of government would be accompanied by such high levels of trust for the news media. Something has changed in the ensuing twenty-three years. The public now tends to see the media as part of the problem, not part of the solution.

The data from our studies indicate that people have strong opinions about media practices, believing that they choose stories that are more strategic than substantive and, once chosen, tend to slant the stories toward more strategic and sensational frames. The same people who hold these beliefs implicitly do not themselves select stories on the basis of more strategic headlines. To the contrary, their choices seem dictated more by topic than frame.

When criticizing the news media, our sample employed the stock topics of sensationalism, bias, and inaccuracy as their chief concerns. Conspicuous by their absence were any mentions of games, horse races, polls, excessive self-interest, conflict, adversity — in short, any of those features of news that have marked our concerns in this book. Preferred news events included those that involved the news media least — debates, lengthy interviews, and unedited speeches.

In the health reform debate, cynicism about the media's handling of this important issue was again associated with perceptions of imbalanced attention to various plans, biased treatment of plans as either too favorable or too unfavorable, and the perception of inaccuracy. Absent from the findings was a concern with negative coverage. Negative coverage seems not to contribute to cynicism about the news media; rather, coverage that is too negative or too positive reflects poorly on the public's trust of news institutions.

When communicating their understanding of the reasons why health care reform did not occur in 1994, our participants seldom mentioned the news media per se in either open-ended essays or in telephone interviews. Instead, their attempts to make sense of this intense debate centered on political matters, not media matters. Implicit in their understanding of the health care reform debate is an acceptance of the way the debate was characterized in the mainstream news media. Also implicit in their understanding is a clear sense that the reform efforts failed in large part because of the uncompromising conflicts engendered by the self-interested motivations of the political and social groups engaged in dispute.

We are not suggesting that these characterizations are accurate, nor that they are inaccurate. This is an undecidable issue in general. Rather, we are claiming that news formats structure the way people

make sense of political events. When one structuring of events pre-
dominates, then so will the public's interpretation be biased toward
one sense than any other. The sense people make is that government
officials, advocates of public policies, and candidates have motives that,
despite appearances, are directed at advancing their own self-interest
and that of their constituents. At the same time, the cynicism that has
undermined every social institution is undermining the institutions of
news, which less than twenty-five years ago were the paragons of trust,
even for those least trusting of the government.

BREAKING THE SPIRAL

OF CYNICISM

POLITICAL EVENTS, like all social events, are the objects of interpretation by the press, the public, and the public through journalistic frameworks of presentation. Our studies are premised on the assumption that understanding the impact of social and political events requires understanding how the events are framed for the public in the stories the press tells. Framing is a kind of sense-making that creates one interpretation of political events while ignoring others.

That framing is done by the press, by the public, and by the public through the press is a widely shared assumption. Murray Edelman describes the framing process this way:

> Interpretation pervades every phase of news creation and dissemination. Officials, interest groups, and critics anticipate the interpretations of particular audiences, shaping their acts and language so as to elicit a desired response. The audiences for news are ultimate interpreters, paying attention to some news stories, ignoring most, and fitting news accounts into a story plot that reflects their respective values. For any audience, then, an account is an interpretation of an interpretation.[1]

Sometimes the frame of reference is relatively common across members of the public as a "particular interpretation of an issue [is] popularized through political discussion"[2] while diversity in interpretive frames may be the norm when personal experiences intersect with mediated frames.[3] Common to each of these positions and central to our own conceptualization is the assumption that interpretive framing is a fact of journalistic practice and public understanding.

In approaching the evaluation of this assumption about the public and the press, our focus has been on the journalistic frame we have called strategic. This pervasive way of characterizing political events has been widely indicted for activating the public's cynicism. We have sought to evaluate it carefully.

We have also examined the effects of the strategic frame on the way the public thinks about political processes. The structure of thought is the locus of the consequences of journalistic frames. If mental frames are the interpretive filters through which citizens understand politics, then to understand the process we need to study the impact of journalistic frames on the audience's acts of framing. Accordingly, to borrow a phrase from Murray Edelman, we have studied how frames affect frames.

Strategic News Frames Thought About Politics

Our most important question asked about the effects of strategic news frames. Unlike some who have studied political alienation from the government or studied distrust of particular leaders or candidates, we studied cynicism about the political process, including candidates, leaders, advocates, practices, and interest groups. Alienation from government taints people's attitudes toward the actions of the agents and agencies of governmental action, usually federal and legislative. Political cynicism has a wider target — the very processes of selection and governance.

When viewed together, our findings offer a coherent picture of the impact of strategy framing on how the public thinks about campaigns and policy debates. We believe that the collection of results is more important than any individual test in establishing a conclusion with confidence. The findings pertinent to strategic framing and cynical response include:

A single strategically framed news story can activate cynical attributions. Large doses are not necessary.

A week of strategic news, whether in broadcast or print form, whether in election campaigns or policy debates, consistently activates cynical response (see Figure 7.1).

Strategic stories prompt the audience's own political stories, which are themselves cynical and loaded with strategic language.

The impact of strategic news across media is additive, with one source neither catalyzing nor canceling the effects of the other.

Those ready and able to receive the media's messages about health care reform experienced increased cynicism over the period of the debate.

Cynicism about the trustworthiness of government explained in part the negative reactions to Clinton's plan for reform.

If the pattern of our results is reliable, media critics' concerns about the consequences of strategic coverage have been on target. It promotes cynical judgments and cynical stories to interpret political actions; it does so readily and in controlled, but realistic, experiments and in surveys over time. Strategic press frames form cynical frames in the citizenry.

The news about strategic news is not all bad, however. Although these news formats can sometimes be highly focused on tactics, maneuvers, and positioning, our content analyses suggest a healthy component of issue-oriented discussion in stories about the political game. The consequences for learning from strategic news include:

A readiness to acquire knowledge about politics in other circumstances that we have called semantic activation.

A propensity to pick up information (e.g., strategic) consistent with the activated frame (e.g., strategic) — which we have called schematic activation.

A tendency for those ready and able to receive information from the mass media (political sophisticates) to acquire knowledge that is strategic, substantive, and both differentiated and integrated.

Political sophisticates are knowledgeable about the positions of ideological groups and personalities, a fact that readies them to store and recall the substance and tactics making up political news. In the same way, exposure to news, even strategic news, has a kind of readying effect on the audience, priming the acquisition of both substantive and strategic information from ensuing political events. In addition to stimulating cynical judgments, strategic news acts like other news forms in readying the consumer for more information.[4]

Issue and Narrative News Frames

Although assessing the effects of strategic news was the most important goal of our research, we harbored the hope that other forms of coverage — specifically issue-oriented ones — would have positive consequences for the public's attitude toward politics. Issue frames emphasize problems and possible solutions to them; engagement with opposing views; alternatives and analysis; critique and reformulation; advocacy and compromise where appropriate. We reasoned that issue coverage invited consideration of the substantive merits of policies and the abilities of leaders to carry them out. It did not invoke, implicitly or explicitly, the motivations of political actors and so we hoped for an amelioration — even a deactivation — of public cynicism in response to this framing of political events. These hopes were unrealized in the study of health care reform.

The real challenge for our future research will be to propose and evaluate news frames that dampen the public's cynicism about politics. During the mayoral study, issue frames for campaign news did not elevate cynicism the way that strategy coverage did. In fact, as Figure 7.1 indicated, in seven of nine cases, cynicism in response to issue coverage was below that of strategy coverage, although few of these differences were reliable. These trends went in the opposite direction in the health care study as issue coverage elevated cynicism in the same way that strategic coverage did.

We attributed this increase to the fact that people believed health care problems to be significant and relevant both to their lives and those of other citizens as well. At the same time, the issue coverage critiqued and rejected all available alternatives. In the actual coverage of the health care debate in the print media, common ground and compromise were at a low point, lower than during the 1992 presidential race. Additionally, people who felt that media coverage of health care was focused too much on conflict were more cynical about the health reform debate. We believe that issue coverage of important, relevant matters that is primarily critical and avoids reporting common ground — thereby focusing exclusively on conflict — marks a social context and a news frame that invites cynicism.

While we think our assessments of the problems with issue coverage are plausible, the challenge remains not only to confirm them but, more importantly, to find reporting frames that correct them. For example, will the inclusion of common ground and compromise in connection with critique of competing solutions ameliorate the effects of critique and rejection? Are relevance, importance, and complexity of the topic contextual factors that activate cynicism in the presence of conflict? We did not see cynicism rise in response to conflicting issue positions in the mayoral study. However, this context was not central to the lives of our participants — it was only a simulation of an election from another city. The problem they were asked to solve was also one they had solved before — for whom should I vote? At heart, this judgment is a judgment about people, and judgments about people are the kinds we make everyday. The issue — who to elect — was neither complex nor unfamiliar.

In contrast, in the health reform study, the issue was real, consequential for everyone, and complex. Our participants were not making a decision about a hypothetical mayoral candidate, but were deciding about a health plan for the country. Only a very few experts were in a position to master the available information, let alone choose among heavily criticized competing alternatives.

The challenge to future research is clear: understanding when and how issue frames activate cynicism. Equally important is the invention and evaluation of news frames that dampen cynical reaction – ones that inform, engage alternatives, critique, but still move toward solution of important problems in a civil way.

The NBC special "To Your Health" was an attempt to create a unique news vehicle about health care reform. We called it "narrative news." Our evaluation of this format was not ideal: one study had a small, unrepresentative sample that was randomly assigned to conditions; the other had a large, representative sample that self-selected to watching and nonwatching groups. Also, those who watched had to be compared to those who did not rather than to another group getting a second news format during the same period. If a second news format had been available, it would have been possible to compare a group getting narrative news about health care to one receiving another format also focused on health care coverage with the non-watching control as baseline. In this hypothetical design, the effect of format could be separated from the effect of content about health care. Future studies of narrative news will have to be sensitive to the confounding of content and format.

Despite these inadequacies in the design and evaluation of the NBC special, we believe that the narrative news frame is worth exploring in future work. It did, after all, produce both an increase in learning about health care and an amelioration of a growing cynicism about the health care reform debate. Narrative news as practiced in the "To Your Health" special had many features: an absence of technical discussion of health reform plans; real people with stories about their own health care concerns; interaction among experts, leaders, and ordinary citizens; little political posturing or pandering by the leaders and experts; little innuendo from reporters about the real, hidden motives of the involved parties; the search for and acknowledgment of common ground when it existed; civility by all parties. This description is not meant to imply that the NBC special was a "love-in" or that narrative news is envisioned as a "New Age" replacement for the Capitol Hill Gang. In fact, there was disagreement among experts, political leaders, and representatives of interest groups; there were moments of conflict and moments inviting empathy. The NBC special was a unique moment in the news history of the health care reform debate.

We cannot be certain if the narrative news format is one that will have replicable effects on learning, cynicism, and other outcomes in different political contexts. But we are certain that it is necessary to experiment with — invent, really — alternative formats to convey the realities of political life without undermining the trust necessary for civic life and sound governance. Although not everyone agreed,[5] in our view, the NBC special created a successful framework for discussing a policy issue of consequence and complexity to the public. We need more experiments like this one in how to frame news.

The Strategy Frame Frames the Messenger

The cynicism that has infected the public about politics has tainted their views of the press as well. Public opinion polls show sharp drops in the public's confidence in the press. Our research indicates that those most cynical about the press are the educated, those following politics closely but cynical of government generally. Informed citizens are those harboring the deepest cynicism.

Beliefs about press practices conform to this cynicism. One of our studies found that most assumed that reporters and editors would offer the public more strategic and lurid stories and that most stories, regardless of topic, would be slanted to emphasize the strategic and lurid. Media cynics held this view more strongly. When given an opportunity to tell us what the news media did well and did poorly, our participants leveled the usual criticisms about lack of objectivity, distortion, inaccuracy, and sensationalism. They also described some journalists as driven by the same kinds of self-interested motives other essayists had attributed to politicians in the mayoral study.

Those most cynical about the media's coverage of health care reform were also most concerned that the press had failed to recognize and report compromise and common ground when they were present. Interestingly, almost no one cited the news media for blame in the failure to pass any legislation regarding health care reform. At the same time, their essays accounting for the impasse recapitulated the conflicting and irreconcilable interests and the failed strategies that constituted the bulk of reporting on health care reform. Whether these beliefs about the press are fair and accurate or not, their attribution to news institutions is consequential in accounting for the public's (lack of) trust and confidence.

In the two plus decades since Watergate and Vietnam, the public has come to a new framing of the activities of the news media and, hence, to new interpretations of their motivations, interests, and contributions to society. Whether justified in general or not, the interpretations are not flattering. The trust and confidence that the public once bestowed on the press have evaporated in part perhaps because the frames that the press has overlaid on campaigns and governance have insinuated themselves into the public's understanding of the fourth estate as well.

Re-framing Press Frames

We opened this book with an extended analysis of the discourse of Clinton and Gingrich at the Senior Center in New Hampshire on June 11, 1995. Its substance and civility made that exchange unusual in contemporary political discourse. Understanding how members of the press reported it was instructive in gauging just how deeply ingrained news norms are in treating this deviant political event.

Just how unique was indicated when, in the weeks that followed, the debate over Medicare reform degenerated into the hyperbolic soundbites indicted by Clinton in the New Hampshire forum. In the subsequent Medicare debate, Republicans impugned the motives of Democrats and vice versa. Reporters detailed those exchanges and added their own accounts of the partisan purposes of the various sides.

Reporters' stuttering response to the original New Hampshire exchange indicates the extent to which this was for them a foreign form of public discourse. At the same time, their superficial reporting revealed the poverty of the dominant journalistic frame.

By contrast, reporters were on familiar ground once the debate veered toward name-calling. There is value in understanding motive and utility in critiquing the inadequacy of the press and public dialogue. The problem occurs when this perspective becomes the dominant one, crowding out the substantive engagement and discussion that helps the public understand the relative merits and practical consequences of political decisions.

The problem with the reporting on the New Hampshire exchange is that it was cynical rather than skeptical. We do not mean to imply that there is no truth to the various perceptions of press, politicians, and public. Among the central and legitimate roles of reporters is exposing the actual workings of government — the good, the bad, and the ugly. We are not arguing that the press should abandon its watchdog function. Following the money trail from lobbyists to legislation is both helpful to readers and useful to voters. So too are investigative reports of illegal or unethical activities. Nor are we arguing that strategic coverage has no place in a reporter's repertoire. Instead, we are claiming that it is appropriate for the press to be skeptical but not cynical.

The distinction is well articulated by *New York Times* Washington Bureau Chief R. W. Apple.

> A person who is cynical thinks everything is bad. To feel that way about politics and government ... is to abdicate the most important thing a journalist can bring to his or her work, which is judgment. If you are just being cynical you are saying they are all sons of bitches. Cynicism is incredibly corrosive of the values we should have as journalists....

Skepticism is using your intelligence and resources to check out what anyone tells you. But you don't begin by believing it not to be true. If you believe that everything they say is lying, you don't bother to check it out. I was in Vietnam for three years. Plenty of people lied to me.... But not everyone in Vietnam lied to us or we never would have found out what happened. The game is finding out what happened — sorting the lies from the truths. Cynicism is a giving up and [saying] a pox on all their houses.... We don't have to passively accept all that politicians or generals or businessmen or economists say to us but we do owe them the right to report what they have to say before we begin interpreting it.

Another is not to assume ... that everything a politician says is part of a game.... Campaigns are a fascinating, often indecipherable mixture of idealism and conniving. They're not one or the other. Sometimes when reading news accounts you feel as if it's all one or the other. I try to the degree that I can to see that that's not the case with our stories.[6]

When skepticism gives way to cynicism, a self-destructive dynamic is created. If reporters believe that the discourse is not substantive, they are justified in approaching it through an alternative filter — for example, the tactical or strategic frame. If political leaders believe that the press responds to a discourse of conflict not consensus, assertion not argument, strategy not substance, then they may be more likely to produce it. We saw evidence of this in the 1994 debate over health care reform when those sponsoring advertising revealed at a July 1994 Annenberg Conference held at the National Press Club that they shifted from ads advocating a position to attack ads when they realized that positive ads were not receiving press coverage.

The first spiral of cynicism we see operating in contemporary politics is one in which reporters and politicians justify their own cynical discourse by saying that it is required by the other. By producing the predicted discourse, each reinforces the assumption the other brought to the exchange.

The second spiral feeds on the first. Witnessing the tactical focus of the press and the conflictive, hyperbolic, dismissive rhetoric of its leaders, the public's own cynicism about the press and the process is confirmed. Polls reflect these attitudes. These surveys license reporters to perpetuate a cynical interpretation of the political process; political leaders read the polls as public rejection of current press practice.

The interrelation of the first two spirals is well expressed by journalist Jim Fallows who writes, "Reporters know that they sound cynical, and they know that people blame them for it. But they say it's not their fault. They are simply reflecting the world they see, They say that their cynical tone is justified — even required — by the relentless 'spin' of the politicians they write about."[7]

A third spiral is fed by perceptions of what the public wants and will reward. News consumers want horse-race coverage, say reporters. The excitement of politics resides in determining who is winning and losing. Votes can be more easily moved by negative than positive ads, report the consultants. Simplified slogans are more easily remembered than nuanced argument, claim the members of executive and legislative branches.

Believing that they are offering the public what it wants, reporters and political leaders minimize public access to substance. Having constrained the citizens' choices, reporters and leaders can then interpret continuing public attention to the impoverished journalistic and deliberative forms as evidence that the public is indeed being given what it wants. The cynicism of those remaining attentive is fed by the resulting diet. Others simply disengage.

In this climate, there is little incentive to enter or hold public office. In an essay titled "Cynicism Run Amok," the *Wall Street Journal*'s Washington bureau chief noted that "The writings of many political reporters today read like a perpetual sneer. Little wonder that truly thoughtful and conscientious politicians from both parties are throwing in the towel."[8]

Among elected officials, reporters, and the public are some hearty voices speaking for alternatives. But a sufficient number embrace these cynical perceptions as truths to play a role in shaping the discourse of campaigns and governance. The perceptions have come to serve a rhetorical purpose as well. Appeals to them assume the form of mantras. They form the final assertions that shut down discussion of the question, How can we do democracy better?

Some deny the existence of a problem. "Americans did not become more disillusioned because the press distorted the workings of government but because the press exposed the workings of government," writes *New York Times* columnist Maureen Dowd.[9] By exposing how the government works, the press may well have contributed to a realistic albeit pessimistic assessment of how the system works. But what our studies have shown is that press structures also can heighten cynicism.

It is undoubtedly true that Americans now have more access to more useful political information that at any time in the nation's history. Although audiences for traditional news are down, the amount of news available to interested citizens is up. In 1960, ABC broadcast two and a quarter hours of weekly news; it aired thirty-five hours in 1994.[10] And in the mix we now have instances of exemplary journalism from such sources as *Nightline, Frontline, The Jim Lehrer News Hour,* and *Meet the Press.* At the same time, CNN has made it possible to locate televised news around the clock and C-SPAN brings live coverage of Congress to those with access to cable.

But, contrary to a claim by the *New Yorker's* Michael Kelly, access does not of itself produce learning, and public cynicism is not the by-product of a higher level of information. "The press does a better job and the public is hugely more informed about what's going on in Washington than it has ever been — and being hugely more informed does have a tendency to make one a little more cynical," notes Kelly.[11] Were that the case, the information level of our participants would have increased after reading fifteen articles about the health care reform debate. Although their cynicism rose, their learning did not.

As our studies suggest, the price for these reinforcing beliefs is ultimately paid in public disengagement both from the political process and from the press. As a starting point, we have focused on the role of the press in feeding these cycles. In the past chapters, we have argued that the tactical structure has become the dominant one through which campaigns and governance are covered and that this structure activates public cynicism and changes the structures through which voters learn to privilege strategic information. We have also shown that those who perceive that the press focuses on strategy are more likely to be cynical about the press itself. And we have responded to the belief that the press is simply satisfying the public's demands with data showing that readers gravitate neither to issue-based nor strategic coverage but toward material they judge to be important to them, regardless of the structure encasing it.

If these spirals of cynicism are mutually reinforcing, intervening at a single point will not produce change. That is the lesson we draw from the forum in New Hampshire. Changing the character of a single meeting did not markedly alter the strategic frame of reporters.

Breaking the spirals will require a consistent change in political discourse with a consistent commitment of the press to cover it differently and a commitment of citizens to give the resulting discourse careful attention.

As we argued in our opening chapters, the public is providing the press and politicians with clear signals that it is unhappy with the status quo. Because that message has gotten through to both, this is a time conducive to change.

Declining readership and viewership of traditional news is one signal. Although more people still read a daily newspaper than don't, the increase in readership has not kept pace with expansion of the U.S. population. Daily newspaper circulation is 59.8 million, 62.6 million on Sundays; 62.1 percent of the households receive a daily paper; 64.9 percent get one on Sunday.[12] By contrast, the 1996 Super Bowl reached an estimated 138.5 million viewers.[13]

The comments of reporters and editors reflect an awareness of public discontent. Evidence that the message has been grasped is easy to come by. When asked by professional journals to characterize public sentiment about news professionals, editors respond with words such as "Mistrustful. Cynical. Resentful"[14] People "view us as hypocritical, privacy-invading, emotionally and practically remote from them, paternalistic and prone to frequent error," comments James Warren, the bureau chief of the *Chicago Tribune*. "And there's ample evidence to support each of these beliefs. All of which melds into what I find a very depressing — visceral almost — disdain of us."[15] "The general tendency in the press to treat all public figures as suspect" is a greater threat than tabloid journalism, notes ABC anchor Peter Jennings.[16]

The *Washington Post*'s media critic Howard Kurtz adds, "I think we bear 95 percent of the responsibility for the low repute in which we are held."[17]

Nor are these comments atypical. A spring 1995 survey of reporters by the Times Mirror Center found a majority agreeing that the anger of the public was justified, either in whole or part.[18] Increasingly, reporters are recognizing that the accountability of those in power is diminished by the strategy structure. In his book, *Breaking the News*, journalist James Fallows includes a statement by a former Clinton aide saying, "[Y]ou almost never have to worry that you'll be called on the substance of an issue."[19] Correspondingly, elected leaders are acknowledging the need for a different kind of discourse. "We can't restore the

American dream unless we can find some way to bring the American people closer together," Clinton said in a speech at Georgetown University on July 6, 1995. "Therefore how we resolve these differences is as important as what specific positions we advocate. I think we have got to move beyond the vision [*sic.*] and resentment to common ground. We've got to go beyond cynicism to a sense of possibility."

There is, however, more consensus about the nature of the problem than optimism about its likely solution. Nonetheless, we are optimistic for several reasons. Among them is the opportunity created quadrennially by general election presidential campaigns. Because it provides a chance for the public at large to give direct feedback to elected officials and indirect feedback to the press, it is one period in the national calendar well suited to breaking the spirals of cynicism. These campaigns include demonstrably beneficial events such as televised debates whose audience size is taken as evidence of public attentiveness to politics in general. By voting or by their apathy, citizens also voice their enthusiasm for the process. During campaigns, aspiring leaders monitor the pulse of the public with diligence. So, for example, by watching two of third-party candidate Ross Perot's half-hour broadcasts in unprecedentedly large numbers in the general election of 1992, citizens sent politicians a signal that the public would embrace longer political forms if the topics were salient and the messenger potentially consequential. When after more than a decade of decline, viewership for presidential debates rose, that too sent a signal as did the uptick in voting in the 1992 campaign.

A campaign provides other advantages. By definition, it involves an extended period of discourse and its attendant press coverage. The two months of general election campaigning afford sufficient time to reinforce positive tendencies in discourse and extinguish negative ones. If political discourse reflects the candidates' understanding of what will be rewarded with press coverage, then changes in press norms — for example, away from the histrionic sound bite and toward the representative one — would have time to influence and reinforce a changed pattern in candidate speeches. The extended time also gives audiences an opportunity to identify channels that are providing helpful coverage.

If the influential national media follow the lead of pioneers in the 1992 general election, 1996 could mark a turning point. Pilot projects in small media markets in 1992 were widely hailed for showcasing an alternative model. *The Charlotte Observer* used polls not to track the horse race but to determine the citizens' issue agenda. Substance was more prominent than strategy in its pages. Problems and their solutions were probed. The truth and accuracy of candidate claims were assessed. In 1996, the model has been adopted by NPR's Election Project. The Pew Civic Journalism Center has also been working aggressively to get media outlets to adopt the alternative perspective as has the Project on Public Life and the Press at New York University, which is headed by Jay Rosen and funded by the Knight Foundation. Among the available guides is *Public Journalism and Public Life* by Davis Merritt, editor of the *Wichita Eagle* and a pioneer in the civic journalism movement. Where in 1992, the civic journalism model was tried primarily in small media markets, in 1995-1996, some major papers have begun experimenting with alternative forms of communication. The *Philadelphia Inquirer*, for example, has opened its op-ed page to citizens whose questions are then answered by candidates.

And in the *New York Times* there is recent evidence of increased use of historical contextualization, decreased reliance on tactical discussion, and increased unmediated access to the actual words of those in power.

So, for example, an article by Robert Pear, creates an historical context by describing alternatives advocated in the past. "No one here expects Congress to pass anything like President Clinton's original [health reform] plan to guarantee health insurance for all Americans — or even Senator Dole's 1993 plan to provide access to insurance for all, with Federal subsidies if necessary for low-income families. Instead, the issue is expected to reach the House floor next Thursday, and the Senate floor next month, in the form of legislation to help workers keep health insurance if they lose or change jobs."[20] In that context, Pear justifies an examination of tactics on the grounds that the failed tactics of the past hobble leaders in the present. "In this debate, legislative tactics are almost as important as the substantive merits of the proposals. Such tactical considerations would ordinarily deserve little notice, but health care is no ordinary political issue. It has tripped up Mr. Gingrich, who failed last year in his efforts to overhaul Medicare. Both stumbled badly after overreaching, and they still bear political scars from the experience."

Similarly an article on Perot's possible 1996 bid reminds readers of the questions currently outside the media frame. "But," writes Adam

Nagourney, "in five television appearances since last Friday. Mr. Perot has yet to be asked about his campaign proposals of four years ago to impose a 50-cent gas tax or cut Social Security to reduce the deficit."[21]

Instead of focusing on its strategic intent or probable electoral effect, another article evaluates Republican candidate Steve Forbes's claim that when the tax burden goes down revenues go up. "The history books do show that in the years following tax cuts, the Government's tax receipts have almost always gone up," writes David E. Rosenbaum. "But they have also risen in the years following tax increases. In fact, except for the recession years of 1971 and 1983, Government tax collections have risen annually ever since the 1960 fiscal year."[22]

A second change is reflected in articles that go beyond accusation and counteraccusation to examine the accuracy of the rhetoric itself. In the debate over Medicare reform, another *Times* story noted, "There is much truth to the claims of both parties. But there is also a good deal of hyperbole. What follows is an attempt to separate the facts from the political hot air."[23] Also evident in the *Times* is an effort to give readers direct access to the words of those campaigning for office and making policy. Under the heading "In Their Own Words," The *New York Times* has increased the amount of space given to direct and extended quotation. So, for example, on Sunday, March 31, 1996, the *Times* included one box quoting extended passages of four Clinton speeches [24] and another, organized by issue, featuring excerpts from speeches delivered by prospective third-party candidate Ross Perot.[25] By inviting readers to evaluate these passages on their own, editors broke past the constraints of the existing structures of coverage. "I want to do some preaching to our folks that one of our big responsibilities ... is to let the candidates come through in their own terms," says *Times* executive editor Joseph Lelyveld.[26]

One reason for hope that journalistic norms can be shifted emerges from our reading of the May 1995 Times Mirror poll comparing the attitudes of reporters with those of the public. To the surprise of the pollsters and to many in journalism, the poll found that, contrary to the impression one would gather from reading and viewing mainstream news, reporters thought that public officials were more honest than the public did. In other words, those with the most contact with the country's leaders were less likely than their readers to see them as venal, self-interested, and corrupt. Journalists also expressed more confidence in the ability of the process to solve problems. It is on that sense of reality rather than the sense conveyed in news that *journalists* can build an alternative model of journalism.

Such efforts are in fact underway. Tom Hamburger of the *Minneapolis Star and Tribune* has crafted and publicized "The Minnesota Compact" — a document that recognizes that citizens, leaders, and reporters must all be part of the solution. The compact was offered in July 1995 as a means of improving the 1996 U.S. Senate election. All provisions of the compact are voluntary. The compact would increase candidate accountability by restoring Lincoln–Douglas-style debates — one in each congressional district. If citizens would turn out to participate, that action of itself would reinvigorate the sense that politics is a communal activity. In Hamburger's compact, candidates would have to speak their own ads directly into camera — a requirement that could circumvent First Amendment concerns only if adopted voluntarily, but would dramatically increase candidate accountability for the content of ads.

Reforming candidate behavior won't matter much if the news media on which most of us rely for most of our political coverage ignore the substance and focus on the strategy. So Hamburger would have news organizations commit to covering substance. In the tradition of civic journalism, he would ask media organizations to devote part of their survey research budget to identifying the concerns of voters. And he would ask citizens to participate in politics at the level of other countries. If adopted, this three-pronged structure with its increased accountability for politicians, the press, and the people could help break the spirals of cynicism this book has explored.

In November 1995, Minneapolis advertising executive Lee Lynch joined the discussion with a six-point advertising code that, consistent with Hamburger's goals, was designed to increase candidate accountability. Candidates signing it would agree to take responsibility for their ads and ask stations to reject PAC ads aired on their behalf. Under Lynch's proposal, candidates would also include their likeness or voice or both in all ads at all times and reject ads using film, video, photos, or illustrations of an opponent.

In early May 1996, the substance of the compact was adopted. Its four planks focus on the obligations of the candidates (to debate with follow-up news conferences, to accept accountability for ads and refrain from false and misleading attacks and unpleasant visuals of the opponent), journalists (a de-emphasis on horse race and coverage of substance), and citizens (participation in organized discussions). The details of the planks of the compact can be found in Appendix I.

Whether the Minnesota Compact and the ad code promoted better campaign discourse is impossible to say. More than 250 candidates statewide signed on.[27] Some of the reporting at the *Minneapolis Star Tribune* offered the kind of in-depth, issue-oriented, comparative analysis of the presidential candidates and their positions that is the antithesis of strategic, cynical, poll-driven coverage. In six news and analysis pieces, reporters treated issues ranging from the role of big government to cross-generational, foreign policy, and urban concerns. The coverage provided background information as well as candidates' positions and records. Former Minnesota Congressman and initiator of the compact, Tim Penny, observed, "From my travels around the state, I am convinced that the standards laid out in the compact have raised awareness among voters that we can expect and demand better conduct from candidates and the news media."[28]

The experiment in Minnesota is less important for its short-term outcome than the principles on which it was based. Although we have focused exclusively on the press's role in *Spiral of Cynicism*, we believe the problem is systemic. By making citizens, the media, and politicians mutually responsible for the quality of public discourse, the compact recognizes the systemic nature of the problem and its possible solutions. The predicate of the compact is that mutual accountability is more effective than finger pointing.

Meanwhile, citizens continue to signal their desire for an alternative form of campaigning and coverage. When given the opportunity to question four of the Republican contenders in the University of Texas's January 1996 National Issues Convention, a randomly selected group of citizens from across the nation asked not about polls or tactics but jobs, taxes, welfare, foreign affairs, and other matters relevant to governance and central to the role of a president. As important was the number of times the citizens responded to pat replies from the politicians by reporting to moderator Jim Lehrer of PBS that the question remained unanswered.

When offered accessible substance, voters have on occasion provided dramatic evidence that it satisfies an appetite. So, for example, when the *Philadelphia Inquirer* published a readable nine-day series "America: What Went Wrong?," it received over 400,000 requests for reprints. The resulting book sold more than half a million copies. The series focused on such topics as "leveraged buyouts, deregulation and the global economy."[29]

However, after an election in which turnout plummeted to a post–World War II low, voters expressed little enthusiasm for the candidates, debates, press, parties, poll-takers, or themselves. The year 1996 had not measured up to 1992.[30] While scholars might debate whether it reflected or reinforced public disinterest, both front page campaign coverage and nightly news reporting were down significantly from 1992 as well.[31]

The good news is that the proportion of the print news devoted to talk about strategy dropped from 51 percent in 1992 to 43 percent in 1996. Correcting for the drop in the amoung of broadcast news, there were half as many references to polls.

But voters still believed that broadcast and print news focused on candidates' strategies for winning over their stands on issues.[32] And in relative terms, they were right. In broadcast news, issue and strategy information got about equal time; in print, there was 17 percent more strategy than issue coverage. These data may explain why, overall, the public gave the press a C in 1996[33] while giving itself a C+, Republican nominee Bob Dole a C, and Democratic nominee Bill Clinton a B–. In sum, voters perceive that there is need for improvement all around.

Although some would say, with Ambrose Bierce, a cynic is simply a dead idealist, we instead read evidence of public concern as a call to resurrection. Evidence that the call is being heard can be found on the subscription order form of *The Washington Monthly*, which promises "Cynicism? No. Solutions"[34] and in the sign that once hung over the desk of *New York Times* editor R. W. (Johnny) Apple: "Skepticism not cynicism."

When journalist James Reston of the *New York Times* died in December 1996, a colleague wrote, "He remained an idealist in a world of cynics."[35] The body politic would be well served if the same could be said of all of us.

Issue and Strategy Versions of Print News

The text of two versions of the same news story appear below. The first is the original story which we assumed was framed in issue terms. The second was a strategy version of the story rewritten from the original. Both stories were set in the type of the original story with the masthead *Philadelphia Examiner* prominently displayed.

Tonight's Debate Gives Rendell Chance to Defend Privatization

By Dorthea Brooke The Philadelphia Examiner

Tonight's debate affords mayoral front-runner Edward G. Rendell his most extensive chance yet to explain to voters his plan to privatize city services.

It will also give challenger Joseph M. Egan Jr. his best chance to shoot down the plan, which has caused great distress among city employees who fear they will be thrown out of work.

Democrat Rendell has the chance tonight to cement voter approval on this issue. Polls show that a majority of taxpayers say they favor contracting out city services such as trash collection to private firms in the hopes of better service but that they worry about private services costing more money.

Rendell has yet to make his case for the plan. He has discussed it only in dribs and drabs, in interviews on the fly and in position papers that the press has ignored.

Tonight's hour-long debate, to be broadcast live on WHYY-TV (Channel 12) and WPVI-TV (Channel 6) at 7 p.m., gives him his first extensive opportunity to tell voters how privatization fits into his overall scheme for staving off bankruptcy and what safeguards he would put in place against cost overruns.

It will give him the opportunity to be specific about the number of workers who might be laid off or retrained, how much money the city might save and what he would do with the savings. It will also allow him to discuss the generous benefits package that city workers enjoy, whether they would retain those benefits under a private plan and what the city's posture would be in the event of a strike.

At the same time, Republican challenger Egan has the chance to make his pitch to the thousands of city workers who will almost certainly lose their jobs under the plan and could go on the unemployment rolls — at greater cost to the city than keeping the services in city hands.

Egan will also have the opportunity to link Rendell with the failures of past Democratic administrations, which have caved into union demands, especially in the face of November elections. Egan's charges on this score have so far been vague. Tonight, viewers should get to see whether Egan can make the case that Rendell and his Democratic allies have run the city for too long and run it into the ground.

But the privatization plan has forced Rendell and Egan into an odd reversal of roles. As a Democrat, Rendell might be expected to favor keeping city services in the hands of the powerful municipal unions, who have traditionally supported Democratic candidates.

And Republican Egan might be expected to support the use of private businesses with their reputation for more efficient service based on the bottom line.

But Rendell has seized the upper hand here by promoting himself as a fiscally responsible Democrat, leaving the role of defending the status quo to Egan, whose business background shows him to be one who hews to the bottom line in making decisions and who can meet a payroll.

The unusual role-reversal is likely to prompt intense debate on managing the city that should provide insights into the candidates' views.

But neither candidate has been comfortable in front of the cameras, which is perhaps why their views are still murky to many voters. Now, with just 14 days to go till Election Day, Rendell has to put forth his plan cogently without drawing attention to himself.

"As in the Democratic primary, Rendell has the most to lose in this debate," said Chris Motolla, a Republican media adviser. "Egan, by comparison, has nothing to lose, and it's safe to assume he'll come out swinging."

David L. Cohen, Rendell's campaign manager, said Rendell toned down his torrid campaign pace the last two days to rest and rehearse. He said the debate format would probably buffer any real clashes.

"The format is sleep-inducing," he said, "but that may play to

Rendell's advantage and he seeks to impress voters with his determination to resolve the city's financial crisis.

Also on stage will be Consumer party candidate Pamela Lawler and independent Dennis Wesley, both long-shots in the race. Their inclusion has irked the Republicans, who were hoping for a clear shot at Rendell. But they could possible turn into allies by helping to poke holes in Rendell's plan. And their presence could muddy the differences between Egan and Rendell, which would serve to confuse voters and thus possible help Egan.

Egan and his advisers retreated yesterday morning to a seminar room at the Pennsylvania Manufacturers Association in Center City for an hour-long dress rehearsal that mimicked the actual debate format.

Later in the afternoon, the candidate and his entourage viewed and critiqued a videotape of the session.

Lawrence Tabes, City Council candidate and veteran campaigner, played Rendell, and Egan's press secretary, Joe Sanchez, a former television reporter, acted as a journalist.

"What we did," said Sanchez, "is try to simulate a debate as much as humanly possible. We tried to make it realistic. We had a panel of reporters, and we just fired away with questions."

Egan also got some advice from former mayoral candidate Sam Katz, whose live performances on TV during the primary were considered instrumental in his quick rise to contention late in the campaign.

Said Katz: "I just told (Egan) to be self-confident and relaxed, not to get overly inundated with enormous numbers of details. My advice was to be as positive as possible, to be forthright, to be conscious of completing all of his thoughts." Egan has been criticized for speaking in half-sentences on the campaign circuit.

The second and final televised debate is scheduled for next Tuesday.

The strategy version of this story follows.

Why Egan Has the Most to Gain, Rendell the Most to Lose Tonight

By S. A. Paolantonio   Examiner Staff Writer

Tonight's first live televised debate of the fall campaign for mayor of Philadelphia holds little drama.

For Republican Joseph M. Egan Jr., trailing badly in the polls, the plan is simple: Give Philadelphia voters a compelling reason to jettison their allegiance to the front-running Democrat, Edward G. Rendell, and choose him instead.

And for Rendell, who has led in every poll since August 1990, the hour-long debate broadcast live on WHYY-TV (Channel 12) and WPVI-TV (Channel 6) at 7 p.m. is fraught with risks.

He has to guard against attacks from Egan, and his other two long-shot adversaries – Consumer Party candidate Pamela Lawler and independent Dennis Wesley.

At the same time, Rendell has his first opportunity this fall to look voters in the eye and tell them how he is qualified to heal Philadelphia's chronic miseries.

Moreover, though Rendell already has spent about $1.5 million in television advertising since Labor Day, the campaign has not featured an ad in which Rendell talks directly to the voters. Strategists from rival campaigns say Rendell is ineffective on camera.

It was only during the latter stages of the primary that Rendell's ads featured the candidate on camera in a speaking role.

Thus, with just 14 days remaining until Election Day, the front-runner has to walk this fine line of being cautious and aggressive without committing a gaffe that alters the shape of the campaign.

"As in the Democratic primary, Rendell has the most to lose in this debate," said Chris Mottola, a Republican media adviser who advised former District Attorney Ronald D. Castille during the spring. "Egan, by comparison, has nothing to lose and it's safe to assume he'll come out swinging."

Rendell's campaign manager, David L. Cohen, said Rendell toned down his torrid campaign pace the last two days to rest and rehearse. He said the debate format likely would buffer any clashes. "The format is sleep-inducing," Cohen said.

First, the moderator will ask a question and each candidate will get 60 seconds to answer. Then each panelist will ask a question, and the candidate will get 60 seconds to answer, then 30 seconds to answer a follow-up question. Each candidate will be allotted 75 seconds for a closing statement.

During the primary, Rendell avoided confrontation on camera with his opponents, because his two warring opponents — former City Councilmen Lucien E. Blackwell and George R. Burrell — were attacking each other.

Indeed, the Egan campaign was disappointed when Lawler and Wesley were included in the debates. The Republicans wanted a clear shot at Rendell.

Still, Egan wanted to be positioned next to Rendell on stage at WHYY's studios — so much so that when he won the right to choose stage position first, he refused until the debate officials would tell him where Rendell would be. Rendell, drawing the third pick, did not have to disclose his choice for position.

Finally, after nearly a two-day delay last week, Egan picked spot number three. Wesley picked two and Rendell chose one, at the far left of the stage. Lawler will be in the fourth spot, at the far right.

Yesterday, the Egan campaign downplayed the importance of stage position.

"It's my guess that because of the format there will not be very wide shots," said Joe Sanchez, Egan's press secretary. "If you think about it, it'll be a close-up of the panelist, close-up of the candidate and a very few wide shots."

The debate — the first of two set up by the League of Women Voters and the Greater Philadelphia Chamber of Commerce — is coming late in the campaign. Rendell's extensive television campaign has been aimed at building his name recognition and making voters familiar with his proposals.

Egan, cash-poor, has been relegated to advertising on cable TV, but more than a third of the city's households are not hooked up to cable, and he recently canceled TV ads to conserve money.

Egan and his advisers retreated yesterday morning to a seminar room at the Pennsylvania Manufacturers Association in Center City for an hour-long dress rehearsal that mimicked the actual debate format. Later in the afternoon, the candidate and his entourage viewed and critiqued a videotape of the session.

Lawrence Tabas, City Council candidate and veteran campaigner, played Rendell, and Egan's press secretary, Joe Sanchez, a former television reporter, stood in as a journalist.

"The real danger is bombarding Joe," said Sanchez. "What we did this morning is try to simulate a debate as much as humanly possible. We tried to make it realistic. We had a panel of reporters and we just fired away with questions."

Egan also got some advice from former mayoral candidate Sam Katz, whose live performances on TV during the primary were considered instrumental in his quick rise to contention late in the campaign.

"Sam Katz was written off as dead, but he did very well on live TV and all of a sudden he was back in the race," said Mottola.

"I just told him to be self-confident and relaxed, not to get overly inundated with enormous numbers of details," said Katz. "My advice would be to be as positive as possible, to be forthright, to be conscious of completing all his thoughts." Egan has been criticized for speaking in halfsentences on the campaign circuit.

The second and final live televised debate is scheduled for next Tuesday.

Examiner staff writers Doreen Carvajal and Marc Duvoisin contributed to this article.

APPENDIX B

Issue and Strategy Versions of Broadcast News

The voice-overs of two versions of the same TV news segment are printed below. Commentary by the candidates, which remained the same in both versions, as did the visuals, is not reproduced. The first is the issue version, the second strategy. The same news anchor and reporter are used in both versions.

Issue Version

Jim Gardner:

But the big story on Action News tonight is the first televised debate among mayoral candidates in Philadelphia. It happened here tonight and Action News Reporter David Henry was there.

David Henry:

As the four candidates assembled for the debate Republican Joe Egan greeted his Democratic opponent Ed Rendell. But Egan spent the rest of the night telling voters why he'd make a better mayor than Rendell.

Independent Dennis Wesley pointed out some other differences among the candidates.

All agreed the city's a mess and needs sweeping changes. The one issue they clearly disagreed on is privatization of city services

And throughout the debate the candidates agreed on the need for fundamental change in the way the city is run.

After the debate all the candidates gave themselves high marks for taking command of the issues.

But don't count out the Independents yet. Dennis Wesley, a former Republican, says he can win if he scores big in the Black community.

Of course, that remains to be seen. The finish line for the race is almost here — the Mayor's office at City Hall.

David Henry, Channel 12 news.

Strategy Version

(An underscore indicates wording repeated verbatim from the issue version)

But the big story on Action News tonight is the first televised debate among mayoral candidates in Philadelphia. It happened here tonight and Action News Reporter David Henry was there.

As the four candidates assembled for the debate Republican Joe Egan greeted his Democratic opponent Ed Rendell. Those were the last kind words Egan had for the acknowledged front-runner all night. Egan went on the attack a dozen times. The others knew they had to score points against Rendell or hope that he would stumble on his own.

All agreed the city's a mess and needs sweeping changes. The one issue they clearly disagreed on is privatization of city services.

While Egan and Rendell slugged it out, the two minor party candidates welcomed the televised exposure.

After the debate all the candidates gave themselves high marks but did the rest of the pack score against the front-runner?

But don't count out the Independents yet. Dennis Wesley a former Republican, says he can win if he scores big in the black community.

Of course, that remains to be seen. The finish line for the race is here — the door to the Mayor's office at City Hall. The smart money in still riding on Ed Rendell but his opponent's still have two more televised chances to knock him off his horse.

David Henry, Channel 12 news.

APPENDIX C

Demographic Characteristics of Campaign and Health Care Samples to National Norms

In the following tables, the distribution of people by age, race, education, and sex for the mayoral campaign and health care studies are compared to the distributions derived from census data and from the National Election Study of voters from 1992.

Table C.1. Percentage of Samples for Race: Campaign Study, Health Reform Study, Census Data, Voters

Race	Percent Campaign	Percent Health ($\underline{N} = 276$)	National %[a] Census ($\underline{N} = 349$)	NES %[b] Voters
White	78.5	74.5	80.3	86.5
Afro-American	12.4	17.8	12.1	9.8
Asian	1.1	1.1	2.9	—
Hispanic	5.8	2.3	9.0	3.8
Native-Am.	0.4	0	0.8	—
Missing	1.5	3.4	-	—

[a] U.S. Bureau of the Census, press release CB91-216—1990.
[b] U.S. Bureau of the Census, "Voting and Registration in the Election of November 1992"—*Current Population Reports*, Series P20-466, Table 2.

Table C.2. Percentage of Samples for Age Groups: Campaign Study, Health Reform Study, Census Data, Voters

Age	Percent Campaign (N = 276)	Percent Health (N = 349)	National %[a] Census %	NES %[b] Voters
18–25	13.5	21.5	16.2	10.8
26–35	23.6	26.1	23.2	20.1
36–45	25.8	21.2	20.2	22.3
46–55	12.7	12.6	13.4	16.0
56–65	5.5	8.3	11.2	13.3
66–75	10.9	5.4	9.4	11.4
75+	5.5	4.9	6.4	6.2
Missing	2.5	0	—	—

[a] U.S. Bureau of the Census, Unpublished Data — 1991
[b] U.S. Bureau of the Census, "Voting and Registration in the Election of November 1992" — *Current Population Reports*, Table 1.

Table C.3. Percentage of Samples for Education: Campaign Study, Health Reform Study, Census Data, Voters

Education	Percent Campaign (N = 276)	Percent Health (N = 349)	National %[a] Census %	NES %[b] Voters
Some high school	1.8	3.8	20.8	12.3
High school	18.2	14.0	36.6	32.9
Some coll/assoc.	26.2	24.4	23.7	28.2
Coll/some grad.	31.3	44.5	11.9	17.6
Masters and Ph.D.	20.0	13.5	5.2	9.0
Missing	5.3	0	—	—

[a] U.S. Bureau of the Census, *Current Population Reports*, Series P-70, No. 21 — 1987
[b] U.S. Bureau of the Census, "Voting and Registration in the Election of November 1992" — *Current Population Reports*, Series P20-466, Table 7.

Table C.4. Percentage of Samples for Gender: Campaign Study, Health Reform Study, Census Data, Voters

Gender	Percent Campaign (N = 276)	Percent Health (N = 349)	National %[a] Census %	NES %[b] Voters
Male	42.9	39.5	48.8	46.8
Female	54.5	59.9	51.2	53.2
Missing	2.5	.6	—	—

[a] U.S. Bureau of the Census, *Current Population Reports*, Series P-70, No. 21 — 1987.
[b] U.S. Bureau of the Census, "Voting and Registration in the Election of November 1992" — *Current Population Reports*, Series P20-466, Table 2.

Titles of Health Reform News Articles

The following is a listing of titles of articles used in field study of health reform by condition. The GSP and IGSP groups are made up of articles from the other groups. Article 5 is the same in all conditions and describes the similarities and differences among plans.

Group 1: Issue (fifteen articles)
1. Health Plan to Hold Array of Benefits
2. Socialized Medicine in America
3. Clinton Gets an Earful on Health Care
4. What Is "Universal" Is Center of Fight Over a Health Plan
5. Breaking Down the Tough Debate on Health Care
6. Health Plan Has Many Layers, Twists
7. "Choice" Belongs to Government
8. Rep. Cooper's Plan
9. Killing Drug Research Kills People
10. Cooper Plan, Clinton Lite
11. The Clintons' Lethal Paternalism
12. Bureaucracy a Target and Product of Clinton's Health-Care Reform
13. No Health-Care Crisis? Nonsense!
14. There is No Health Care Crisis
15. Carefully Into the Breach

Group 2: Groups (fifteen articles)
1. Winners and Losers in Health Reform
2. Clinton Fighting Rich Lobbies on Health Revisions
3. AMA Urging its Physicians to Enlist Patients as Health Reform Lobbyists
4. Paying for Precious Access
5. Breaking Down the Tough Debate on Health Care
6. Health-Care Industry Had Raised its Donations to Congress
7. Doctors Soften Criticism of Health Plan
8. Reform Plan too Restrictive, Pharmaceutical Firms Charge
9. A.M.A. to Seek Major Changes in Clinton Plan

10. Surgeon Group Backs Canada-Style Health Care
11. Big, Small Businesses Reject Plan
12. Business Leaders Reject Health Plan
13. Business Delivers Another Blow to Health Plan
14. Plan's Effects on Unions Will Vary
15. Manufacturers Oppose Clinton Plan

Group 3: Strategy (fifteen articles)
1. The Guns of February
2. Administration Fumbles on Health Plan
3. Hillary Clinton Opens Campaign to Answer Critics of Health Plan
4. Clinton Aide Says Poll Had Role in Health Plan
5. Breaking Down the Tough Debate on Health Care
6. Perot Attacks Clinton's Health Plan and Flirts with an Alternative
7. Clinton Seeks Support of Doctors
8. Gephardt Goes After Critics of Clinton's Health-Care Plan
9. Administration Rethinks Health Plan Strategy
10. Budget Office Gives Clinton's Health Plan a Lift, With a Catch
11. Clintons Campaign to Scuttle Endorsement of Rival Health Plan
12. Health Care Splitting GOP
13. Odd Couple Behind Health Plan That Rivals Clinton's
14. GOP Tones Down Rhetoric on Health Care
15. Administration Opens Talks with Chief Rival on Health Compromise

Group 4: Process (fifteen articles)
1. Health Reform Promises to be a Capitol Hill Circus
2. How to Work a Congressman
3. The Game's Afoot
4. "Big John" Is Key to the Health of the Clinton Plan
5. Breaking Down the Tough Debate on Health Care
6. The Real Health Care Issue: Turf
7. Hope, Risks Run High in Health Plan Equation
8. Republicans Engage in Factional Warfare over Health Reform
9. Moynihan Shakes White House with Stance on Health Reform
10. Congressional Republicans Nip at Heels of the President
11. Ickes to Coordinate Health Care Drive

12. Old Republican Fissures Feel Strain as Health Care Debate Grows
13. Long Legislative Route for Clinton Health Plan
14. Health-Care Reform Faces Deadlock in Congress as Lawmakers Wrangle Over Rival Proposals
15. Health Care's Power Player

Group 5: GSP—Selected articles from groups 2,3,4, and 5 (fifteen articles)
1. Winners and Losers in Health Reform
2. Clinton Fighting Rich Lobbies on Health Revisions
3. Health-Care Industry Has Raised its Donations to Congress
4. AMA Urging its Physicians to Enlist Patients as Health Reform Lobbyists
5. Breaking Down the Tough Debate on Health Care
6. Business Delivers Another Blow to Health Plan
7. The Guns of February
8. Administration Fumbles on Health Plan
9. Hillary Clinton Opens Campaign to Answer Critics of Health Plan
10. Clinton Aide Says Polls Had Role in Health Plan
11. Clinton's Campaigning to Scuttle Endorsement of Rival Health Plan
12. Health Reform Promises to be a Capitol Hill Circus
13. The Game's Afoot
14. Health Care's Power Player
15. Hope, Risks Run High in Health Plan Equation Congress

Group 6: IGSP—Selected articles from groups 1,2,3, and 4 (fifteen articles)
1. Health Plan to Hold Array of Benefits
2. Clinton Gets an Earful on Health Care
3. There Is No Health Care Crisis
4. Carefully into the Breach
5. Breaking Down the Tough Debate on Health Care
6. Winners and Losers in Health Reform
7. Clinton Fighting Rich Lobbies on Health Revisions
8. Health-Care Industry Has Raised its Donations to Congress
9. The Guns of February

10. Administration Fumbles on Health Plan
11. Hillary Clinton Opens Campaign to Answer Critics of Health Plan
12. Clinton Aide Says Poll Had Role in Health Plan
13. Health Reform Promises to be a Capitol Hill Circus
14. The Game's Afoot
15. Health Care's Power Player

Group 7: Control (fifteen articles)
1. Federal Budget Process May Focus on Proposed Cuts
2. Federal Agencies Focus on Achieving Environmental Justice
3. CIA Failure to Unmask Traitors Assailed
4. Scientists Say Mutant HIV Strains Could Resist Their Promising Drug
5. Breaking Down the Tough Debate on Health Care
6. Party Finances Do Not Reflect the Victors and the Vanquished
7. Critics Say "Three Strikes" Proposal Would Do Little to Reduce Crime
8. How School Choice Improves Public Schools
9. Cable Rate Cut: Don't Count on the Savings Yet
10. Law Firms Begin Reining in Sex-Harassing Partners
11. Balancing-Budget Showdown Is Nearing
12. Business Criticizes Administration Plan to Speed High-Tech Exports Licensing
13. The Wooing of American Investors
14. Stop Violence Before It Begins
15. Term Limits for Officeholders Favor the Rich and Unprincipled

APPENDIX E

Structural Characteristics for Health Reform News Articles

Table E.1 gives the average structural characteristics of the news stories across experimental conditions including readability, number of sentences, number of passives, number of long sentences, number of words, and average word length. Significant differences are found in readability $[F(6,98)= 3.31, p < .005]$, number of long sentences $[F(6,98) = 3.23, p < .006]$, and average word length $[F(6,98) = 4.34, p < .001]$. Although only three differences emerge by a Scheffe's test (primarily involving the control group), the pattern of means giving rise to the differences is clear.

Control is the least readable of all conditions primarily as a result of having longer words and more passives. Control has fewer long sentences in opposition to its lower readability. Since there is only one difference among experimental groups by the Scheffe's procedure (Group has longer words than Process on average), we can safely conclude that news stories are structurally similar across the experimental conditions. The lower readability of the control works against hypothesis about cynicism and does not affect learning scores directly.

Table E.1. Structural Characteristics of News Stories across Experimental Conditions

	Readability	No. of Sentences	No. of Passives	No. of Long Sentences	No. of Words	Average Word Length
Issue	47.1	51.4	5.53	9.27	1029.7	5.09
Group	44.3	38.5	3.73	6.87	782.2	5.20
Strategy	48.4	42.8	4.87	8.80	894.7	5.01
Process	51.5	55.3	4.87	10.93	1136.9	4.94
GSP	47.8	47.5	4.87	10.80	1002.5	5.04
IGSP	48.8	47.1	4.80	10.20	989.5	5.03
Control	43.1	48.0	6.87	5.0	984.7	5.17
Overall	47.3	47.3	5.08	8.84	974.3	5.07

Table E.2. Mean Judgment of Types of News Stories

	Issue	Group	Strategy	Process
Easy to understand?	4.69	4.99	4.83	5.20
Knowledge of HC debate?	4.32	3.89	3.49	3.80
HC debate will benefit powerful interests?	3.00	3.65	3.40	3.41
Interesting article?	3.89	3.78	3.37	4.28
Favorable to HCR? (=7)	3.73	4.06	4.25	4.36
Knowledge of which proposal is ahead?	2.32	2.96	2.94	3.05
Relevant to you?	3.44	2.85	2.49	2.76
Knowledge of support of HCR by groups	2.47	4.58	4.19	4.23
Knowledge of HCR's benefits?	2.40	3.03	2.83	2.91
Which plan will pass Congress?	2.00	2.78	2.99	3.83
Which group will win and which will lose?	3.36	4.15	3.07	3.38
HC reform good for special interests only?	4.44	4.81	4.92	4.60
Knowledge about maneuvering through Congress?	2.11	3.39	3.57	5.59

Note: All questions are scored from strongly disagree (= 1) to strongly agree (= 7) except as noted.

Table E.3. Ranking of Stories from Most to Least on Five Criteria

		Issue		Group		Strategy		Process	
		F	%	F	%	F	%	F	%
Told abouts	Most	21	14.8	26	18.3	23	16.2	72	50.7
tactics	Least	66	46.5	28	19.7	31	21.8	17	12.0
Which plan	Most	79	59.8	25	18.9	14	10.6	14	10.6
to support?	Least	9	6.8	24	18.2	31	23.5	68	51.5
How groups	Most	53	41.4	50	39.1	12	9.4	13	10.2
affected?	Least	20	15.6	15	11.7	29	22.7	64	39.5
Read most	Most	71	53.5	18	13.4	7	5.2	38	28.4
closely?	Least	23	17.3	29	21.8	33	24.8	48	36.1
Makes you	Most	34	25.8	30	22.7	27	30.5	41	31.1
feel cynical	Least	51	39.8	23	18	28	21.9	26	20.3

Note: F is frequency of selection; % is percentage selecting news story.

Proportion of Recall: Health Reform

Table F.1 gives the means, standard deviations, and sample sizes for recall accuracy (substantive, strategic, factual) of the seven groups in the health care reform study. We found no significant differences between experimental and control groups or between issue and strategy groups.

Table F.1. Comparison of Mean Recall Scores Between Experimental Condition and Control Across Three Measures of Recall

	Issue (N = 49)	*Group* (N = 47)	*Strategy* (N = 45–46)	*Process* (N = 47)	*GSP* (N = 50)	*IGSP* (N = 47)	*Control* (N = 49)
Strategic recall	.60 (.23)	.55 (.21)	.58 (.24)	.56 (.20)	.61 (.19)	.52 (.23)	.56 (.24)
Substan recall	.73 (.25)	.71 (.24)	.74 (.25)	.71 (.21)	.72 (.21)	.73 (.24)	.72 (.23)
Factual recall	.53 (.21)	.56 (.24)	.59 (.24)	.51 (.21)	.56 (.22)	.60 (.25)	.52 (.25)

APPENDIX G

Constructing Cynicism Scales

This appendix provides information on the reliability and validity of our measures of political cynicism. Reliability is evaluated with the standard techniques of factor analysis* and internal scale reliability. We assessed validity through patterns of association with other, established measures and with questions whose content obviously taps some component of cynical reaction.

Campaign Study

Ten agree-disagree and six forced-choice questions were the initial group of items we employed to assess political cynicism about the simulated mayoral campaign. The agree-disagree items and the forced choice items were analyzed both separately and together.

Image factor analysis of the ten agree-disagree items indicated three factors with eigenvalues greater than 1.0 but examination of the plot of eigenvalues suggested that a single factor (33 percent of variance) was primary, with subsequent factors dropping off rapidly in variance explained. Based on an alpha reliability analysis, two of the ten items were dropped from the scale leaving an eight-item scale with internal reliability of .77. A similar analysis of the six forced choice items yielded a single factor (49 percent of variance) of five items with an internal reliability of .80 (Cronbach's alpha).

The sixteen cynicism items were also factored together using image techniques. Four factors with eigenvalues greater than 1.0 emerged, but the first factor predominated (31 percent of variance) with the others tailing off rapidly. A single scale of thirteen items (the same eight agree-disagree and five forced-choice as before) resulted, with an internal reliability of .85.

*Image factor analysis is used instead of the more common principal components. Some recent simulation studies suggest that image techniques can more readily reveal the underlying structures of association among items than principal components. Jerry L. Buley, "Evaluating Exploratory Factor Analysis: Which Initial Extraction Techniques Provide the Best Factor Fidelity," *Human Communication Research*, 21 (1995), pp. 478–93.

A listing of the items follows; those starred remained in the final scales.

Political Cynicism (FC)

• The campaign was concerned with policies to meet the city's needs. *or* The campaign was concerned with standing in the polls.
• The candidates were grandstanding. *or* The candidates were focused on problems.
• The candidates' concerns were getting elected. *or* The candidate's concerns were the city's problems.
The candidates told the voters what they *needed* to hear. *or* The candidates told the voters what they *wanted* to hear.
• The candidates were lying about their goals. *or* The candidates were telling the truth about their goals.
• The candidates were being manipulative in their campaigning. *or* The candidates were being direct and straightforward in their campaigning.

Political Cynicism (AD)

• What they said depended on who was listening.
• They only took chances when they were behind in the polls.
• Nobody would talk about the hard issues, such as taxes, because that would lose voters.
• Money bought the best advisers and advisers won the election.
• The candidates were willing to do whatever it took to win.
• Who is elected won't make much difference because the major candidates' positions were determined by the interests of those who gave them campaign funds.
• The campaign gave voters a real choice among candidates with different positions.
• The candidates seriously discussed the major problems facing the city and offered detailed solutions to those problems.
• The candidates explained what is was about their backgrounds that qualified them for mayor.
• It makes a difference who is elected mayor in a large city.

Two other measures of cynicism were also created. The first attempted to directly measure attributions of self-interest and dishonesty versus the common good. This was named Cynical Motive and had the following items.

> One candidate proposed that he would establish ten little city halls around the city, mostly because (1) he thought this would appeal to voters *or* (2) he wanted to make city government more responsive to neighborhoods.

> One candidate proposed to privatize city services primarily to (1) separate him from the other major candidates *or* (2) solve a problem with the cost of city services.

> One candidate said that, if elected, he would reappoint Police Commissioner Willie Williams, mostly because (1) Williams had done a good job as Police Commissioner *or* (2) the candidate needed a way to appeal to the black vote.

These three items had an internal reliability of .53.

Cynical learning asked people to choose three of the following six items indicating what they learned about the Philadelphia mayoral race.

> I learned which candidates looked most mayoral in the debate.

> I learned how the candidates differ on at least one important issue.

> I learned of one area in which Egan and Rendell hold the same position.

> I learned who acted like the person who was ahead in the polls.

> I learned the strategy used by the front runner to appeal to Blacks.

> I learned who was ahead and behind in the polls.

The four components of cynicism correlated from .29 to .59 and were all significant at $p < .001$.

Survey of Beliefs about the Press

During fall 1993, we conducted a survey of people's beliefs about the press, their cynicism about politics in general, political alienation (specifically mistrust and government inefficacy), and their cynicism about the media. The questions about political cynicism were parallel in content and structure to the forced choice and agree-disagree questions from the study of the mayoral campaign. Approximately 125 people participated in this study and were roughly representative of the Philadelphia metropolitan area, except that they were somewhat more educated.

The standard measure of political alienation correlated with our measure of political cynicism at r = .51, p < .001, suggesting that a general measure of political cynicism is associated with mistrust and assumed unresponsiveness of elected officials. This correlation indicates that our measure of political cynicism has some construct validity but is not highly redundant with previous measures of mistrust of government.

Health Care Reform Debate

As in the mayoral study and the survey of reactions to the press, we employed a variety of measures of cynicism. These included agree-disagree scales, forced-choice questions, questions about actors' motivations for their actions, and a question about what people thought they learned from the articles they read. The questions are not repeated here, but they are close in format to those of the campaign study. Instead of referring to "the candidates" as in the campaign study, questions referred to "advocates," who were defined as "any group or individual which actively campaigns for or against certain health care plans."

Cynical Learning had the same form as in the campaign study: three of six possible statements about what they believed they learned form the materials they read. The six alternatives were:

I learned how lobbying takes place.

I learned how the health care plans differ on at least one important issue.

I learned which plan was ahead and behind in the polls.

I learned at least one reason why Clinton's health care plan should pass or not pass.

I learned the strategy used by advocates to appeal to the middle class.

I learned at least one possible solution to this country's health care problems.

A set of four questions attempted to ascertain the attributions that people made to the motivations of advocates in the health care reform debate. This measure of *Cynical Motivation* was not very reliable. A three item index had an internal consistency of .42.

The health reform plans that don't require that businesses pay for the employee's health benefits take this position because (1) they think this appeals to voters. *or* (2) they think that requiring businesses to pay for health will hurt the economy and jobs.

The health reform plans that would insure all Americans do so because (1) people have a right to have their health needs met. *or* (2) this is popular with the voters who don't have health coverage.

Some insurers have attacked Clinton's health reform plan, because (1) they would be harmed economically by the plan *or* (2) they believe that the quality of health care delivery will be hurt by the plan.

Two other groups of questions aimed at assessing general cynicism about the health care debate using a six-point agree disagree format (eight questions) and a forced-choice method (five questions). These questions focused on the manipulativeness of advocates, dishonesty, winning and getting ahead, looking good, using fear, the absence of real choice, and the role of big money. The agree-disagree items were:

What the advocates of various plans say depends on who is listening.

Fear tactics by advocates rather than reasoned discussion drive the debate.

Nobody will talk honestly about the hard issues, such as taxes and costs, because that would lose support.

Money will buy the votes that will win the debate on health care.

The campaign gives people an important choice among different health care plans.

Advocates of various health care plans are willing to do whatever it takes to look good even if it means deceiving the public.

Advocates of various health care plans explain in detail why their plan offers the best solutions to the country's problems.

The advocates of various plans are attacking each other without offering clear solutions to the country's health care problems.

The forced-choice items were:

Health care advocates are concerned with policies that meet the country's needs.   *or*   Health care advocates are concerned with approval ratings.

Advocates are focused on winning.   *or*   Advocates are focused on problems.

The advocates tell the people what people *need* to hear.   *or*   The advocates tell the people what they *want* to hear.

The advocates are lying about their goals.   *or*   The advocates are telling the truth about their goals.

The advocates are being manipulative in their campaigning.   *or*   The advocates are being direct and straightforward in their campaigning.

The full set of thirteen cynicism questions were factor analyzed to determine if they grouped together or into smaller groups. Image factor analysis suggested five factors using an eigenvalue greater than one criterion. However, the scree plot indicated that the first factor explained most of the variation in the questions (24.7 percent) and the others tailed off markedly in a linear fashion. Based on this and a follow-up varimax rotation, either one or two groups could be justified. The groups were made up of the agree-disagree questions (alpha = .72) and the forced choice questions (alpha = .76). Together the two groups had a standardized alpha of .83.

Two measures were retained for analysis. The eight agree-disagree questions are *Political Cynicism (AD)* and five forced-choice questions are *Political Cynicism (FC)*. The two groups together are simply called *Political Cynicism*.

The four distinct measures of cynicism correlate positively and significantly with one another (range from .11 to .61) and with a two-item measure of government efficacy taken from the NES survey. The correlations are reported in Table G.1. Learning Cynicism correlates positively but not reliably with government efficacy; all other measures show the positive, significant correlations of a valid measure. They correlate with one another at modest levels and they correlate with other measures of presumed validity.

Individuals higher on our measures of cynicism also agree more with claims that government cannot do anything right and is ineffective in making people's lives better. Further construct validity is provided by another question internal to the survey, a question about which type of plan the participant would vote for if he or she were a member of Congress. Four plans are described in terms of their chief characteristics, not their ideology or association with a particular political actor. A fifth option is "I'd vote against all of the plans." This option is strongly worded and in the negative rather than the positive (e.g., I'd work for a better alternative). People who chose this option tended to be higher in Cynical Motivation ($p < .0001$), Political Cynicism (FC) ($p < .002$), and Political Cynicism (AD) ($p < .0005$) than those who chose other options. Cynical Learning was in the right direction, but not significantly so.

In sum, the measures of cynicism used in our study of the health care reform debate show acceptable internal reliability, patterns of correlation among components, and construct validity.

Correlations to Measures of Trust

We have argued that the conceptual roots of cynicism are found in the absence of trust. If so, then measures of mistrust should correlate with measures of political cynicism. In an experimental study with 57 students who were evaluating clear and confusing news articles, questions about trusting people in Washington to do the right thing on four issues (e.g., the balanced budget amendment and welfare reform) were correlated with five questions assessing political cynicism on the balanced budget process (the topic of the news articles). An index of distrust correlated with an index of cynicism (using both forced choice and agree-disagree measures) at $r = .26$ ($p < .05$), suggesting that at least a part of what is operating in cynicism is mistrust of government to do what is right.

Table G.1. Correlations Among Measures of Cynicism and with Government (In)efficacy: Health Care Reform

	Government (In)efficacy	Health Care Cynicism	Health Care Cynicism (AD)	Health Care Cynicism (FC)	Learning Cynicism
Cynicism	.323				
	p = .000				
Cynicism (AD)	.314	.923			
	p = .000	p = .000			
Cynicism (FC)	.260	.868	.610		
	p = .000	p = .000	p = .000		
Cynical learning	.068	.207	.207	.163	
	p = .214	p = .000	p = .000	p = .003	
Cynical	.317	.329	.296	.293	.109
Motive	p = .000	p = .000	p = .000	p = .000	p = .047

APPENDIX H

Describing the Media Cynics

Table H.1. Demographic and Political Characteristics of Media Cynics: Direction of Effect and Probability Level for Five Samples

	MARKLE Fall, '93 (N = 125)	HCR Fall, '94 (N=230)	TIMES MIRROR Unfavor (N=1800)[a]	TIMES MIRROR Cynic (N=1800)[a]	HARVARD Panel (N=1200)	HARVARD Indep. (N=700)
AGE						
Linear	nsd[b]	nsd	nsd	nsd	pos .01	pos .05
Quadratic	pos .04[c]	nsd	neg .0004	nsd	neg. .05	neg. .05
PARTY	R,D > I	R > I,D	R > I > D	R > I > D	R,I > D	nsd
	.04	.15	.0001	.0001	.07	
EDUCATION						
Linear	neg .07	pos .11	pos .0001	pos .0001	pos .0001	pos .01
Quadratic	nsd	nsd	nsd	neg .05	nsd	neg .05
GENDER	nsd	nsd	M > F	F > M	M > F	nsd
			.0001	.003	.0001	
IDEOLOGY	L,C > I	C > L,I	C > I > L	C > I > L	C > I,L	C,I > L
	.01	.11	.04	.0001	.04	.04
WHITE/BLACK	nsd	nsd	W > B	nsd	W > B	nsd
			.002		.05	
HISPANIC/NON	—	—	nsd	Non > His	Non > His	Non > His
				.06	.07	.01
INCOME						
Linear	—	—	pos .0001	nsd	pos .0001	pos .0001
Quadratic	—	—	neg .004	neg .01	nsd	nsd

[a] Sample size for Times Mirror varies as a function of interview protocol. C is conservative, I independent or moderate, L liberal. R Republican, I independent or no party, D Democrat.

[b] nsd is "no significant difference."

[c] A positive quadratic effect has the shape of a U; a negative quadratic effect has the shape of an inverted U. When a linear and a quadratic effect are present, the shape of the relationship is the sum of the two shapes added together.

Table H.2. Media Exposure and Attention to Political Events of Media Cynics: Direction of Effect and Probability Level for Five Samples

	MARKLE Fall, '93 (N = 125)	HCR Fall, '94 (N=230)	TIMES MIRROR Unfavor (N=1800)[a]	TIMES MIRROR Cynic (N=1800)[a]	HARVARD Panel (N=1200)	HARVARD Indep. (N=700)
NEWSPAPERS						
Linear	nsd[b]	nsd	nsd	nsd	pos .006	nsd
Quadratic	nsd	nsd	—	—	nsd	nsd
TV NEWS						
Linear	nsd	nsd	No>Yes .0001	No>Yes .006	neg .01	nsd
Quadratic			—	—	nsd	nsd
CLOSE FOLLOW						
Linear	—	pos .20	pos .0001	pos .001[c]	pos .05	pos .01
Quadratic	—	nsd	nsd	neg .002	pos .05	nsd
LIMBAUGH						
Linear	—	pos .11	pos .0001	nsd	—	—
Quadratic	—	pos .004	nsd	pos .03	—	—
CALL-IN						
Linear	pos .06	nsd	pos .02	Hi > Lo .05	pos .0003	pos .01
Quadratic	pos .03	nsd	nsd	—	nsd	nsd

[a] Sample size for Times Mirror varies as a function of interview protocol.
[b] nsd is "no significant difference."
[c] A positive quadratic effect has the shape of a U; a negative quadratic effect has the shape of an inverted U. When a linear and a quadratic effect are present, the shape of the relationship is the sum of the two shapes added together.

The Minnesota Compact

Plank 1: Candidate Agreement

Recognizing that democratic elections require the open exchange of ideas, as a candidate for United States Senate (House of Representatives) I agree:

1. to participate in a minimum of two public debates;
2. to abide by the ground rules, format, and criteria set forth by a sponsoring organization which does not support or endorse political parties or candidates;
3. that such debates may incorporate a series of newspaper point/counterpoint articles;
4. that such debates may be carried on-line;
5. that the debates may include live audience participation and follow-up news conferences;
6. that one or more debates will be broadcast statewide (or district-wide) on radio and television

Plank 2: The Campaign Advertising Code

The General Principles

I recognize that some standards of practice in campaign communications are essential if we are to maintain a well-functioning democracy in Minnesota, rather than degrade that democracy. I recognize that campaign advertising should present meaningful information on the candidates and their records, philosophies, issue stands and leadership capabilities. I recognize that emphasis on mere personal attacks or sensational "issues" and demeaning photos or video of my opponent increases public cynicism, decreases voter participation and degrades democracy. I recognize that at times it is appropriate to criticize my opponents' record, beliefs and positions and that these criticisms must be fully documents and must not be false, misleading or taken out of context. I recognize that any appeal to discrimination based on race, gender or religious belief violates acceptable standards of campaign communication.

I further recognize that some of these general principles will be subject to various interpretations and therefore I commit myself and my campaign staff to the following specific principles.

Specific Principles

1. I take full responsibility for all advertising created and placed by my campaign staff, committees or groups connected with my campaign. I will review and approve all such advertising and will publicly rebuke advertising created and placed in support of my candidacy by independent groups.

2. In television advertising my voice and likeness will be in the commercial at least 50% of the time.

3. In radio advertising my voice will be in the commercial at least 50% of the time.

4. In print advertising, including newspapers, direct mail, brochures, posters and fundraising materials, I will display the logo of the Code in a legible fashion.

5. I will not use any photo of my opponent that has been retouched or modified; I will not use any cartoons, illustrations or drawings that are representative of my opponent; all film or video of my opponent will be run in real time and will not be distorted, retouched, colorized or morphed in any way.

6. I will request, by certified mail, that broadcast stations turn down any independent expenditure, political action committee or special interest advertising that supports my candidacy. If the stations, in their own interest, reject my request, then I will ask them to at least run advertising that is in keeping with the spirit of the general and specific principles of this code.

You have my word that I will be true to this Campaign Advertising Code.

Signature of candidate _____

Candidate for the office of _____

The Campaign Advertising Code is to be signed 50 days or more prior to the general election and sent certified mail to:

     Campaign Advertising Code
     800 Hennepin Avenue, Suite 200
     Minneapolis, MN 55403

Plank 3: The Role of Journalists

Journalists agree:

1. To identify through polling and other methods the issues that concern their readers, viewers and listeners. To emphasize those issues in campaign coverage by:

> Covering the candidates' proposals and other policy options for dealing with citizen concerns. Providing in-depth, explanatory articles on significant issues, such as taxes, health care, crime, and education.

2. To de-emphasize the "horse race," or predictions about the outcome of the election in their stories and broadcasts.
3. To write and broadcast stories about candidate debates, citizen reaction to these debates, and follow-up news conferences.
4. To inform audiences of opportunities for participation in public discussion of campaign issues.
5. To review campaign ads for fairness and accuracy and publish and broadcast stories detailing their findings.
6. To describe to readers the news organization's decision-making process on ethically challenging or controversial campaign stories.

Plank 4: Citizen Participation Code

1. As citizens, we acknowledge a responsibility to play an active role in the political process;
2. we expect candidates, as fellow citizens, to engage in constructive discussion of public concerns;
3. and we expect the news media to support this constructive discussion of public concerns.
4. Believing that public dialogue is essential to democracy, we commit to participating in both informal conversation and at least one organized discussion to be held in conjunction with the Minnesota Congressional or Senate debates (scheduled for fall 1996).

"As citizens, we acknowledge a responsibility to play an active role in the political process...." This is how the citizen participation code (plank 4 of the Minnesota Compact) begins. While all the components of the

Minnesota Compact are inextricably linked and mutually reinforcing, the success of the Compact depends heavily on the involvement of concerned, active, informed citizens.

The goal of the Minnesota Compact Coalition is to involve at least 10,000 individuals statewide in group conversations focusing on the candidates, campaign issues, and other concerns related to the 1996 election. This would require identifying at least 1000 individuals who would each be willing to involve a group of ten individuals in political discussion. Each group would be asked to participate in at least one organized discussion to be held in conjunction with the Minnesota Congressional or Senate debates scheduled for late September/early October 1996. These groups would also be encouraged (though not required) to participate in informal conversation about politics in the weeks and months leading up to the general election. The format could range from a formalized studio setting to informal conversations in private homes.

Conversation groups will be formed in two ways. First, organizations and institutions throughout the state (churches, community organizations, service groups, the Minnesota Extension Service, labor unions, professional associations, etc.) will be encouraged to form groups comprised of their members. Other already existing groups (such as study circles, book clubs, block clubs ... *even bowling leagues*) will be asked to dedicate two to three hours of their meeting time to discussion of the campaigns and issues of public concern. Many of these groups already meet on a regular basis but do not necessarily discuss politics. Second, individuals will be invited through the media to form their own discussion groups made up of family members, friends, coworkers, neighbors, etc.

All groups will be provided with a conversation-starter packet and, if desired, facilitator training. Some new materials for the conversation packets ill be developed which will be specific to the 1996 campaign. Resources which have already been developed through the League of Women Voters, the Citizens League, the Kettering Foundation and others will also be made available. Packets might also include "tip sheets" which will provide background on how to watch a debate and what to look for in terms of how candidates are conducting their campaigns and how news organizations are covering them. (Since food and conversation are so closely linked, the Minnesota Compact will also try to identify a donor to provide pizzas to conversation groups on the occasion of their first meeting.)

The Minnesota Compact Coalition will serve as an information center/clearinghouse for all conversation groups meeting around the state. In addition, the Coalition will work with the media to (1) inform the public about the opportunities for participation and (2) to publish and broadcast stories about the issues and ideas raised by the conversation groups.

NOTES

CHAPTER 1 *The President, the Speaker, and the Press*

1. *National Journal's Congressional Daily*, June 12, 1995.
2. *New York Times*, June 12, 1995.
3. Cited in *The Independent*, June 12, 1995, p. 12.; see also *Austin American-Statesman*, June 12, 1995, p. A7.
4. *Baltimore Sun*, June 12, 1995.
5. Ibid.
6. June 12, 1995, p. A1.
7. *International Herald Tribune*, June 12, 1995 (from *Washington Post* wire).
8. *Boston Globe*, June 12, 1995.
9. *Boston Globe*, June 12, 1995.
10. *Boston Globe*, June 12, 1995.
11. *New York Times*, June 12, 1995.
12. *Boston Globe*, June 12, 1995, p. 1.
13. U.S. Newswire, June 12, 1995.
14. *The Independent*, June 12, 1995, p. 12.
15. *The National Journal*, June 12, 1995.
16. *National Journal's Congressional Daily*, June 12, 1995.

17. *National Journal's Congressional Daily*, June 12, 1995.

18. *Financial Times*, June 12, 1995.

19. *New York Times*, June 12, 1995.

20. *Dallas Morning News*, June 12, 1995.

CHAPTER 2 *Cynicism or Realism?*

1. David S. Broder, "War on Cynicism," *Washington Post*, July 6, 1994, p. A19.

2. Richard Morris and David S. Broder, "Six Out of 10 Disapprove of Way Hill Does Its Job," *Washington Post*, July 3, 1994, pp. A1/A8.

3. "Can Congress Ever Be a Popular Institution," in Joseph Cooper and G. Calvin Mackenzie, *The House at Work* (Austin: University of Texas Press, 1981), p. 31.

4. Eric Uslaner, *The Decline of Comity in Congress* (Ann Arbor: University of Michigan Press, 1993), p. 94.

5. Chicago: National Opinion Research Center, February–April, 1973; 1993.

6. Timothy J. Conlan, "Federal, State, or Local? Trends in the Public's Judgment," *The Public Perspective*, January/February 1993, p. 4.

7. Richard Morin, "Anger at Washington Cools in Aftermath of Bombing," *Washington Post*, May 18, 1995, pp. A1, A12.

8. R. W. Apple, Jr., "Poll Shows Disenchantment with Politicians and Politics," *New York Times*, August 12, 1995, pp. 1/8 and 8.

9. July 10, 1995, p. 22.

10. "Popular Support for Congress," in Thomas Mann and Norman J. Ornstein, eds. "Introduction," *Congress, the Press, and the Public* (Washington, DC: American Enterprise Institute and The Brookings Institute, 1994, p. 22.

11. Peter G. Brown, *Restoring the Public Trust* (Boston: Beacon Press, 1994), p. 11.

12. *The Wit and Wisdom of Benjamin Franklin*, James C. Humes, ed. (New York: HarperCollins, 1995), p. 55.

13. James Bryce, *American Commonwealth*, Vol. 2, p. 146.

14. "On the Relation of Altruism and Self-Interest," in *Beyond Self-Interest*, Jane Mansbridge, ed. (Chicago: University of Chicago Press, 1990), p. 133.

15. Jeff Fishel, *Presidents and Promises* (Washington, DC: Congressional Quarterly, 1985), p. 2.

16. Ibid., p. 187.

17. Gerald Pomper with Susan S. Lederman, *Elections in America: Control and Influence in Democratic Politics* (New York: Longman, 1980), p. 161.

18. Ian Budge and Richard I. Hofferbert, "Mandates and Policy Outputs: U.S. Party Platforms and Federal Expenditures," *American Political Science Review*, 84, No. 1 (March 1990), p. 111.

19. Mansbridge, *Beyond Self-Interest*, p. 196.

20. Ibid., pp. 198–99.

21. Lynda W. Powell, "Issue Representation in Congress," *Journal of Politics*, Vol. 44 (1982), p. 676.

22. Cited by Mansbridge, op. cit., p. 260.

23 John Wright, "PACs, Contributions, and Roll Calls: An Organizational Perspective," *American Political Science Review* 79 (June 1985), pp. 403–4.

24. Gary C. Jacobson, "Parties and PACs in Congressional Elections," in *Congress Reconsidered*, 3rd Ed, Lawrence C. Dodd and Bruce I. Oppenheimer, eds. (Washington, DC: Congressional Quarterly Press, 1985), pp. 131–58 at p. 151.

25. Stephen G. Bronars and John R. Lott, "Do Campaign Donations Alter How a Politician Votes?" Paper. January 11, 1995, p. 2.

26. Ibid., p. 17.

27. Frank Sorauf, *Inside Campaign Finance* (New Haven: Yale University Press, 1992), p. 166.

28. Wright, op. cit., pp. 400–414.

29. Martin Schram, *Speaking Freely: Former Members of Congress Talk About Money in Politics* (Washington, DC: Center for Responsive Politics, 1995), p. 93.

30. Mansbridge, op. cit, p.205.

31. Joseph P. Kalt and Mark A. Zupan, "The Apparent Ideological Behavior of Legislators: Testing for Principal-Agent Slack in Political Institutions," *Journal of Law and Economics* (April 1990), Vol. XXXIII, pp. 103–32.

32. Alan Murray, "Cynicism Run Amok," *Wall Street Journal*, January 31, 1996.

33. Mann and Ornstein, op. cit., p. 1.

34. Simon Blackburn, *The Oxford Dictionary of Philosophy* (New York: Oxford University Press, 1994), p. 311.

35. *A Campaign to Epistemology*, Johnathan Dancy and Ernest Sosa, eds. (Cambridge, MA: Blackwell, 1993), p. 457.

36. Frederick Copleston, *A History of Philosophy*, Vol. I (New York: Doubleday Image Books, 1993), p. 439.

37. Ibid., p. 458.

38. Ibid., p. 412.

39. Ibid., p. 414.

40. *OED*, p. 636.

41. *OED*, p. 636.

42. *Webster's New Collegiate Dictionary* (Springfield, MA: G. C. Merriam Co., 1961), p. 793.

43. Ibid., pp. 206–7.

44. Quoted in David Shaw, *Los Angeles Times*, April 17, 1996, p. 1.

45. Jean Bethke Elshtain, *Democracy on Trial* (New York: Basic Books, 1995), p. 2.

46. Ibid., p. 24.

47. Arthur H. Miller, "Political Issues and Trust in Government: 1964–1970," *American Political Science Review*, Vol, 68 (1974), pp. 951–72.

48. Samuel Barnes and Max Kaase et al., *Political Action: Mass Participation in Five Western Democracies* (Beverly Hills: Sage, 1979).

49. Seymour Lipset and William Schneider, "The Confidence Gap During the Reagan Years, 1981–1987," *Political Science Quarterly*, Vol. 102 (1987), pp. 1–23 at p. 22.

50. Robert N. Bellah, Richard Madsen, William M. Sullivan, Ann Swidler, and Steven M. Tipton, *Habits of the Heart: Individualism and Commitment in American Life* (New York: Harper & Row, 1985), p. vii.

51. Robert Coles, *The Mind's Fate: A Psychiatrist Looks at His Profession* (New York: Little Brown, 1995), p. 129.

52. James Carey, "Why: The Dark Continent of American Journalism," in *Reading the News*, Robert K. Manoff and Michael Schudson, eds. (New York: Pantheon Books, 1986).

53. Joseph Schumpeter, *Capitalism, Socialism and Democracy* (New York: Harper Colophon, 1950, 1975).

54. Miller, 1974, op. cit.

55. Jack Citrin, "Comment: The Political Relevance of Trust in Government," *American Political Science Review*, Vol. 68 (1974), pp. 973–88.

56. George Will, "The Last Word," *Newsweek*, July 11, 1994, p. 60.

57. Dwight D. Eisenhower, "Annual Message to the Congress on the State of the Union," in *Public Papers of the Presidents of the United States, Dwight D. Eisenhower, 1960–61* (Washington, DC: Government Printing Office, 1961), January 7, 1960, pp. 3–17 at p. 17.

58. Ibid., p. 13.

59. Richard F. Fenno, Jr., *Home Style: House Members in Their Districts* (Boston: Little Brown, 1978), p. 168.

60. George F. Will, "The Pollution of Politics," *Newsweek*, November 6, 1989, p. 92.

61. Ruth Shalit, "Uncle Bob," *New York Times Magazine*, March 5, 1995, p. 37.

62. Ibid., p. 57.

63. William J. Gilmore, *Reading Becomes a Necessity of Life* (Knoxville: University of Tennessee Press, 1989), p. 84.

64. Alex De Tocqueville, *Democracy in America* (New York: Vintage Books, 1945), Vol. II, p. 119.

65. H. R. Haldeman, *The Haldemann Diaries: Inside the Nixon White House* (New York: Berkley Books, 1994), p. 163.

66. *Rolling Stone* interview, December 9, 1993, p. 40.

67. Nolan Walters, "Gingrich Now Keeps the Media at Arm's Length," *Philadelphia Inquirer*, January 15, 1995, p. E3.

68. David Shaw, *Los Angeles Times*, April 19, 1996.

69. Business Wire, "Freedom Forum Releases Report on Congress and Media," April 17, 1996.

70. H. Zucker, "The Variable Nature of News Media Influence," *Communication Yearbook*, 2 New Brunswich, NJ: Transaction, 1978.

71. D. Nimmo and J. Combs, *Mediated Political Realities* (New York: Longman, 1983).

72. Seymour Lipset and William Schneider, *The Confidence Gap* (Baltimore: Johns Hopkins University Press, 1983, 1987), p. 437.

73. Richard C. Leone, "What's Trust Got to Do With It?," *The American Prospect*, No. 17 (Spring 1994), pp. 78–83.

74. *Los Angeles Times*, April 17, 1996.

75. Mary Matalin and James Carville, *All's Fair* (New York: Random House, 1994), pp. 184–5.

76. David Shaw, *Los Angeles Times*, April 17, 1996.

77. Paul Taylor, *See How They Run* (New York: Knopf, 1990), p. 23.

78. Larry Sabato, *Feeding Frenzy: How Attack Journalism Has Transformed American Politics* (New York: Free Press 1991).

79. Matalin and Carville, op. cit., p. 163.

80. Joseph D. Younger, "Al Neuharth Covers the USA," *Amtrack Express* (March/April 1995), pp. 33–35 at p. 35.

81. "The News Media and the National Interest," Cecil Lectures on Moral Values in a Free Society, University of Texas at Dallas, November 1992.

82. See Hofstetter's analysis of the 1972 campaign's network news: C. Richard Hofstetter, *Bias in the News* (Columbia: Ohio State University Press, 1976).

83. Arthur Miller, Edie Goldenberg, and Lutz Erbring, "Type-Set Politics: Impact of Newspapers on Public Confidence," *American Political Science Quarterly*, 94 (Fall 1979), pp. 412–17.

84. Michael J. Robinson and Margaret A. Sheehan, *Over the Wire and on TV* (New York: Russell Sage, 1983), Ch. V.

85. See Thomas Patterson, *Out of Order* (New York: Knopf, 1993), p. 7.

86. Michael Robinson, "Just How Liberal Is the News," *Public Opinion* (June-July 1983), pp.2–3; Charles M. Tidmarch and John J. Pitney, Jr., "Covering Congress," *Polity*, Vol. XVII, No. 3 (Spring 1985), pp. 481–82.

87. Michael J. Robinson, "Three Faces of Congressional Media," in Thomas E. Mann and Norman J. Ornstein, eds., *The New Congress* (Washington, DC: American Enterprise Institute, 1981), p. 73.

88. "Press Coverage of Congress" in Mann and Ornstein, 1994, op. cit., p. 109.

89. Patterson, op. cit., p. 20.

90. Ibid., pp. 7–8.

91. Kathleen Hall Jamieson, *Dirty Politics* (New York: Oxford University Press, 1992); Patterson, op. cit.

92. An important aspect of the experiment was that each set of stories con-

tained a common core of factual issue-relevant information. In the first set, regardless of structure, the reader could learn that Rendell plans to keep the police commissioner and support a black City Council president. In the second, both articles reveal that Egan plans to set up little city halls.

Indeed, in the broadcast condition, we only changed the words of the reporter:

Issue	*Strategy*
But on AM Philadelphia today with host Wally Kennedy, Rendell confronted Egan with the issue.	But on AM Philadelphia . . . it was Egan who was on the defensive concerning political baggage.
Rendell claims that he fought Mayor Wilson Goode while Egan did not.	Rendell quickly hit saying he challenged Wilson Goode in the 87 primaries while Egan was part of a nonprofit development company worked hand in glove with democratic city hall

Rendell: Joe who has been part of the last four administrations as a patronage employee — Tate, Rizzo, and Goode. Joe endorsed Wilson Goode in 1987 when I was standing there fighting Wilson Goode and fighting the mess.

Egan: Well obviously that's horse dip. Joe Egan was employed by the business community in Philadelphia. I worked with the Philadelphia Industrial Development Corporation and I was put on loan to the city. . . .

rpt: Both camps want to dissassociate themselves from the mistakes of the present administration. The key question is what each would do for Phila. that mayor Wilson Goode did not do.	This was Egan's first lengthy live TV appearance. While at times he made solid points, he often appeared less relaxed than Rendell. But as one observer pointed out, Rendell has been campaigning for years. Egan has been a candidate for thirty-three days.

As part of one of our studies, we determined that news consumers believed that the materials they were shown and read were similar to the news they regularly receive.

93. Larry Bartels, "The Impact of Electioneering in the United States," in *Electioneering: A Comparative Study of Continuity and Change*, Ed. David Butler and Austin Ranney (Oxford: Clarendon Press, 1992), p. 264 ff. "In a world

where most campaigners make reasonably effective use of reasonably similar resources and technologies most of the time, much of their effort will necessarily be without visible impact, simply because every campaigner's efforts are balanced against more or less equally effective efforts to produce the opposite effect (p. 267)."

94. "Introduction," in *Under the Watchful Eye: Managing Presidential Campaigns in the Television Era*, Matthew D. McCubbins, ed. (Washington, DC: Congressional Quarterly Press, 1992), p. 50.

95. Lutz Erbring, Edie N. Goldenberg, and Arthur Miller, "Front Page News and Real World Cues: A New Look at Agenda Setting by the Media," *American Journal of Political Science* (1980), 16–49; Doris Graber, *Processing the News* (New York: Longman, 1984; Shanto Iyengar and Donald Kinder, *News That Matters: Television and American Opinion* (Chicago: University of Chicago Press, 1987); Shanto Iyengar, *Is Anyone Responsible? How Television Frames Political Issues* (Chicago: University of Chicago Press, 1991); W. Russell Neuman, Marion R. Just, and Ann N. Crigler, *Common Knowledge: News and the Construction of Political Meaning* (Chicago: University of Chicago Press, 1992).

96. Samuel C. Patterson and Gregory Caldeira, "Standing Up for Congress: Variations on Public Esteem Since the 1960s," *Legislative Studies Quarterly* (1990), 25–47; Asher and Barr, in Mann and Ornstein, 1994 op. cit.; Lichter and Amundson, in Mann and Ornstein, 1994 op. cit.; Rozell, in Mann and Ornstein, 1994, op. cit.

97. Transcript from tape.

CHAPTER 3 *Framing the News*

1. James H. Kuklinski, Robert C. Luskin, and John Bolland, "Where Is the Schema? Going Beyond the "S" Word in Political Psychology," *American Political Science Review,* 85(4) (1991), pp. 1341–56.

2. Paul Watzlawick, Janet Beavin-Bavelas, and Donald D. Jackson, *The Pragmatics of Human Communication.* (New York: W.W. Norton, 1967).

3. Marvin Minsky, "A Framework for Representing Knowledge," In P. H. Winston, ed., *The Psychology of Computer Vision,* (New York: McGraw Hill, 1975), pp. 211–77.

4. Daniel Kahneman and Amos Tversky, "Choices, Values, and Frames," *American Psychologist,* 28, (1984).pp. 107–28.

5. John D. Bransford and Nancy S. McCarrell, "A Sketch of a Cognitive Approach to Comprehension," In W. B. Weimar and D. S. Palermo, eds., *Cognition and the Symbolic Processes* (Hillsdale, NJ: Lawrence Erlbaum, 1974), pp. 189–229.

6. R. A. Sulin and D. J. Dooling, "Intrusion of a Thematic Idea in Retention of Prose," *Journal of Experimental Social Psychology,* 104 (1974), pp. 255–62; D. J. Dooling and R. E. Christiaansen, "Episodic and Semantic Aspects of Memory for Prose," *Journal of Experimental Psychology: Human Learning*

and Memory, 3 (1977), pp. 428–36. Walter Knitsch, *The Representation of Meaning in Memory* (Hillsdale, NJ: Lawrence Erlbaum, 1974).

7. G. H. Bower, J. B. Black, and T. J. Turner, "Scripts in Memory for Text," *Cognitive Psychology*, 2 (1979), pp. 331–50.

8. Thomas Gilovich, "Seeing the Past in the Present: The Effect of Associations to Familiar Events on Judgments and Decisions," *Journal of Personality and Social Psychology*, 40 (1981), pp. 797–808.

9. Galen V. Bodenhausen, "Stereotypic Biases in Social Decision Making and Memory: Testing Process Models in Stereotypic Use," *Journal of Personality and Social Psychology* 55, (1988), pp. 726–37.

10. Mark Snyder and Seymour W. Uranowitz, "Reconstructing the Past: Some Cognitive consequences of Person Perception," *Journal of Personality and Social Psychology*, 36 (1978), pp. 941–50.

11. P. G. Devine, "Stereotype and Prejudice: Their Automatic and Controlled Components," *Journal of Personality and Social Psychology*, 56 (1989), pp. 5–18; S. L. Gaertner and J. P. McLaughlin, "Racial Stereotypes: Associations and Ascriptions of Positive and Negative Characteristics," *Social Psychology Quarterly*, 46 (1983), pp. 23–40.

12. Paul Slovic, Baruch Fischoff, and Sarah Lichtenstein, "Informing the Public about the Risks of Ionizing Radiation," *Health Physics*, 41 (1981), pp. 589–98.; Richard H. Thaler, "Illusions and Mirages in Public Policy," *The Public Interest*, 73 (1983), pp. 60–74.; Tuen A. van Dijk and Walter Knitsch, *Strategies of Discourse Comprehension* (New York: Academic Press, 1983).

13. W. Russell Neuman, Marion R. Just, and Ann N. Crigler, *Common Knowledge: News and the Construction of Political Meaning* (Chicago: University of Chicago Press, 1992); William Gamson, *Talking Politics* (Cambridge: Cambridge University Press, 1992).

14. Shanto Iyengar, *Is Anyone Responsible? How Television Frames Political Issues* (Chicago: University of Chicago Press, 1992).

15. June W. Rhee, The Interaction Between News Frames and Schemata: A Theory of News Interpretation and a Simulation. Paper presented at the Annual Conference of the Association for Education in Journalism and Mass Communication, Washington, DC, August, 1995; Sonia Livingstone; *Making Sense of Television* (New York: Pergamon, 1990); Walter Knitsch, "The Role of Knowledge in Discourse Comprehension: A Construction-Integration Model," *Psychological Review*, 95 (1988), pp. 163–82; Doris Graber, *Processing the News: How People Tame the Information Tide*, 2nd ed. (New York: Longman, 1988).

16. Erving Goffman, *Frame Analysis: An Essay on the Organization of Experience* (New York: Harper & Row, 1974).

17. Todd Gitlin, *The Whole World is Watching* (Berkeley: University of California, 1980), p. 7.

18. Both Tuchman and Gans adopt the position that frames reside in the news text: Herbert J. Gans, *Deciding What's News: A Study of the CBS Evening*

News, NBC Nightly News, Newsweek, and Time (New York: Vintage Books, 1979); Gaye Tuchman, *Making News: A Study in the Construction of Reality* (New York: Free Press, 1978).

19. William A. Gamson and A. Modigliani, "Media Discourse and Public Opinion: A Constructionist Approach," *American Journal of Sociology,* 95 (1989), pp. 1–37.

20. William A. Gamson, *Talking Politics.* (Cambridge: Cambridge University Press, 1992).

21. Robert M. Entman, "Framing: Toward Clarification of a Fractured Paradigm," *Journal of Communication,* 43 (1993), pp. 51–58.

22. James Tankard, Laura Hendrickson, Jackie Silberman, Kriss Bliss, and Salma Ghanem, Media Frames: Approaches to Conceptualization and Measurement. Paper presented to Communication Theory and Methodology Division, Association for Education in Journalism and Mass Communication, Boston, MA, 1991.

23. Entman, 1993, op. cit., p. 52.

24. Zhongdong Pan and Gerald M. Kosicki, "Framing Analysis: An Approach to News Discourse," *Political Communication,* 10 (1993), pp. 55–75; Guy Tuchman, op cit.

25. Marvin Minsky, "A Framework for Representing Knowledge," in P. H. Winston, ed., *The Psychology of Computer Vision* (New York: McGraw-Hill, 1975), pp. 211–77; Donald E. Rummelhart, "Schemata and the Cognitive System," in Robert S. Wyer and Thomas K. Srull, eds., *The Handbook of Social Cognition,* Vol. 1 (Hillsdale, NJ: Lawrence Erlbaum, 1984), pp. 161–88.

26. W. Lance Bennett, *News: The Politics of Illusion* (New York: Longman, 1988); Doris Graber, *Mass Media and American Politics* (Washington, DC: Congressional Quarterly Press, 1993); Vincent Price and David Tewksbury, "News Values and Public Opinion: A Theoretical Account of Media Priming and Framing," in George Barnett and Franklin J. Boster, eds., *Progress in Communication Sciences* (Norwood, NJ: Ablex, in press); C. MacDougall, *Interpretive reporting* (New York: Macmillan, 1982).

27. A fourth criterion called representational validity is introduced in the next chapter.

28. Patterson, 1993, op cit; Chapter 2 of this book; The Times Mirror Center for the People and the Press reported that in the health care reform debate fully 66 percent of the coverage across print and broadcast news concerned "the politics of health reform" rather than other issues (The Times Mirror Center, 1995, Media Coverage of Health Care Reform: A Final Report. Supplement to the March/April issue of the *Columbia Journalism Review*).

29. Robert Huckfeldt and John Sprague, *Citizens, Politics, and Social Communication* (New York: Cambridge University Press, 1995).

30. Donald R. Kinder and D. O. Sears, "Prejudice and Politics: Symbolic Racism Versus Racial Threats to the Good Life," *Journal of Personality and*

Social Psychology, 40 (1981), pp. 414–31; Laura Stoker, "Interest and Ethics in Politics," *American Political Science Review*, 86 (1992), pp. 369–80. Most of the research on the effects of self-interest on public opinion takes as measures of self-interest personal involvement with issue. For example, opinions on health care reform were related in part to whether people had pre-existing conditions, recent experience with the health care system, and so on. See Robert Y. Shapiro, Lawrence R. Jacobs, and Lynn K. Harvey, Influence on Public Opinion Toward Health Care Policy. Unpublished paper, Department of Political Science, Columbia University, New York, 1995.

31. Richard Nisbett and Lee Ross, *Human Inferences: Strategies and Shortcomings of Social Judgment* (Englewood Cliffs, NJ: Prentice-Hall, 1980).

32. Gamson, op. cit.; W. Russell Neumann, Marion R. Just, and Ann N. Crigler, *Common Knowledge* (Chicago: University of Chicago Press, 1992).

33. Entman, 1993, op. cit.

34. Patterson, 1993, op. cit.

35. Ibid., p. 63.

36. Ibid., p. 89.

37. Ibid., p. 93

38. Jamieson, op. cit., makes similar claims, holding that strategy coverage invites "public cynicism" (p. 186), disengagement from the electoral process (p. 188), and minimized learning (p. 187) without the kinds of effects studies necessary to back these suppositions.

39. Hal R. Arkes and Kenneth R. Hammond, eds., *Judgment and Decision-Making: An Interdisciplinary Reader* (Cambridge: Cambridge University Press, 1986); Susan T. Fiske and Shelley E. Taylor, *Social Cognition*, 2d ed (New York: McGraw-Hill, 1991); Daniel Kahneman, Paul Slovic, and Amos Tversky, eds., *Judgment Under Uncertainty: Heuristics and Biases* (London: Cambridge University Press, 1982).

40. Howard Schuman and Stanley Presser, *Questions and Answers in Attitude Surveys: Experiments on Question Form, Wording, and Context.* (New York: Academic Press, 1982); John Zaller, *The Nature and Origins of Mass Opinion* (New York: Cambridge University Press, 1992). Jon Krosnick and Donald Kinder, "Altering the Foundations of Support for the President Through Priming," *American Political Science Review*, 84 (1990), pp. 497–512; Joanne M. Miller and Jon A. Krosnick, "News Media Impact on the Ingredients of Presidential Evaluations: A Program of Research on the Priming Hypothesis," in Diana C. Mutz, Paul M. Sniderman, and Richard A. Brody, eds., *Political Persuasion and Attitude Change* (Ann Arbor: University of Michigan Press, 1996), pp. 79–101.

41. Maxwell E. McCombs and Donald L. Shaw, "The Agenda Setting Function of the Mass Media," *Public Opinion Quarterly*, 36 (1972), pp. 176–87. Maxwell E. McCombs and Donald L. Shaw, "The Evolution of Agenda Setting

Research: Twenty-five Years in the Marketplace of Ideas," *Journal of Communication*, 43 (1993), pp. 58–67.

42. Shanto Iyengar and Donald R. Kinder, *News That Matters* (Chicago: University of Chicago Press, 1987).

43. James Watt, M Mazza, and L. Snyder, "Agenda-setting Effects of Television News Coverage and the Effects Decay Curve," *Communication Research*, 20 (1993), pp. 408–35.

44. Iyengar and Kinder, 1987, op. cit.

45. For a review, see E. Tory Higgins, "Knowledge Accessibility and Activation: Subjectivity and Suffering from Unconscious Sources," in James S. Uleman and John A. Bargh, eds., *Unintended Thought* (New York: Guilford Press, 1989), pp. 75–123.

46. In a recent article, Lawrence R. Jacobs and Robert Y. Shapiro, "Issues, Candidate Image, and Priming: The Use of Private Polls in Kennedy's 1960 Presidential Campaign," *American Political Science Review*, 88 (1994), pp. 527–40] used priming effects in a unique way. They argued that in Kennedy's 1960 presidential campaign, polling information about what issues the public felt were important was the basis for both the frequency and direction of Kennedy's comments about those issues. As detailed polling data became available, Kennedy's subsequent speeches and debates focused on those issues of highest priority to the public and made statements whose valence matched that of the public. The authors argue that these patterns represent a kind of strategic use of priming by the Kennedy campaign — altering candidate impressions by speaking to those issues likely to receive the most weight in the public's judgments of favorability.

47. Iyengar and Kinder, 1987, op. cit.; Jon A. Krosnick and Donald R. Kinder, "Altering the Foundations of Popular Support for the President Through Priming," *American Political Science Review*, 84 (1990), pp. 497–512. Shanto Iyengar and Adam Simon, "News Coverage of the Gulf Crisis and Public Opinion: A Study in Agenda-setting, Priming, and Framing," *Communication Research*, 20 (1993), pp. 365–83.

48. Iyengar and Kinder, 1987, op. cit.

49. Shanto Iyengar, *Is Anyone Responsible? How Television Frames Political Issues.* (Chicago: University of Chicago Press, 1992).

50. Lee Ross, "The Intuitive Psychologist and his Shortcomings: Distortions in the Attribution Process," in L. Berkowitz, ed., *Advances in Experimental Social Psychology*, Vol. 10 (New York: Academic Press, 1977), pp. 174–221.

51. Jamieson, op. cit.

52. Michael Pfau and Allan Louden, "Effectiveness of Ad Watch Formats in Deflecting Political Attack Ads," *Communication Research*, Vol. 21 (June 1994), pp. 325–41.

53. Stephen Ansolabehere and Shanto Iyengar, "Can the Press Monitor Campaign Advertising?," *The Harvard International Journal of Press/ Politics*, 1(1) (1996), pp. 72–86; Kathleen Hall Jamieson and Joseph N. Cappella, "Setting the Record Straight: Do Ad Watches Help or Hurt," *The Harvard International Journal of Press/Politics*, in press.

54. The study is reported fully in Joseph N. Cappella and Kathleen Hall Jamieson, "Broadcast Adwatch Effects: A Field Experiment," *Communication Research*, 21, No. 3 (June 1994), pp. 342–65.

55. Entman, 1993, op. cit., pp. 51–58; William A. Gamson, *Talking Politics* (Cambridge: Cambridge University Press, 1992).

56. John N. Bassili, ed., *On-Line Cognition in Person Perception* (Hillsdale, NJ: Lawrence Erlbaum, 1989); Reid Hastie and Bernadette Park, "The Relationship Between Memory and Judgement Depends on Whether the Judgement Task Is Memory Based or On-Line," *Psychology Review*, 93 (July 1986), pp. 258–68.

57. Lutz Erbring, Edie N. Goldenberg, and Arthur Miller, "Front Page News and Real World Cues: A New Look at Agenda Setting by the Media," *American Journal of Political Science* (1980), pp. 16–49; Doris Graber, *Processing the News* (New York: Longman, 1984); Shanto Iyengar and Donald Kinder, 1991, op. cit.; Neuman, Just, and Crigler, 1992, op. cit.

58. Samuel C. Patterson and Gregory Caldeira, "Standing Up for Congress: Variations on Public Esteem Since the 1960s,"
Legislative Studies Quarterly (1990), pp. 25–47; Asher and Barr, in Mann and Ornstein, 1994, op. cit.; Lichter and Amundson, in Mann and Ornstein, ibid.; Rozell, in Mann and Ornstein, ibid., 1994)

59. Michael J. Robinson, "Public Affairs Television and the Growth of Political Malaise," *American Political Science Review*, 70 (June 1976), pp. 409–32 at pp. 420–21.

60. Miller, Goldenberg, and Erbring, op. cit., p. 70.

CHAPTER 4   *The Cognitive Bases for Framing Effects*

1. Price and Tewksbury, in press, op. cit.; Shanto Iyengar, "Shortcuts to Political Knowledge: The Role of Selective Attention and Accessibility," in John A. Ferejohn and James H. Kuklinski , eds., *Information and democratic Processes* (Chicago: University of Illinois Press, 1990), pp. 160–85 ; Milton Lodge and Patrick Stroh, "Inside the Mental Voting Booth: An Impression-Driven Model of Candidate Evaluation," in Shanto Iyengar and William J. McGuire, eds., *Explorations in Political Psychology* (Durham, NC: Duke University Press, 1993), pp. 225–63.

2. Allan Paivio, *Imagery and Verbal Processes* (New York: Holt, Rinehart and Winston, 1971).

3. Zenon W. Pylyshyn, *Computation and Cognition.* (Cambridge, MA: MIT Press, 1984).

4. A. M. Collins and M. R. Quillian, "Retrieval Time from Semantic Memory," *Journal of Verbal Learning and Verbal Behavior,* 8 (1969), pp. 240–47.

5. Reid Hastie and P. A. Kumar, "Person Memory: Personality Traits as Organizing Principles in Memory for Behaviors," *Journal of Personality and Social Psychology,* 37 (1979), pp. 25–38; Thomas Srull, "Person Memory: Some Tests of Associative Storage and Retrieval Models," *Journal of Experimental Social Psychology: Human Learning and Memory,* 7 (1981), 440–62.

6. John R. Anderson, *The Architecture of Cognition,* (Cambridge, MA: Harvard University Press, 1983).

7. A. Collins and Elizabeth Loftus, "A Spreading Activation Theory of Semantic Processing," *Psychological review,* 82 (1975), pp. 407–28.

8. E. Tory Higgins, W. S. Rholes, and C. R. Jones, "Category Accessibility and Impression Formation," *Journal of Experimental Psychology,* 13 (1977), pp. 141–54. Srull and Wyer, op. cit.; P. M. Herr, S. J. Sherman, and R. H. Fazio, "On the Consequences of Priming: Assimilation and Contrast Effects," *Journal of Experimental Social Psychology,* 19 (1983), pp. 323–40; E. T. Higgins, J. Bargh, and W. Lombardi, "Nature of Priming Effects on Categorization," *Journal of Experimental Psychology: Learning, Memory and Cognition,* 11 (1985), pp. 59–69; G. McKoon and R. Ratcliff, "The Comprehension Process and Memory Structures Involved in Anaphoric Reference," *Journal of Verbal Learning and Verbal Behavior,* 19 (1980), pp. 668–82. G. McKoon and R. Ratcliff, "Inferences About Predictable Events," *Journal of Experimental Psychology: Learning, Memory, and Cognition,* 12 (1980), pp. 82–91.

9. Edward E. Jones, *Person Perception* (New York: W.H. Freeman, 1990).

10. Thomas Gilovich, "Seeing the Past in the Present: The Effect of Associations to Familiar Events on Judgments and Decisions," *Journal of Personality and Social Psychology,* 40 (1981), 797–808.

11. Galen V. Bodenhausen, "Stereotypic Biases in Social Decision-Making and Memory: Testing Process Models of Stereotype Use," *Journal of Personality and Social Psychology,* 55 (1988), 726–37; Galen V. Bodenhausen and Robert S. Wyer, "Effects of Stereotypes on Decision-Making and Information Processing Strategies," *Journal of Personality and Social Psychology,* 48 (1985), 267–82.

12. Mark Snyder and S. W. Uranowitz, "Reconstructing the Past: Some Cognitive Consequences of Person Perception," *Journal of Personality and Social Psychology,* 36 (1976), pp. 941–50.

13. Susan T. Fiske and Shelley E. Taylor, *Social Cognition,* 2nd ed. (New York: McGraw-Hill, 1991).

14. D. J. Dooling, and R. E. Christiaansen. "Episodic and Semantic Aspects of Memory for Prose," *Journal of Experimental Psychology: Human Learning and Memory,* 3 (1977), pp. 428–36.

15. Roger C. Schank and Robert P. Abelson, *Scripts, Plans, Goals, and Understanding: An Inquiry into Human Knowledge Structures* (Hillsdale, NJ: Lawrence Erlbaum 1977).

16. Ibid.; Fiske and Taylor, 1991, op. cit.

17. Robert Huckfeldt and John Sprague, *Citizens, Politics, and Social Communication* (Cambridge: Cambridge University Press, 1995).

18. Hayden White, "The Value of Narrativity in the Representation of Reality," in *On Narrative*, ed. W. J. T. Mitchell (Chicago: University of Chicago Press, 1981); Paul Ricoeur, *Time and Narrative*, trans. Kathleen McLaughlin and David Pellauer (Chicago: University of Chicago Press, 1984–86); Jerome Bruner, *Actual Minds, Possible Worlds* (Cambridge, MA: Harvard University Press, 1986); W. Lance Bennett and Murray Edelman, "Toward a New Political Narrative," *Journal of Communication*, 35, (1985), pp. 156–71.

19. Bruner, 1986, op. cit.; Jerry R. Hobbs, *Literature and Cognition* (Stanford, CA: Center for the Study of Language and Information, 1990); W. Thorndyke, "Cognitive Structures in Comprehension and Memory of Narrative Discourse," *Cognitive Discourse*, 9 (1977), pp. 77–110.

20. Roger C. Schank and Robert P. Abelson, "Knowledge and Memory: The Real Story," in Robert S. Wyer, ed., *Knowledge and Memory: The Real Story. Advances in Social Cognition*, Vol. VIII (Hillsdale, NJ: Lawrence Erlbaum, 1995), p. 1.

21. John D. Bransford and Nancy S. McCarrell, "A Sketch of a Cognitive Approach to Comprehension," in W. B. Weimar and D. S. Palermo, eds., *Cognition and the Symbolic Processes* (Hillsdale, NJ: Lawrence Erlbaum, (1995); Teun A. van Dijk, "Semantic Macro-structures and Knowledge Frames in Discourse Comprehension," in Marcel A. Just and Patricia A. Carpenter, eds., *Cognitive Processes in Comprehension* (Hillsdale, NJ: Lawrence Erlbaum, 1977), pp. 3–33.

22. Schank and Abelson, 1995, op. cit., p. 17.

23. Ibid., p. 23.

24. Nancy Pennington and Reid Hastie, "Evidentce Evaluation in Complex Decision-Making," *Journal of Personality and Social Psychology*, 51 (1986), pp. 245–287; Nancy Pennington and Reid Hastie, "Explaining the Evidence: Tests of the Story Model for Juror Decision-making," *Journal of Personality and Social Psychology*, 62 (1992), pp. 189–206.

25. Nancy Pennington and Reid Hastie,"Reasoning in Explanation-based Decision-Making," *Cognition*, 49 (1993), pp. 123–63.

26. Reid Hastie and Nancy Pennington,"The Big Picture: Is It a Story?" in Wyer, op. cit., pp. 133–38.

27. Hastie and Pennington, 1989, op. cit., p. 135.

28. Schank and Abelson, 1995, op. cit., p. 40.

29. Ibid.

30. Research by Tulving [Endel Tulving, *Elements of Episodic Memory* (New York: Oxford University Press, 1983)] on episodic structures for memory contains suggestive evidence for the Schank and Abelson claim but is far from definitive.

31. M. Linton, "Memory for Real World Events," in D. A. Norman and D. E. Rumelhart, eds., *Explorations in Cognition* (San Francisco: Freeman, 1995); W. A. Wagenaar, "My Memory: A Study of Autobiographical Memory over Six Years," *Cognitive Psychology*, 18 (1986), pp. 225–52. For a review, see Alan Baddeley, *Human Memory: Theory and Practice* (Boston: Allyn and Bacon, 1990).

32. Gordon H. Bower and Margaret C. Clark, "Narrative Stories as Mediators of Serial Learning," *Psychonomic Science*, 14 (1969), pp. 181–82.

33. A. C. Graesser, N. L. Hoffman, and L. F. Clark, "Structural Components of Reading Time," *Journal of Verbal Learning and Verbal Behavior*, 19 (1980), pp. 131–51. K. Haberlandt and L. C. Graesser, "Component Processes in Text Comprehension and Some of Their Interactions," *Journal of Experimental Psychology: General*, 114 (1985), pp. 357–74; A. C. Graesser, K. Haupt-Smith, A. D. Cohen, and L. D. Pyles, "Advanced Outlines, Familiarity, Text Genre, and Retention of Prose," *Journal of Experimental Education*, 48 (1908), pp. 209–20.

34. S. Y. Suh and T. Trabasso, "Global Inferences in the On-line Processing of Texts: Converging Evidence from Discourse Analysis, Talk Aloud Protocols, and Recognition Priming," *Journal of Memory and Language*, 32 (1993), pp. 279–300; T. Trabasso and S. Y. Suh, "Using Talk-aloud Protocols to Reveal Inferences During Comprehension of Text," *Discourse Processes*, 16 (1993), pp. 3–34. T. Trabasso, and P. van den Broek, "Causal Thinking and the Representation of Narrative Events," *Journal of Memory and Language*, 24 (1985), pp. 612–30.

35. N. E. Sharkey and D. C. Mitchell, "Word Recognition in a Functional Context: The Use of Scripts in Reading," *Journal of Memory and Language*, 24 (1985), pp. 253–70.

36. C. M. Seifert, G. McKoon, R. P. Abelson, R. Ratcliffe, "Memory Connections Between Theoretically Similar Episodes," *Journal of Experimental Psychology: Learning, memory and cognition*, 12 (1986), pp. 220–31.

37. Tuen A. van Dijk and Walter Knitsch, *Strategies of Discourse Comprehension* (New York: Academic Press, 1983).

38. Bernadette Park, "A Method for Studying Development of Impressions of Real People," *Journal of Personality and Social Psychology*, 51 (1986), pp. 907–17.

39. Bernadette Park, "Trait Attributes as On-line Organizers in Person Impressions," in Bassili, 1989, op. cit., pp. 39–59.

40. John R. Anderson, "Retrieval of Propositional Information from Long term Memory," *Cognitive Psychology*, 5 (1974), pp. 451–74; John R. Anderson, *Language, Memory, and Thought* (Hillsdale, NJ: Lawrence Erlbaum, 1976).

41. See also Wyer and Srull, 1989, op. cit., especially chapter 7 for a review.

42. A. C. Graesser, M. Singer, and T. Trabasso, "Constructing Inferences During Narrative Text Comprehension," *Psychological Review*, 101 (1994), pp. 371–95.

43. Richard R. Lau, "Political Schemata, Candidate Evaluations, and Voting Behavior," in Richard R. Lau and David O. Sears, eds., *Political Cognition* (Hillsdale, NJ: Lawrence Erlbaum, 1986), pp. 95–126.

44. Arthur H. Miller, Martin P. Wattenberg, and Oksana Malanchuk, "Schemata Assessments of Presidential Candidates," *American Political Science Review*, 71 (1986), pp. 11–30.

45. Kathleen M. McGraw, Neil Pinney, and David Neumann, "Memory for Political Actors: Contrasting the Use of Semantic and Evaluative Organizational Strategies," *Political Behavior*, 13 (1991), pp. 165–89.

46. Richard R. Lau, "Cognitive Ability and Electoral Choice," *Political Behavior*, 11 (1989), pp. 5–32.

47. Wendy M. Rahn, John H. Aldrich, Eugene Borgida, John L. Sullivan, "A Social-Cognitive Model of Candidate Appraisal," in John A. Ferejohn and James H. Kuklinski, eds., *Information and Democratic Processes* (Urbana, IL: University of Illinois Press, 1990), pp. 136–59..

48. Ibid.

49. Donald R. Kinder and Susan T. Fiske, "Presidents in the Public Mind," in Margaret G. Hermann, ed., *Political Psychology* (San Francisco: Jossey-Bass, 1986).

50. Rahn et al., 1990, op. cit.

51. Rahn et al., 1990, op. cit., also report that political sophistication does not play a role in this process, working the same for those who are more and less sophisticated. Political sophisticates would be expected to base their judgments more on substantive and policy concerns than character, but this assumption is not required of political sophisticates.

52. Wyer and Srull, 1989, op. cit.

53. Norman H. Anderson, "Functional Memory and On-line Attribution," in John N. Bassili, ed., *On-line Cognition in Impression Formation* (Hillsdale, NJ: Lawrence Erlbaum, 1989), pp. 175–220. Fritz Heider, *The Psychology of Interpersonal Relations* (New York: Wiley, 1958).

54. E. E. Jones, and K. E. Davis, "From Acts to Dispositions: The Attribute Process in Person Perception," in L. Berkowitz, ed., *Advances in Experimental Social Psychology*, Vol 2, (New York: Academic Press, 1965), pp. 220–66; H. H. Kelley, "Attribution Theory in Social Psychology," in D. Levine, ed., *Nebraska Symposium on Motivation*, Vol. 15 (Lincoln: University of Nebraska Press, 1967), pp. 192–240.

55. Ross, op. cit.

56. John N. Bassili ("Traits as Action Categories Versus Traits as Person Attributes in Social Cognition," in Bassili, 1989, op. cit., pp. 61–90) argues that trait categories may not imply trait attributions. But his argument concerns automatic trait attributions versus automatic trait categorization. We readily agree that the evidence is not yet conclusive about *automatic* trait attributions,

even though the evidence about automatic trait categorization is strong. We doubt that automatic categorization would not lead to trait attributions in light of the sloppy way that most of us interpret other's actions in news and ordinary accounts. Leonard S. Newman and James S. Uleman, "Spontaneous Trait Inferences," in James S. Uleman and John A. Bargh, eds., *Unintended Thought* (New York: Guilford, 1989), pp. 155–88, make similar arguments.

57. John A. Bargh, in Uleman and Bargh, op. cit. pp. 3–51; E. Tory Higgins, "Knowledge Accessibility and Activation: Subjectivity and Suffering from Unconscious Sources," in Uleman and Bargh, op. cit. , pp. 75–123.

58. L. Winter and J. S. Uleman, "When Are Social Judgments Made? Evidence for the Spontaneousness of Trait Inferences," *Journal of Personality and Social Psychology*, 47 (1984), pp. 234–52; J. S. Uleman, L. S. Newman, and L. Winter, "Making Spontaneous Trait Inferences Uses Some Cognitive Capacity at Encoding," Unpublished manuscript, New York University, cited in Uleman and Bargh, op. cit.; L. Winter, J. S. Uleman, and C. Cunniff, "How Automatic are Judgments?" *Journal of Personality and Social Psychology*, 49 (1985), pp. 904–17.

59. Endel E. Tulving and D. M. Thompson, "Encoding Specificity and Retrieval Processes in Episodic Memory," *Psychological Bulletin*, 30 (1973), pp. 352–73.

60. Paul Whitney, Douglas A. Waring, and Brian Zingmark, "Task Effects on the Spontaneous Activation of Trait Concepts," *Social Cognition*, 10 (1992), pp. 377–96.

61. Whitney, Waring, and Zingmark, 1992, op. cit., p. 387.

62. Robert Lau, "Negativity in Political Perception," *Political Behavior*, 4 (1982), pp. 353–77; R. Lau, "Two Explanations for Negativity Effects in Political Behavior," *American Journal of Political Science*, 29 (1985), pp. 119–38; K. Kellermann, "The Negativity Effect and Its Implications for Initial Interaction," *Communication Monographs*, 51 (1984), pp. 37–55.

63. B. Reeves, E. Thorson, and J. Schleuder, "Attention to Television: Psychological Theories and Chronometric Measures," In J. Bryant and D. Zillman, eds., *Perspectives in Media Effects* (Hillsdale, NJ: Lawrence Erlbaum 1986), pp. 251–79; John E. Newhagen, "The Evening's Bad News: The Effects of Compelling News Images on Memory," *Journal of Communication*, 42 (1992), pp. 25–41.

64. Felicia Pratto and Oliver P. John, "Automatic Vigilance: The Attention-Grabbing Power of Negative Social Information," *Journal of Personality and Social Psychology*, 61 (1991), pp. 180–91.

65. Ibid., p. 390.

66. Vincent Price and David Tewksbury, "News Values and Public Opinion: A Theoretical Account of Media Priming and Framing," in George Barnett and Franklin J. Boster, eds., *Progress in Communication Sciences* (in press);

67. Milton Lodge, "Toward a Procedural Model of Candidate Evaluation," in Milton Lodge and Kathleen M. McGraw, eds., *Political Judgment: Structure and Process* (Ann Arbor: University of Michigan Press, 1995); Milton Lodge, Marco R. Steenbergen, and Shawn Brau, "The Responsive Voter: Campaign Information and the Dynamics of Candidate Evaluation," *American Political Science Review*, 89 (1995), pp. 309–26. Milton Lodge, Kathleen M. McGraw, and Patrick Stroh, "An Impression-driven Model of Candidate Evaluation," *American Political Science Review*, 83 (1989), pp. 399–419. Lodge and Stroh, 1993, op. cit.

68. E. Tory Higgins, W. S. Rholes, and C.R. Jones, "Category Accessibility and Impression Formation," *Journal of Experimental Social Psychology*, 13 (1977), pp. 141–54. Thomas Srull and Robert S. Wyer, "The Role of Category Accessibility in the Interpretation of Information about Persons: Some Determinants and Implications," *Journal of Personality and Social Psychology*, 37 (1979), pp. 1660–72; Srull and Wyer, op. cit.

69. E. Tory Higgins, John A. Bargh, and W. Lombardi. "Nature of priming effects on categorization," *Journal of Experimental Psychology: Learning, Memory, and Cognition*, 11 (1985), 59–69.

70. John A. Bargh and R. D. Thein, "Individual Construct Accessibility, Person Memory, and the Recall-Judgment Link: The Case of Information Overload," *Journal of Personality and Social Psychology*, 49 (1985), pp. 1129–46. John A. Bargh, R. N. Bond, W. L. Lombardi, M. E. Tota, "The Additive Nature of Chronic and Temporary Sources of Construct Accessibility," *Journal of Personality and Social Psychology*, 50 (1986), pp. 869–79.

71. Norman H. Anderson and S. Hubert, "Effects of Concomitant Verbal Recall on Order Effects in Personality Impression Formation," *Journal of Verbal Learning and Verbal Behavior*, 2, (1963), pp. 379–91.

72. See Norman H. Anderson, "Functional Memory and On-line Attribution," in Bassili, op. cit., pp. 175–220, for a summary.

73. Martin Fishbein and Icek Ajzen, *Belief, Attitude, Intention, and Behavior* (Reading, MA: Addison-Wesley, 1975).

74. Much research is consistent with the lack of correlation between what is remembered and the judgment based on the memory [see Reid Hastie and Bernadette Park, "The Relationship Between Memory and Judgment Depends on Whether the Judgment Task is Memory-based or On-line," *Psychological Review*, 93 (1986), pp. 258–68, and Fiske and Taylor, 1991, op. cit., for summaries].

75. Hastie and Park, 1986, op. cit.

76. One has to be careful to distinguish between memory-based tasks and memory-based processes, and on-line tasks and on-line processes. The tasks required of information processors will favor one type of processing rather than another, but the point we will make is that both processes are normally

active in realistic tasks like judging who won a debate but trying to remember some of the details in order to chat about it the next day at work over coffee.

77. Lodge, McGraw, and Stroh, 1989, op. cit.; Lodge, Steenbergen, and Brau, 1995, op. cit.

78. Lodge, McGraw, and Stroh, 1989, op. cit.

79. Ibid., p. 416.

80. F. I. M. Craik and I. S. Lockhart, "Levels of Processing: A Framework for Memory Research," *Journal of Verbal Learning and Verbal Behavior*, 11 (1972), pp. 671–76.

81. Lodge, Steenberge, and Brau, 1995, op. cit.

82. Ibid., p, 316

83. Ibid., p. 321.

84. Fishbein and Ajzen, 1975, op. cit.

85. Stanley Kelley, *Interpreting Elections* (Princeton: Princeton University Press, 1983); Stanley Kelley and Thadeus Mirer, "The Simple Act of Voting," *American Political Science Review*, 61 (1974), pp. 572–91.

86. Vincent Price and John Zaller, "Who Gets the News? Alternative Measures of News Reception and Their Implications for Research," *Public Opinion Quarterly*, 57 (1993), pp. 133–57. John Zaller, *The Nature and Origins of Mass Opinion* (New York: Cambridge University Press, 1993); Iyengar and Kinder, op. cit.

87. Schank and Abelson, 1977, op. cit.; Jerome Bruner, *Actual Minds, Possible Worlds* (Cambridge, MA: Harvard University Press, 1986).

88. Doris A. Graber, "Seeing Is Remembering: How Visuals Contribute to Learning from Television News," *Journal of Communication*, 40 (1990), pp. 134–55.

89. Jamieson, 1992., op. cit.

90. Lodge, Steenbergen, and Brau report that their levels of recall are similar to those reported in the 1988 NES study. However, the levels of education in the Lodge study are much higher than those in the NES study, suggesting that the conditions of the experiment made recall especially difficult.

91. Our reasons are somewhat technical and cautionary, rather than definitive, and so they are relegated to a footnote. The correlations that Lodge, Steenbergen, and Brau, 1995, report in their Table 1 for the Democratic candidate show that the relationships between on-line judgment and candidate evaluation are lower than those for memory and evaluation *but not significantly so.* This means that both processes have a role in the evaluation of the Democratic candidate when considered separately. When considered together and with party identification, memory effects are reduced, but they remain borderline significant (their Table 2). Missing from this prediction model is the experimental condition that, according to Table 1, clearly interacts with the key predictors — memory and on-line evaluation. Our suspicion is that with the

experimental condition included, the memory effect would remain significant for the deep processing condition but not for the superficial processing condition. We suspect that the same would hold true for the evaluation of the Republican candidate because the correlations in the deep processing condition for that candidate are almost identical to those for the Democratic candidate.

The bottom line is not that on-line evaluation is not operating. Rather, we think that memory-based evaluation is also operating in candidate judgment at least under conditions that allow deeper processing of campaign messages in what is otherwise a set of conditions that make recall of anything rather difficult.

92. Lodge et al., 1989, op. cit., p. 416.

93. Lodge, 1995, op. cit.

94. Ibid., p. 135.

95. James Tankard, Laura Henderson, Jackie Silberman, Kriss Bliss, and Salma Ghanem, Media Frames: Approaches to Conceptualization and Measurement. Paper presented to the Communication Theory and Methodology Division, Association for Education in Journalism and Mass Communication, Boston, 1991.

96. Susan Fiske and M. A. Pavelchak, "Category-based Versus Piecemeal-based Affective Responses: Developments in Schema-triggered Affect," in R. M. Sorrentino and E. T. Higgins, eds., *Handbook of Motivation and Cognition: Foundations of Social Behavior* (New York: Guilford, 1986), pp. 167–203.

97. Norman H. Anderson, *Foundations of Information Integration Theory* (New York: Academic Press, 1981).

98. Lola Lopes, Towards a Procedural Theory of Judgment (Technical Report #17, pp. 1–49). Information processing program, University of Wisconsin, Madison, 1982; H. J. Einhorn and R. M. Hogarth, "Ambiguity and Uncertainty in Probabilistic Inference," *Psychological Review*, 92 (1985), pp. 433–61.

99. Lodge, 1995, op. cit.; Price and Tewksbury, 1995, op. cit.; Robert S. Wyer and Victor C. Ottati, "Political Information Processing," in Shanto Iyengar and William J. McGuire, eds., *Explorations in Political Psychology* (Durham, NC: Duke University Press, 1993); Victor C. Ottati and Robert S. Wyer, in Ferejohn and Kuklinski, (1990), op. cit., pp. 186–216.

100. Fiske and Taylor, 1991, op. cit., see especially p. 329.

101. Ibid.

102. Wyer and Srull, 1989, op. cit., p. 8.

103. Hastie and Park, 1986, op. cit.

104. Baddeley, 1990, op. cit., discusses some of the complexities of retrieval under different testing conditions, evaluating the question of recall versus recognition.

105. Hastie and Park, 1986, p. 266, op. cit.

106. Maxwell McCombs and Donald Shaw, "The Agenda Setting Function of Mass Media," *Public Opinion Quarterly,* 36 (1972), pp. 176–87. Maxwell McCombs and Dixie Evatt, Issues and Attributes: Exploring a New Dimension in Agenda Setting. English version of a paper published in *Comunicacion Y Sociedad,* 8, (1985), pp. 7–32.

107. Iyengar and Kinder, 1987, op. cit.; Shanto Iyengar, "Shortcuts to Political Knowledge: The Role of Selective Attention and Accessibility," in Ferejohn and Kuklinski, 1990, op. cit., pp. 160–85.

108. Shanto Iyengar, "Shortcuts to Political Knowledge: The Role of Selective Attention and Accessibility," in John A. Ferejohn and James H. Kuklinski, eds., *Information and Democratic Processes* (Urbana: University of Illinois Press, 1990), pp. 160–85.

109. George Gerbner, Larry Gross, Michael Morgan, and Nancy Signorelli, "Growing Up with Television: The Cultivation Perspective," in Jennings Bryant and Dolf Zillamn, eds., *Media Effects: Advances in Theory and Research* (Hillsdale, NJ: Lawrence Erlbaum, 1986), pp. 17–41; George Gerbner, Larry Gross, Michael Morgan, and Nancy Signorelli, "Living with Television: The Dynamics of the Cultivation Process," in Bryant and Zillamn, Ibid.

110. L. J. Schrum, "Assessing the Social Influence of Television: A Social Cognition Perspective on Cultivation Effects," *Communication Research,* 22, (1995), pp. 402–29.

111. L. J. Schrum and T. C. O'Guinn, "Processes and Effects in the Construction of Social Reality: Construct Accessibility as an Explanatory Variable," *Communication Research,* 20 (1993), pp. 436–71.

112. Charles M. Judd, Roger A. Drake, James W. Downing, and Jon A. Krosnick, "Some Dynamic Properties of Attitude Structures: Context Induced Response Facilitation and Polarization," *Journal of Personality and Social Psychology,* 60 (1991), pp. 193–202; Abraham Tesser, "Self-generated Attitude Change," in Leonard Berkowitz, ed., *Advances in Experimental Social Psychology* Vol 11) (San Diego, CA: Academic Press, 1978), pp. 289–338.

113. Some of this research was reviewed in Chapter 3. Seel also Iyengar, 1987, op. cit., pp. 5 and 14.

114. Lee Ross, "The Intuitive Psychologist and His Shortcomings: Distortions in the Attribution Process," in Berkowitz, op. cit., Vol. 10, pp. 174–221. For a review see Susan T. Fiske and Shelley E. Taylor, *Social cognition,* 2nd ed. (New York: McGraw Hill, 1991).

115. D. T. Gilbert, B. W. Pelham, and D. S. Krull, "On Cognitive Busyness: When Person Perceivers Meet Persons Perceived," *Journal of Personality and Social Psychology,* 54 (1988), pp. 733–39; D. T. Gilbert, and D. S. Krull, "Seeing Less and Knowing More: The Benefits of Perceptual Ignorance," *Journal of Personality,* 54 (1988), pp. 593–615.

116. Iyengar, 1987, op. cit., p. 134.

117. So does the data on what is remembered from descriptions of people's behavior. Park, 1986, op. cit., found open-ended descriptions of others to focus almost immediately on traits instead of behaviors. Robert S. Wyer and Thomas K. Srull [*Memory and Cognition in Its Social Context* (Hillsdale, NJ: Lawrence Erlbaum, 1989)] argue that the evidence for the priority of processing tasks in impression formation has the encoding of traits and their evaluation at the top of the list and encoding of behaviors — which confirm the traits — at the bottom of the list (Chapter 7, p. 193).

CHAPTER 5   *Designing the Studies*

1. Donald T. Campbell and Julian C. Stanley, *Experimental and Quasi-experimental Designs for Research* (Chicago: Rand-McNally, 1966); Donald R. Kinder and Thomas R. Palfrey, "On Behalf of an Experimental Political Science," in Donald R. Kinder and Thomas R. Palfrey, eds., *Experimental Foundations of Political Science* (Ann Arbor: The University of Michigan Press, 1992), pp. 1–39.

2. Kathleen Hall Jamieson and Joseph N. Cappella, Media in the Middle: Fairness and Accuracy in the 1994 Health Care Reform debate. Report of the Annenberg Public Policy Center of the University of Pennsylvania prepared for the Robert Wood Johnson Foundation, 1995.

3. J. P. Folger and M. S. Poole, "Relational Coding Schemes: The Question of Validity, in Michael Burgoon, ed., *Communication Yearbook*, Vol. 5 (New Brunswick, NJ: Transaction, 1982), pp. 235–48.

4. L. Edna Rogers and Frank Millar, "The Question of Validity: A Pragmatic Response," in Michael Burgoon, ed., *Communication Yearbook*, Vol. 5 (New Brunswick, NJ: Transaction, 1982), pp. 249–57.

5. S. T. Fiske, R. R. Lau, and R. A. Smith, "On the Varieties and Utilities of Political Expertise," *Social Cognition*, 8 (1990), pp. 31–48. June W. Rhee and Joseph N. Cappella, Political Sophistication, Media Exposure, and Learning: Measuring Schema Development. Unpublished paper, Annenberg School for Communication, University of Pennsylvania, Philadelphia, 1996.

6. To find out whether the random assignment was successful, we compared conditions within each experiment on demographics, and two other measures from the pre-test: political sophistication and political cynicism.

No significant differences across conditions (experimental and control) were found on age, gender, education, or race. The experimental conditions were comparable demographically. Political sophistication was measured to assess both accuracy of political positions and ideological knowledge. The measure is based on the work of John Zaller and is described in Chapter 8. Political cynicism was measured during the pre-test phase and focused on the 1992 presidential election. Comparisons across experimental conditions showed no significant differences among experimental groups or between experimental and control

The absence of differences in demographic features and in measures of political sophistication and cynicism across experimental conditions means that any subsequent findings of difference across experimental conditions cannot be attributed to spurious factors related to an unsuccessful random assignment to condition. In short, random assignment to condition within study was successful.

7. We distinguished two types of articles that focused on groups affected by health reform. One concerned how groups advanced their own agendas, positioning their constituency to its best advantage. These articles were clearly more strategic. A second type examined the problems and solutions activated by the current health care system or the proposed reforms for specific groups in society. This type was more substantive and much less frequent. The groups articles used in the study were chosen from the strategic category.

8. Michael Pfau and Henry Kenski, *Attack Politics: Strategy and Defense* (New York: Praeger, 1990); Michael Pfau and Allan Louden, "Effectiveness of Ad Watch Formats in Deflecting Political Attack Ads," *Communication Research*, 21 (1994), pp. 325–41; Stephen Ansolabehere and Shanto Iyengar, *Is Anyone Responsible? How Television Frames Political Issues* (Chicago: University of Chicago Press, 1991); Shanto Iyengar and Donald Kinder, *News That Matters* (Chicago: University of Chicago Press, 1987).

CHAPTER 6   *Learning from Strategic and Issue Coverage*

1. Kathleen Hall Jamieson and Joseph N. Cappella, 1995, op. cit. The percentage of strategy articles included both strategic and "legislative process" frames. The latter focus on the tactics employed in moving bills through committee and into Congress for consideration. The number of print stories coded was 1,929 and included news reports, analyses, and question and answer but not op-eds or editorials. Ten national and local newspapers were coded from January 16, 1994, through October 5, 1994. Nine weekly televised news programs were also coded for a total of 934 segments.

Coding procedures allowed for three levels of coding for print stories: headline and sub-heading (level 1); first three to four paragraphs (level 2); and remainder of the story (level 3). Two levels were employed with broadcast stories: the primary and secondary foci of the news segment. The numbers reported here refer to the level 2 codes of print stories and the primary code of the broadcast stories.

For more complete information on coding procedures and results please contact the authors.

2. Richard M. Perloff, "Perceptions and Conceptions of Political Media Impact: The Third Person Effect and Beyond," in Ann N. Crigler, ed., *the Psychology of Political Communication* (Ann Arbor: University of Michigan Press, 1996), pp. 177–98.

3. William McGuire, "The Myth of Massive Media Impact: Savagings and

Salvagings," in G. Comstock, ed., *Public Communication and Behavior*, Vol. 1 (New York: Academic Press, 1986), pp. 173–257.

4. John P. Robinson and Dennis K. Davis, "Television News and the Informed Public: An Information Processing Approach," *Journal of Communication*, 40 (1990), pp. 106–19.

5. Jack M. McLeod, and Donald G. McDonald, "Beyond Simple Exposure: Media Orientations and Their Impact on Political Processes," *Communication Research*, 12 (1985), pp. 3–33.

6. Steve Chaffee, and Joan Schleuder, "Measurement of Effects of Attention to Media News," *Human Communication Research*, 13 (1986), pp. 76–107.

7. Steve H. Chaffee, X. Zhao, and G. Leshner, "Political Knowledge and the Campaign of 1992," *Communication Research*, 21 (1994), pp. 305–24.

8. Ibid., p. 217.

9. Ibid., p. 318.

10. Barrie Gunter, "Responding to News and Public Affairs," in Jennings Bryant and Dolf Zillman, eds., *Responding to the Screen* (Hillsdale, NJ: Lawrence Erlbaum, 1991), pp. 229–60; J. P. Robinson, "Long-term Information and Media Usage," in J. P. Robinson and Mark R. Levy, eds., *The Main Source* (Beverly Hills, CA: Sage, 1986), pp. 57–85; John P. Robinson and Dennis K. Davis, "Comprehension of a Single Evening's News," in Robinson and Levy, Ibid., pp. 107–132.

11. Robinson and Davis, 1990, op cit.

12. Vincent Price and John Zaller, "Who Gets the News? Alternative Measures of News Reception and Their Implications for Fesearch," *Public Opinion Quarterly*, 57 (1993), pp. 133–64; D. Graber, 1988, op. cit.; McLeod and McDonald, 1985, op. cit.

13. Chaffee and Schleuder, 1986, op. cit.

14. McLeod and McDonald, 1985, op. cit.

15. Larry M. Bartels, "Messages Received: The Political Impact of Media Exposure," *American Political Science Review*, 87(2) (1993), pp. 267–85.

16. Neuman, Just, and Crigler, 1992, op. cit.

17 .This section is a summary of the more detailed discussion in Chapter 4.

18. Vincent Price and David Tewksbury, "News Values and Public Opinion: A Theoretical Account of Media Priming and Framing," in George Barnett and Franklin J. Boster, eds., *Progress in Communication Sciences* (in press); E. Tony Higgins, "Knowledge Activation: Accessibility, Applicability, and Salience," in E. Tony Higgins and Arie W. Kruglanski, eds., *Social Psychology: Handbook of Basid Principles* (New York: Guilford, 1996)pp. 133–68.

19. Price and Tewksbury, op. cit.

20. Jon A. Krosnick, "Expertise and Political Psychology," *Social Cognition*, 8 (1990), pp. 1–8; Kuklinski, Luskin, and Bolland, 1991, op. cit.; R. C. Luskin, "Measuring Political Sophistication," *American Journal of Political Science*, 31 (1990), pp. 857–99; K. M. McGraw and N. Pinney, "The Effects of General and

Domain Specific Expertise on Political Memory and Judgment," *Social Cognition*, 8 (1990), pp. 9–30.

21. Jamieson, 1992, op. cit.

22. Patterson, 1993, op. cit.

23. All reported probability levels will be two-tailed even when specific, directional hypotheses are being tested. When a directional hypothesis is being tested, we will treat probability levels as high as .20 (two-tailed) as borderline effects when their direction is correct. If this level seems overly liberal to purists, consider that multiple tests of the same hypothesis will suffer from excessive Type II error if individual tests are too conservative. Many of our tests of hypothesis are replicated across experiments.

24. Determinants of ability to process information largely consist of knowledge and/or experience indicators, such as civics knowledge, education, political involvement, political sophistication, and attention to political issues (and, more specifically, following the health care debate). To see if there were indeed significant interactions between experimental condition and these third variables, we conducted two-way analyses of variance, splitting the knowledge indicators at approximately the mean, and comparing the high's and low's across conditions versus the high's and low's in the control on the three indices of recall.

Of all the indicators of knowledge tested, only two significantly interacted with experimental condition on factual recall information. No other significant interactions obtained for strategic or substantive recall. Specifically, political involvement and attention to political issues interacted with condition on the recall of factual material. Those high in political involvement were not advantaged by news articles about health care, while those low were; we obtained a similar finding with attention to political issues. The interactions are reported in the following tables.

	Issue vs. Control			*Strategy vs. Control*		
	Issue	*Control*	*Prob.*	*Strategy*	*Control*	*Prob.*
Follow	.48	.36		.44	.36	
(LOW)			.06			.13
Follow	.46	.49		.46	.49	
(HIGH						

	Issue vs. Control			Strategy vs. Control		
	Issue	Control	Prob.	Strategy	Control	Prob.
Involve	.43	.30		.41	.30	
(LOW)			.03			.04
Involve	.50	.53		.49	.53	
(HIGH						

What seems to be happening is that either involvement in political affairs or attention to political issues in general provided participants with resources they could use to recall information regardless of condition. For those not involved politically or not attending to political issues, exposure to news improved recall of information from the news articles. However, this pattern was observed only for factual recall and not strategic or substantive recall.

25. Joseph N. Cappella and Kathleen Hall Jamieson, "Tuning in to NBC's 'To Your Health,'" *Journal of American Health Policy* (September/October 1994), pp. 36–40.

26. The majority of the participants were post-tested within three days of the NBC special. There were a few instances, however, in which a few participants were interviewed after the three-day period because interviewers were unable to reach them for their scheduled interview. No participant was interviewed after six days following the program.

27. In this study, we did not ask questions like the strategic knowledge questions of previous studies. The focus was on gains in substantive knowledge about health care reform and the telephone interviews offered limited time to query participants.

28. Examples of the questions in the various categories follow. Health Care Knowledge (five questions):

Would you say that health care spending is an important reason for the size of the federal deficit, or not?

Term Knowledge (five questions):

How about the term *managed care plan*? Do you know what this term means?

Political Knowledge (four questions):

Who takes the position that . . . The cost of health care reform should come mostly from taxes taken through payroll deductions. President Clinton, Republicans like Bob Dole, Democrats like Wellstone, or none of them?

Show Knowledge (3 questions):

What part of the dollar spent on health care goes to pay for paperwork? About 5–10 cents of the dollar, 20–25 cents, or 35–40 cents?

The four measures correlate positively and range from .21 to .37, $p<.001$ in all cases.

29. We used logistic regression that successfully categorized 64 percent of the cases into the watch and no watch categories.

30. The Harvard data can also be analyzed in a completely different way. The pre-test panel scores could be compared to the post-test independent sample scores to rid the comparison of the effects of sensitization and non-random attrition. When done this way, the effects of the NBC special on health care learning disappear.

We believe that this alternative technique is less precise than the pre-post procedure we employed. Our procedure allows each person to serve as his or her own control. Also, the analysis can be shown to be a result of the amount of watching. People who watched an hour or more learned from the special, while those watching less actually showed lowered learning levels.

31. A sign test of sixteen comparisons all of which are in the same direction would be very highly significant; so too would be a sign test of eight comparisons.

CHAPTER 7   Activating the Public's Cynicism about Politics

1. Kevin Chen, *Political Alienation and Voting Turnout in the United States, 1960–1988* (San Francisco: Mellen Research University Press, 1992).

2. J. Citrin, "Comment: The Political Relevance of Trust in Government," *American Political Science Review*, 68 (1974), pp. 973–88; A. H. Miller, "Political Issues and Trust in Government, 1964–1970," *American Political Science Review*, 68 (1974), p. 951.; S. C. Craig, R. G. Niemi & G. E. Silver, "Political Efficacy and Trust: A Report on the NES Pilot Study Items," *Political Behavior*, 12 (1990), p. 289–314.; D. B. Hill and N. R. Luttberg, *Trends in American Electoral Behavior*, 2nd. ed. (Itasca, IL: F.E. Peacock, 1983).

3. Hill and Luttberg, Ibid.; R. Travis, "On Powerlessness and Meaninglessness," *The British Journal of Sociology*, 37 (1986), pp. 61–73; Mason, House, and Martin, 1985, op. cit.; Craig, Niemi, and Silver, 1990, op. cit.

4. Chen, op cit.

5. Hill and Luttberg, 1983, op. cit.

6. Chen, op. cit., p. 93.

7. Ibid.

8. D. Easton and J. Dennis, *Children in the Political System* (New York: McGraw Hill, 1967).

9. Defending what a term means is the process of concept explication

[Steven H. Chaffee, *Explication* (Newbury Park, CA: Sage, 1991] and is in many senses arbitrary [see Carl G. Hemple, *Fundamentals of Concept Formation in Empirical Science* (Chicago: University of Chicago Press, 1952), on nominal definition]. More important, explication is the process of constructing social reality [Klaus Krippendorff, "On the Ethics of Constructing Communication," in Brenda Dervin, Lawrence Grossberg, Barbara J. O'Keefe, and E. Wartella, eds., *Rethinking Communication*, Vol. 1 (Newbury Park, CA: Sage, 1989)] where the effectiveness of the construction is only found in the predictive and theoretical validity the construct shows in making sense of the social world.

10. Roderick P. Hart, *Seducing America* (New York: Oxford University Press, 1994).

11. Chen, op cit., reports three correlation matrices for 1968, 1980, and 1988. Correlations for distrust, apathy, and meaninglessness are near zero and nonsignificant for all three periods. Distrust and personal inefficacy are present only in the 1988 data.

12. Chen, op. cit.

13. Actually, the analyses reported in this chapter were carried out both with a single index (presented here) and with two separate indices, one using only forced choice questions and one using only agree-disagree questions. The substantive conclusions are not different whether the two measures are combined or kept separate. Readers may request the alternative analysis by writing to the authors.

14. We wish to remind readers that all t-tests reported are two-tailed, even when specific directional hypotheses are being tested. For directional hypotheses, any two-tailed significance test whose probability is less than .20 is considered a trend. Statistical purists are reminded of the trade-off between type I and type II error. Since multiple tests of the same hypothesis are being conducted, excessive conservatism might lead us to conclude that small differences are not reliable when they are in fact present.

15. No significant interactions were found in univariate or multivariate tests.

16. The significant or near significant univariate effects for print included cynical learning and cynical motive. For broadcast, the univariate effects involved political cynicism and cynical learning. The effects on cynical learning were consistent and very strong.

17. Groups were combined for both conceptual and empirical reasons. Conceptually, we had no reason to expect the different types of coverage that had emphasized self-interest (S, G, P, and GSP) to differ in their effects on cynicism and empirically there were no differences across these groups by a Scheffe's test. Similar conceptual and empirical claims hold for the two groups that include issue coverage. In fact, none of the six experimental groups receiving coverage of health care differed by a Scheffe's test.

18. This assumption is based on interpretations of our findings from the previous study. If oppositional issue coverage can raise cynicism in a complex policy debate, then perhaps such a structure of information transmission ought to be avoided in televised news as well, unless directed at a highly informed audience.

19. Hart, 1994, op cit

20. Neuman, Just, and Crigler, 1992, op. cit.

21. If a candidate does not acknowledge the existence of a problem, then his or her comments would be directed at the problem statement that would be the locus of the disagreement. Typically, such commentary would provide reasons why there is no real problem and, hence, no solutions are warranted.

22. Copies of the coding manual and reliability procedures are available from the authors.

23. Coding proceeded as it did in the health care reform debate with one significant exception. A large number of statements were attributed to the presidential candidates, the vice presidential candidates, and their wives. The statements were difficult to code as neutral as opposed to positive since many were descriptions of policy stands given in language intended to be read as positive by the electorate, but couched in relatively neutral language. To attain good reliabilities on evaluation, these statements were coded separately as self-statements with the understanding that they were uniformly positive or, at worst, neutral. No differences in coding advocacy or compromise were necessary.

24. Four questions were directed at the focus on conflict. They were agree-disagree questions worded as follows:

Media coverage focused mostly on the conflict and attacks.

Media coverage did a good job reporting where the various players agreed.

When there is some disagreement as well as some agreement among groups, the media tends to focus on criticism and avoid areas of agreement.

Those who offer a solution are more likely to get media attention than those who argue against a solution.

Their intercorrelation ranged from .11 to .28 and their internal reliability was .47. A single scale was formed to obtain a measure of the media's focus on conflict.

Favorability toward various plans and health care reform in general was determined with four separate questions directed at the single payor plan, the Clinton plan, the Republican plans, or toward the need for health care reform. For example,

Next please think about the Republican alternatives for health care reform (for example, Gramm, Michel, or Dole). Do you think that media coverage mostly favored the Republican alternatives, mostly opposed them, or was balanced?

The responses to these four questions were not summed because the target of the question determined response more than the media did.

25. The F values ranged from 11.9 to 20.1; all were significant at $p < .001$ at least.

26. The F values were 13.2 for health care in general; 1.44 (not significant for the Clinton plan; 4.5 for the Republican alternatives; 2.6 ($p = .07$) for the single payer plan.

CHAPTER 8 *The Workings of the Cynical Public Mind*

1. The sample was well educated with 33 percent having some graduate education or a graduate degree and 32 percent having a college degree. Thirty-two percent were African American and 66 percent were Caucasian. The high number of African Americans is representative of the Philadelphia metropolitan area. About one in six were not currently employed and the remainder were. Females made up 48 percent of the group. The median age was thirty-six. People identifying themselves as more Democrat outnumbered Republicans 71 percent to 12 percent, with the remainder independents. Self-identified liberals (41 percent) and moderates (43 percent) vastly outnumbered conservatives (16 percent). Overall, the sample was representative of the electorate in age, gender, and employment status but was more educated, less conservative, and less Republican than the population at large. The high proportion of African Americans and Democrats in the Philadelphia area is reflected in our sample as well.

2. No significant differences across condition were found for age, education, gender, or race, suggesting a successful random assignment.

3. The analysis of data from this experiment is done more conservatively than in the learning and cynicism studies reported in Chapters 6 and 7. There the opportunity to replicate tests invited more liberal testing so that type I errors would not take precedence over type II errors. The present study employs new methods and techniques and stands alone.

The method employed is multivariate analysis of Covariance (MANCOVA), with the five exposures to news stories as the multiple measures, experimental condition (Issue-first or Strategy-first), and three covariates (age, education, and reading time for the stories). The five stories were not grouped because at this early stage of research it was not clear that they would all work in the same way.

4. On two other key questions relating to the strategic character of the stories, the strategy version was read as significantly "contributing to knowledge regarding campaign strategies." And the issue version was greater than the

strategy version on "policies the candidates would implement," but not significantly so. Story 2 did not produce as clean a manipulation of issue and strategy framing as we might have wished. This problem does not jeopardize our findings in the field experiments since, if anything, the mix of issue and strategy framing works against our hypotheses. Also, this story was one of five print stories whose cumulative effect was the focus. However, in the reaction time study, the issue and strategy versions of story 2 were directly tested against one another where differences (or their absence) matter a great deal more.

5. L. J. Shrum ("Assessing the Social Influence of Television: A Social Cognition Perspective on Cultivation Effects," *Communication Research*, 22 (1995), 402–29, page 416) notes a similar effect called *confirmatory hypothesis testing* or *feature positive effect*. Basically, people are more adept at searching for and recognizing positive instances of a criterion than at searching and recognizing disconfirming instances. The consequence is that positive instance of cynical interpretations are recognized and recognized more quickly than disconfirming instances of actions taken for the public good.

6. The possibility that those who were more cynical about politics or government might have faster reaction times than those less cynical was also investigated (see Hazel Markus, "Self-schemata and Processing Information About the Self," *Journal of Personality and Social Psychology*, 35 (1977), pp, 63–78). No such effects were found either as main effects or in interaction with the experimental conditions.

7. A complete listing of words by category can be obtained from the authors.

8. Both event and category reliability were checked [K. K. Krippendorff, *Content Analysis: An Introduction to Its Methodology*. (Newbury Hills, Ca: Sage, 1980)]. Events were identified consistently across coders with chi squareds showing no significant differences ($p > .95$ in all tests). Category reliability was acceptable, averaging an alpha of .65.

9. Actually, negative trait words increased in the strategy condition in the broadcast-only study. In this study (and the broadcast-print study) people wrote an essay about the presidential campaign of 1992 following directions identical to those for the mayoral study. Changes from pre- to post-test scores in the number of negative trait words increased from first to second testing for twenty-one people in the strategy condition and decreased for thirteen. The opposite pattern of change was observed in the issue condition (twenty-one decreased and fourteen increased) and in the control (sixteen decreased and eight increased). These differences are significant by a chi squared ($df = 2$) = 5.49, $p < .05$. These results were not replicated, however, in either of the other campaign studies.

10. The means reported in Table 8.2 are means adjusted for a covariate that is the number of strategy words in pre-test essays.

11. Roderick Hart, *Seducing American: How Television Charms the Modern Voter* (New York: Oxford University Press, 1994).

12. Neither can the differences in effects of the two media be attributed to the words used in the print or broadcast stories. The strategy, issue, and trait words were proportionally distributed across the news articles and TV segments in a way to reflect the experimental condition. The following table shows this distribution. Although there are many more strategy words in the print condition than the broadcast condition, befitting the nature of the medium, the proportions within conditions are roughly the same.

Number (and proportion) of Trait, Issue, and Strategy Words in News Stories by Experimental Condition

	Print Strategy (% col)	*Print Issue (% col)*	*Broadcast Strategy (% col)*	*Broadcast Issue (% col)*
Strategy Words	274	174	67	38
	33.7%	20.2%	36.0%	21.6%
Issue Words	428	601	103	125
	52.6%	69.9%	55.4%	71.0%
Trait Words	111	85	16	13
	13.6%	9.9%	8.6%	7.4%

13. Of the approximately 240 essays, seventy-three were subject to conceptual coding as well as word counts. These were coded in two of the conditions of the broadcast-print study — the II and SS conditions. Change scores in the number of strategic conceptual codes from pre to post essay were calculated. The change scores show that twenty-three increased and thirteen decreased in the SS condition while twenty-two decreased and fifteen increased in the II condition, significant at chi squared ($\underline{df} = 1$) = 4.1, $\underline{p} < .05$. The analysis at the level of propositions parallels the word analysis in the effects observed at least for the II and SS conditions.

14. R. Petty, and J. Cacioppo, *Communication and Persuasion* (New York: Springer-Verlag, 1986).

15. This evaluation was not a content analysis and coding reliability was thus not established. The results should be viewed as one reading of the essays by an expert with considerable experience with health care reform coverage.

16. A series of rating scales were developed to evaluate the essays for the attribution of cynical motives, mistrust of the process of health care reform, and ineffectiveness of government. Ratings were done on a 1 (= no cynicism)

to 9 (= extreme cynicism) scale. Reliabilities were very good with 163 of 210 comparisons between two coders differing by one or no scale points; 35 comparisons differing by 2 scale points; 12 comparisons differing by 3, 4, or 5 scale points.

17. These percentages reflect the presence of at least some cynicism, mistrust, or ineffectiveness in the essays. The percentages do not sum to 100 because the same essay could have two or more elements of cynicism.

18. Kathleen Hall Jamieson and Joseph N. Cappella, *Media in the Middle: Fairness and Accuracy in the 1994 Health Care Reform Debate.* Report of the Annenberg Public Policy Center of the University of Pennsylvania prepared for the Robert Wood Johnson Foundation, 1995.

19. Ibid.

20. B. Gunter, "Responding to News and Public Affairs," in J. Bryant and D. Zillman, eds., *Responding to the Screen* (Hillsdale, NJ: Lawrence Erlbaum, 1990), pp.229–260; J. P. Robinson, "Long-term Information and Media Usage," in J. P. Robinson and M. R. Levy, eds., *The Main Source* (Beverly Hills, CA: Sage, 1986), pp. 57–85; J. P. Robinson, and D. K. Davis, "Comprehension of a Single Evening's News," in J. P. Robinson and M. R. Levy, *The Main Source* op. cit., pp. 107–132.

21. John R. Zaller, *The Nature and Origins of Mass Opinion* (Cambridge: Cambridge University Press, 1992).

22. Other researchers have suggested similar measures calling them political sophistication [M. E. Crone, The nature of political sophistication in mass publics. Paper presented to the annual meeting of the American Political Science Association, Washington, DC, (1993); R. C. Luskin, "Measuring Political Sophistication," *American Journal of Political Science, 31* (1990), pp. 857–899.], political expertise [S. T. Fiske, R. R. Lau, and R. A. Smith, "On the Varieties and Utilities of Political Expertise," *Social Cognition, 8* (1990), pp. 31–48], public affairs knowledge [D. M. McLeod, and E. M. Perse, "Direct and Indirect Effects of Socioeconomic Status on Public Affairs Knowledge," *Journalism Quarterly, 71* (1994), pp. 433–442; V. Price, and J. Zaller, "Who Gets the News? Alternative Measures of News Reception and Their Implications for Research," *Public Opinion Quarterly, 57* (1993), pp. 133–164], awareness [J. Zaller, "The Diffusion of Political Attitudes," *Journal of Personality and Social Psychology, 53* (1987), pp. 821–833], and political schema [J. H. Kuklinski, R. C. Luskin, and J. Bolland, "Where Is the Schema? Going Beyond the "S" Word in Political Psychology," *American Political Science Review, 85* (1991), pp. 1341–1355]. We will use the phrase "political sophistication."

23. Price and Zaller, 1993, op. cit.

24. Ibid., p. 153.

25. In those cases where the relative positions did not yield a clear answer in terms of acknowledged public positions, the comparison was ignored. For example, Clinton is not clearly more liberal or clearly more conservative than

most liberals on the issue of pro-choice versus pro-life so this comparison does not enter the index of political sophistication.

26. For each topic, a question on confidence about the placements was obtained. An index weighting the answers by a person's confidence produced no substantial differences in correlation with other measures without the confidence weights.

27. B. R. Burleson, and M. S. Waltman, "Cognitive Complexity: Using the Role Category Questionnaire Measure," in C. H. Tardy, ed., *A Handbook for the Study of Human Communication* (Norwood, NJ: Ablex, 1988), pp. 1–35.

28. H. M. Schroder, M. J. Driver, and S. Streufert, *Human Information Processing* (New York: Holt, Rinehart, & Winston, 1967).

29. P. E. Tetlock, "Integrative Complexity of American and Soviet Foreign Policy Rhetoric: A Time Series Analysis," *Journal of Personality and Social Psychology, 49* (1985), pp. 1565–1585.

30. P. E. Tetlock, and K. Hannuum, Integrative complexity coding manual. Unpublished manuscript, University of California, Berkeley, 1984; Burleson and Waltman, 1988, op. cit. A copy of the coding rules is available from the authors. We are very grateful to Cass Conrad and Robin Nabi for their work in this portion of the study.

31. Deanna Kuhn, *The Skills of Argument* (Cambridge: Cambridge University Press, 1991).

32. Ibid., p. 12.

33. This notion is consistent with Jamieson's claim that good political discourse should argue, engage the opponent's arguments, accept accountability for claims, and forecast governance.

34. Emory H. Woodard, Argumentative skill: A measure of schema development. Paper presented to International Communication Association Conference, Albuquerque, New Mexico, 1995.

The following table summarizes the coding rules, percentage agreement, and reliability of coding quality of argument.

Definition, Description, and Intercoder Reliability for a Measure of Argument Quality

Coding Label	Coding Description	Alpha	Agree % or (Correlation)
Reasoning question	Did the participant provide reasons?	1.00	100.0%
No. of Reasons	The number of distinct and relevant claims	.63	(.67)
Quality of reasons	The number of claims with coherent reasoning	.74	70.9%
Counter present?	Did the participant provide counterreasoning?	.56	78.2%
Rejoinder present?	Did the participant provide a rebuttal of counter?	.56	80.0%
Argument quality	The sum of the above responses	.78	

Not only is this coding scheme reliable between coders, but it is internally reliable. Reliability analysis of the variables constituting the depth of processing score (reasoning, number of reasons, quality of reasons, counter, rejoinder) indicates that the scale was reliable with a standardized item $\alpha = .719$. The correlation between subcomponents and total score indicates that each subcomponent of the index is necessary to the overall measure of argument quality.

Argument quality is positively correlated with civics knowledge ($r = .23$, $p < .001$), education ($r = .25$, $p < .001$), political sophistication ($r = .22$, $p < .001$), and political involvement ($r = .25$, $p < .001$). It is also related to the closed-ended recall measures substantive recall ($r = .16$, $p < .003$), cynical recall ($r = .08$, $p = .12$), and factual recall ($r = .24$, $p < .001$). Together these correlations suggest that the skill measure has construct validity.

35. The index took the following form: elaboration = (number of events $*$ (1 + number of claims)) / c where c is a constant indicating the maximum of events times one plus claims.

36. Two measures of news reception are employed. One is attention to public affairs and the other is a measure of political sophistication. The attention measure has been shown to be an important component of measures of media exposure to news. This evidence is reviewed in June W. Rhee and Joseph N. Cappella, Media Exposure versus Political Sophistication: Explaining

Learning and Schematicity in the 1994 Health Care Debate, under review. Together, attention plus reception, should produce a valid and predictive measure of uptake of media news.

37. Two other measures of learning from the March study were shown not to be significant predictors of any learning in June. Controls for watching the NBC special were included in both regressions but are not shown in Tables 8.3 or 8.4.

38. The first three of these measures are discussed in Chapter 6. The last is a measure of health care plan knowledge based on correctly placing various plans on a liberal-conservative continuum relative to one another.

39. W. McGuire, "The Myth of Massive Media Impact: Savagings and Salvagings," in G. Comstock ed., *Public Communication and Behavior*, Vol. 1 (New York: Academic Press, 1986), pp. 173–257.

40. R. Petty, and J. Cacioppo, *Communication and Persuasion* (New York: Springer-Verlag, 1986).

41. W. R. Neuman, M. R. Just, and A. N. Crigler, *Common Knowledge: News and the Construction of Political Meaning* (Chicago: University of Chicago Press, 1992).

42. Political party preference was tested in each model with no effect for party on cynicism. The coefficients and their levels of significance were not appreciably different with party in the equation or not. The reason for this may simply be that baseline levels of cynicism about health care already capture the effects of party preference.

43. Analysis of covariance was used to covary out the effects of pre-test measures of distance from the Clinton plan. Results do not change if the covariate is entered first or simultaneously with the experimental factor.

44. Each condition was compared to the control using difference scores between pre-test and post-test distance from the Clinton plan. Each condition separately showed more distance after news exposure than without exposure. All differences were at or near conventional levels of statistical significance.

45. When all four measures of political cynicism about health care reform (along with pre-test distance) were entered as predictors of distancing first, then the effect of experimental condition was reduced from an F of 5.5 to 3.1, still significant at $p < .05$. When cynicism about government was entered as the first predictor, F dropped to a nonsignificant 1.82, indicating that most of the variance in distancing from the Clinton plan was accounted for by government cynicism. Both types of covariates were significant predictors of distancing but government cynicism was a powerful $F(1,316) = 86.7$.

46. Cynicism toward the health care reform process and party identification do not interact in predicting distancing.

47. Samuel L. Popkin, *The Reasoning Voter* (Chicago: University of Chicago Press, 1991).

48. McGuire, 1986, op. cit.

CHAPTER 9 *Contagious Cynicism*

1. *New York Times,* November 3, 1994, p. A28.

2. *The American Enterprise,* Roper Public Perspective, November/December 1993, pp. 94–95.

3. Ibid., p. 92.

4. In the News Study, three groups of questions were asked of the participants to assess their cynicism about government, politics, and the media. Some of the questions included:

Broadcast news tells audiences what they *need* to know.

or

Broadcast news tells audiences what they *want* to hear.

TV news is geared toward the needs of its audiences.

or

TV News is geared toward high audience ratings.

Being first with a news story is more important to reporters than being accurate.

In general, the press is fair and objective in the way it covers politics.

The usual procedures for obtaining reliable clusterings of questions were used. These included image factor analysis and internal reliability.

The government cynicism questions were taken from the NES survey questions about political alienation [William E. Miller and the National Election Studies, *National Election Studies 1952–1988 Cumulative Data File* (Ann Arbor, MI: Center for Political Studies, 1989)] tapping dimensions of trust and responsiveness [Kevin Chen, *Political Alienation and Voting Turnout in the United States, 1960–1988,* (San Francisco: Mellen Research University Press, 1992)]. These questions have been shown to be both reliable and valid. We included them primarily to validate our own measures of trust in the media and trust in politicians and the political process. The six questions grouped into a single factor with an internal reliability of .69.

The media cynicism questions were of two types: forced choice (five) and agree-disagree statements (nine) and paralleled the political cynicism questions of previous chapters. The final measure of cynicism about the media consisted of eight questions in one group with an internal reliability of .79 (standardized alpha). The political cynicism questions were parallel to the media cynicism ones with six forced choice and eight agree-disagree items. The final measure consisted of all fourteen questions in a single group with an internal reliability of .77 (standardized alpha).

In the third wave of the health care study, we employed a seven-item scale of cynicism about the political process of health care reform. Three of the questions were forced choice and four were agree-disagree in format. The scale had an internal reliability of .66 (standardized alpha). A set of three forced choice and four agree-disagree questions constituted a scale of cynicism about the media's handling of health care reform (internal reliability of .74).

5. The first two items correlated at .38 and were combined into a single measure of *un*favorability to the news media. It is important to note that this question concerns the mainstream news media. The second item correlated at .20 with the index and was held as a separate measure of news cynicism. These two measures of media favorability and cynicism correlated at .16 and .18 with standard measures of alienation from the government (e.g., elected officials care and elected officials lose touch) in this survey.

6. The pre-test sample from the panel are people's media cynicism scores before exposure to the NBC special. The other sample mixes those who watched and did not watch the special. However, there are no effects on media cynicism for this sample at all, so the post scores are not contaminated by watching the special.

7. The relationships among the three types of cynicism are linear.

8. In the Times Mirror data of summer and fall 1994, alienation from government correlates at .16 with media cynicism and .18 with unfavorability toward the media ($p < .001$). In the third wave of our health care study, media cynicism correlates with cynicism about the politics of health care reform at .48 ($p < .001$). In the Harvard samples before and after the NBC special, the correlations between cynicism about media and about health care were .17, $p < .0001$ in the panel sample before the special (increasing to .299 after), and .21, $p < .0001$ in the independent sample taken after the special.

9. Before selecting the headline wordings, we pre-tested them with a group of eleven experts who had been coding print and broadcast materials for strategy and issue differences. The final set of examples that we used had the agreement of a high percentage of informed judges.

10. Only five of the nine items were retained in a final measure of the strategic slant of stories. These five loaded on a single factor in an image factor analysis and had a standardized reliability of .45. The full set of nine items correlates at .81 with the five-item scale used here.

11. An index of the strategic versus issue event selection was significantly different from neutral [(t (124) = 3.67, $p < .001$)].

12. This percentage is significantly different from .50, t (125) = 7.14, $p < .001$).

13. Larry J. Sabato, *Feeding Frenzy: How Attack Journalism Has Transformed American Politics* (New York: Free Press, 1993).

14. As a part of that survey we asked seven questions tapping into media cynicism during the health care reform debate. Four questions were in agree-

disagree format and three in forced-choice style. The group of seven clustered together and had a standardized reliability of .74.

15. The same analyses were done with party affiliation (Democrat, Independent and other, and Republican) with the same results.

16. A model with all nine predictors in the equation accounts for 51.6 percent of the variance and the pattern of significant and nonsignificant predictors is the same as in the final model from the stepwise regression. Regressions using party affiliation in place of ideology yield the same predictors and about the same variance explained.

17. Times/Mirror survey of 1,513 participants reported in Public Opinion Online, October 20, 1994; Internet site.

18. Paul M. Sniderman, *A Question of Loyalty* (Berkeley University of California Press, 1980).

CHAPTER 10   *Breaking the Spiral of Cynicism*

1. Murray J. Edelman, *Constructing the Political Spectacle* (Chicago: University of Chicago Press, 1988), p. 95.

2. Dennis Chong, "Creating Common Frames of Reference on Political Issues," in Diana C. Mutz, Paul M. Sniderman, and Richard A. Brody, eds., *Political Persuasion and Attitude Change* (Ann Arbor: University of Michigan Press, 1996), pp. 195–224.

3. William A. Gamson, "Media Discourse as a Framing Resource," in Ann N. Crigler, ed., *The Psychology of Political Communication* (Ann Arbor: University of Michigan Press, 1996), pp. 111–32.

4. W. Russell Neuman, Marion Just, and Ann Crigler, *Common Knowledge: News and the Construction of Political Meaning* (Chicago: University of Chicago Press, 1992).

5. Joseph N. Cappella and Kathleen Hall Jamieson, "Tuning in 'To Your Health,'" *Journal of American Health Policy* (September/October 1994), pp. 36–40.

6. Interview, April 3, 1996.

7. *Breaking the News: How the Media Undermine American Democracy* (New York: Pantheon Books, 1996), p. 62.

8. David Shaw, "Beyond Skepticism," *Los Angeles Times*, April 17, 1996, p. 1.

9. "Raffish and Rowdy," *New York Times*, March 31, 1996, p. E15.

10. Max Frankel, "Summer Musings," *New York Times*, June 25, 1995, p.24.

11. Quoted by Dowd, p. E15.

12. *Marketer's Guide to Media* (New York: BPI Communications, Spring/Summer 1995), p. 179.

13. Lee Margulies, "Super Bowl XXX Breaks Record for Audience Size," *Los Angeles Times*, January 30, 1996, p. F2.

14. "Under Siege," *American Journalism Review* (September 1995), p. 16.

15. Ibid., p. 18.

16. Shaw, 1996, op. cit., p. 1.

17. Ibid., p. 20.

18. "The People, The Press and Their Leaders," May 1995.

19. Fallows, *op. cit.*, p. 197.

20. "Politics and the Health Care Bill," *New York Times*, March 24, 1996, p. 32.

21. "Both Rival Camps Expect To Be Wild Card," *New York Times*, March 27, 1996, p. A16.

22. "A Forbes Tax Argument Proves Hard to Confirm," *New York Times*, February 3, 1996, p. 9.

23. David E. Rosenbaum, "The Medicare Brawl: Finger-Pointing, Hyperbole and the Facts Behind Them," *New York Times*, October 1, 1995, p. 18.

24. *New York Times*, p. E3.

25. Ibid., p. 26.

26. Shaw, 1996, op. cit., p. A1.

27. Bob von Sternberg, "Campaigns not up to code or compact," *Minneapolis Star Tribune*, October 31, 1996.

28. Tom Hamburger, "Minnesota Compact: What's the impact?" *Minneapolis Star Tribune*, October 31, 1996, p. 14A.

29. "The Love-Hate Relationship Between Politicians and the News Media," *The Forum* (September 1994), p. 7.

30. The Pew Research Center for the People and the Press, "Campaign '96 Gets Lower Grades From Voters," November 15, 1996, pp. 1–5.

31. These data were collected and analyzed as part of the Annenberg School for Communication's Campaign Mapping Project funded by The Ford Foundation and the Carnegie Corporation of New York.

32. The survey was conducted by Chilton Research for the Annenberg Public Policy Center of the University of Pennsylvania from October 17–22, 1996. Details can be found on the Annenberg School homepage at http://www.asc@upenn.edu.

33. "Campaign Gets Lower Grades from Voters," p. 2.

34. March 1996.

35. R. W. Apple, Jr., "James Reston, A Journalist Nonpareil, Dies at 86," *New York Times*, December 8, 1995, p. 1.

INDEX

Printed in the United States
5224